A Beautiful Restoration

*A Story of
Faith, Fellowship
and Discovering
the Father's Heart*

Kelly A. Williams

STONES
PUBLISHERS

A Beautiful Restoration, A Story of Faith, Fellowship and Discovering the Father's Heart

Copyright © 2013 by Kelly A. Williams. All rights reserved.
Published by Five Stones Publishers
1341 Laurel Oak Drive, IN 46123
5stonespublishers.com

No part of this publication may be reproduced, stored in a retrieval system or transmitted in any way by any means, electronic, mechanical, photocopy, recording or otherwise without the prior permission of the author, except as provided by USA copyright law.

All Scripture quotations, unless otherwise indicated, are taken from the New King James Version. Copyright © 1982 by Thomas Nelson, Inc. Used by permission. All rights reserved.

ISBN: 978-0-9883452-4-9 (Paperback Edition)
Library of Congress Control Number: 2012917011

Cover design: Robin Black, Inspirio Design LLC
Cover photo: Voren1
Author photo: Rick McIntyre

To the YaYa's

In my heart you will always be my forever friends.

Foreword

*E*choes of growth tremble through change, so faint their exact moments pass until only their fragrance lingers. New realities sweep through our lives and we find ourselves on the other side of a journey we did not know we began. What we see—all we see—is that our life has changed. Suddenly we are different.

Most often this journey is casual and progressive. But sometimes it is rapturous, absorbing all we are and staking claim to the things we never wanted to lose. It leaves us with endings we never foresaw and demands a degree of surrender to which we never subscribed. Wish as we may, this change never seeks our permission; it refuses to wait for our unwillingness to give. Instead, it engulfs us until we are left standing holding the pieces of crumbled foundations.

Our weary hearts yearn for rest from the courage required to face the stones life throws. They lash and take more. . . always more. Once tall we hunch, battered from the sorrow of unwelcomed new. And from ashes a quivering faith struggles to believe beauty will rise, unable to see beyond the grey of heartache that covers the falsehoods we once enshrined. Because how does the one whose eyes are still swollen in heartache see how tears uncover grey to reveal pale, new skin?

This, however, is among the most unique and autonomous moments we have in our lives: What will we elect to do with the change? How will we respond to that which has left us so dramatically different than we imagined? When change ravages our hearts, taking all it could desire and leaving us in bits, to whom- or to what- will we look as we seek to join the pieces into a whole once again?

Journeying through heartache teaches a person a great many things. This is the continuation of one woman's story where change and the unforeseen left her battered and aching, robbing the things she never surrendered and demanding what she never thought she could live without. Here Kelly details the trials and lessons that came after *A Gradual Redemption*, setting an example in what she chose to do with the pieces she was left, but more importantly, to whom she chose to look to restore them.

—**Anna M. Williams**

Behold what manner of love the Father has bestowed on us, that we should be called children of God!

—1 John 3:1a

CHAPTER ONE

A Fresh Start

*The lines have fallen to me in pleasant places;
Yes, I have a good inheritance*
—Psalm 16:6

I sat, my eyes scanning the small burgundy living room of our new home, awestruck by the surreal nature of it all. It still felt dreamlike, as if at any moment I would hear someone tell me this move wasn't real, that the events of the past six months didn't *really* happen. And yet they did—after three long years and what felt like a lifetime of regret, we had finally returned to the community we loved and had always felt an unexplainable connection with.

I glanced out the front window remembering the number of people who had said, "Your house is lovely, just be patient it will sell," understanding for the first time that their words had served as landmarks along the way—as if they were God's personal way of encouraging us to stay the course.

After three long years of agony and struggling under the weight of purchasing a house that God never intended us to buy and a decision that clearly God had not blessed, I marveled at how on the very day my husband Randy was scheduled to start the refinancing paperwork we had reluctantly resigned ourselves to, his car had broken down on the way to the appointment, preventing him from making a huge step in the wrong direction—*oh yeah, that was just a coincidence.* Just as much of a coincidence as the buyer who had miraculously come forward only once we removed the "For Sale" sign from the yard as a willful act of obedience after years of living out my rebellion.

I leaned back on the couch, full from my last plate of food and closed my eyes, relishing God's sovereignty and the way He made Himself known. *This house is like His personal gift to us,* I thought, *not grand or spectacular, but perfectly ours.* My ears absorbed the distant soft chatter that filled the room and I couldn't help but grin as an abiding contentment enveloped my soul.

I savored the warmth that came from allowing the internal guard of the past few years to come down. The comfort from knowing my family's self-induced exile into Egypt was over let me sink deeper into the billowy cushions of the couch. *I've finally returned to the place I belong—I'm home.*

Like a traveler weary from being on the road for far too long, moving into this house felt like at long last I could finally sleep in my own bed with my own pillow. Reminiscing over the three-year journey one last time, I traveled over each memory until I returned to the present—moving day—and grinned, quietly telling my inner companion Silence, "This is it; we did it. We actually crossed the finish line."

CHAPTER TWO

OFF AND RUNNING

An unbelieved truth can hurt a man much more than a lie.
—John Steinbeck—*East of Eden*

Two weeks after we moved in, school started. Back were the days when I could walk Matthew, now a fifth-grader, to school instead of leaving him at the mercy of the school bus and all of its limitless influences. The single difference was that this year Anna would be joining us. And while I was completely comfortable with the hometown environment my two children would encounter, knowing Anna was already five and ready to start the next chapter of her life was bittersweet. Even Aaron, at only two and a half, was beginning to make sense of different things, and losing his sister for half the day was not something he took to very well.

Aaron was accustomed to Matthew being gone since Matt was already school-age by the time Aaron was born, but in the short two-plus years Aaron had been with us Anna was always right next to him. . . until now. Despite our multiple attempts of explanation, he spent most of those initial mornings wandering through the house repeating, "Where's my Nawna? Where's my Nawna?" with his shoulders shrugged, his hands upturned and the question marks evident in his saucer-sized brown eyes.

Those were sweet days as my family and I readjusted to a lifestyle we were already quite familiar with and had yearned to have back. Within weeks of returning to our former community and school starting, Matthew began junior league football practice, Anna became a cheerleader and Aaron willingly went to whatever gym, football field or school event we needed to attend. Our involvement and acclimation back into the old community was nearly immediate, which allowed my emotional roots to not only reestablish in the soil of our small town, but to penetrate and spread just as quickly.

Though I could see part of the downtown Indianapolis skyline from my house, the small-town feel of the area kept me from feeling completely overwhelmed. Fear, my constant enemy, seemed to reside more in the shadows as I grew increasingly comfortable with my familiar surroundings and I remembered why I loved this place so much. Strangers no longer terrified me as they once had, and although defeating Fear and Intimidation remained a constant struggle, I also knew the security and ambiance of Mayberry was alive and well in my three square mile community. Besides, with Matthew's involvement in sports and his extracurricular activities after school, it didn't take long to get to know the parents in his twelve-student class. Each time he wanted to play kickball or football after school and a new name was mentioned, I had no choice but to walk through the proverbial open door and meet another parent of one of Matthew's school-aged friends.

The security and stability that came from the town's familiarity and friendliness soon overflowed into a prayer group called "Moms-In-Touch" that met weekly, where I had the privilege of not only meeting parents of my children's peers, but faith-filled, like-minded people as well. With two women in particular, Kerri and Lori, the spiritual connection was nearly instant. What had started as a prayer ministry for our school system began to quickly develop into deep abiding personal friendships.

These were the women who soon introduced Randy and me to their respective husbands and families. Before we were even aware of what was happening our three individual families were bonding together, forging friendships that paralleled those I had once enjoyed as a young girl in Ohio. Although our geographical connection is what initially linked us together, it was our shared faith and commitment to live in the trenches with one another that continued to hold us together.

We were like-minded in every way, so as time passed and trust was securely built between our three families, an increased confidence to share our full story was built as well: Yes, there were five of us, and yes, Randy and I had been married for almost eight years, and though I had come to terms with so much of my past and my previous choices, each time I shared that Matthew was mine biologically and that Randy had adopted him when he was four, inevitably the prick of shame and regret would pierce my heart and I always found myself wishing things were different.

Undoubtedly the Lord had put much of my heart back together. Yet there were still days when it felt like it existed in sections rather than as a whole—almost as if things had been systematically compartmentalized—which meant blending things was not always easy, including our family.

Despite a cohesive outward appearance, my past and its subsequent choices often blared in front of me, preventing me from seeing things, or us, as fully united. There were still fragments of my inner self that lived in the small steel town in Ohio while others had been left back in the hospital room—alone—trying to grasp the concept that regardless of what I had believed or hoped about his biological father, all Matthew really had was me.

Even now, nearly ten years later, my heart struggled to relinquish full control where Matthew was concerned. Remnants of his biological father's rejection lingered and I wasn't fully convinced that anyone could walk fully in his place. It was as if my feet stood in two different worlds—one trapped in the world of yesteryear and the other treading on ground that ached for Matthew's life to be defined by paternal normalcy and traditionalism. I never wanted him or my family to be known as the "blended" one—I had grown up with that label defining me my whole life. I grieved at the thought that one of my children would bear the same marking.

So as we became known within our community, I recommitted to not having *any* visible lines of division in my own family structure—there would be no difference among any of my children, not in the way they were treated nor in the way they were loved. And at any perceived or potential threat of disparity, I leapt to Matt's defense as if I was saving his life. Whether I knew it or not, somewhere along the journey it became my job to protect Matthew from feeling any notion of separation or inferiority. Just like in the hospital room almost eleven years ago, I still felt that the overarching responsibility to protect and defend Matt rested squarely on my shoulders.

Desperation helped define the need for my children to have an altogether different childhood than the one I experienced as a young girl growing up with a stepfather in a blended family where two of the seven children followed a different set of rules than my mother's own five children. Although I could readily acknowledge my understanding of father/son relationships was severely limited, I vowed to make sure that with every achievement or setback Matthew experienced, Randy's response would be equal to the one I had conjured up in my own self-created version of the ideal family. I was determined to make the relational environment in my own home as seamless as possible, even if that included sifting Randy's relationship with Matthew through an unseen grid of idyllic expectation and interpretation of how Matt's biological father would have behaved if only had he been here.

CHAPTER THREE

DESPERATE LONGINGS

For what I am doing, I do not understand. For what I will to do, that I do not practice; but what I hate, that I do.
—Romans 7:15

Despite all that Randy had been and done for our family, sporadic moments of mental flashbacks plagued me, and in the quietest times my mind revisited the fringes of things that remained unresolved. It had been thirteen years since life first became chaotic and a variety of choices brought me out of my childhood state of Ohio and back to Indiana and to life with my mother.

I was now almost 30 years old, and while those days no longer taunted me like they once did, in the deepest recesses of my heart the longing for my childhood friends never fully subsided. Oftentimes my curiosity would take me for long walks down imaginary trails if I allowed it. *What would my life be like if I lived back there? Would I still fit in? Would Matthew's biological father still be there?*

Without question I was quickly growing to cherish my newfound Indiana friends, and certainly our collective families were doing more and more things together. But a part of me still ached for my childhood home and the people I still loved. I missed being able to see a lifelong friend in the grocery store or to just walk into any number of homes where I had spent so much of my childhood. There was a culture or a way of life that existed in northeast Ohio that just didn't transfer with my family or me when we moved to central Indiana. Years later I still found it odd to not be able to find authentic Italian bread in the grocery store or hear the old Italian men and women speaking in the native tongue as they gathered together on a Saturday afternoon at the local butcher shop. Thirteen years later I still missed northeast Ohio's personality, and although so much of me had adjusted, there were still parts of me that remained tethered to the place that for eighteen years I had called home.

That subtle longing would resurface each time a special occasion arose or a major milestone was accomplished, and especially whenever Matthew succeeded in something. Invariably with each success a question regarding his biological father who had abandoned us would arise: *What would he think . . . Would he care?*

Thankfully those questions weren't rooted in any false hope or vision of he and I being together. That fantasy had somehow been dispelled years ago, months before Randy and I were married, back when the counselor walked me through giving away the personal gifts he had given to me as a way of letting him go.

Instead those reoccurring questions, subtle though they were, were equally profound because they were rooted in my heart's desire for Matthew's childhood to be normal. I never wanted him to hurt or feel lack because of his biological father's absence so every time I suspected Randy's response was inferior to how I believed his biological father would have reacted, an onslaught of comparisons would barrage me: *How would he respond? What would he think? Would he be requiring the same thing?*

It was as if I was living a great juxtaposition—the prouder I felt over who Matthew was becoming as a person, the deeper my internal struggle grew. With each sensitive and compassionate act he did, coupled with the accolade he was receiving athletically and academically, my heart would swell with the desire to "ooh and aah" over Matthew and his accomplishments. I desperately wanted to be able to look at Randy and share that moment that all proud parents share over their children. But something in me was hesitant. Yes, my head knew he loved Matt, and yes, he had been the one person who in the midst of so much rejection and neglect said, "I want him." Yet deep inside there remained a hidden parameter or boundary that I just couldn't get across. I tried and though there were momentary breakthroughs, I've discovered that sin isn't logical, and for me, deception has been a difficult thing to expose, let alone understand and navigate.

In my case, the facts were clearly the facts: Randy was here and "he" wasn't. But the reality was, his absence didn't change what my heart believed; in the part that no one could see and I didn't disclose, I still defined the relationship as authentic and justified his behavior. Anything less was too painful to consider. *If he didn't love me why did he stick around for as long as he had?* But it wasn't really a question; rather, a silent source of reassurance that I clung to as I wrestled with the truth of my ongoing situation. *And, since he loved me he had to love Matt.* To me, we were a package deal.

On and on it went—not all the time, but enough. And once again I was trapped in a vortex of confusion: mentally, emotionally and spiritually. I had grown to deeply love and respect Randy and the life we had; I wasn't interested in putting that in jeopardy. Yet, as Matthew entered adolescence I found myself amid various authoritative conflicts that can arise between a father and son, with no understanding as to how to cope or where to put them. In my utopic world where families aren't blended and idyllic fathers are without flaws, relational tensions didn't exist. So when the first signs of tension between Randy and Matthew erupted, the aftershock created ripples of desire in me to share Matthew with the one person I still believed had a natural vested interest in him—his biological father.

Like a revolving door, I'd step in and out of the swirling thought vortex until the day my mother asked me to go to northeast Ohio with her for a few days. Something about the thought of going "home" and seeing my childhood friends and becoming, once again—even if just for a weekend—a part of what I still so desperately missed made me walk a bit lighter as if a weight was being lifted. Then when Randy offered to keep all three children so I could have the weekend away, my heart soared with excitement.

Similar to when I was in high school, the six-hour car drive lent itself to a mental journey down memory lane, interrupted only by my mother's narrative on how things used to be. When there were lulls in conversation, I would let my mind drift through the seas of memories: playing hide-n-seek in Nancy's backyard or taking long walks with friends to Mike's Party Shop to buy five cent candy, all the while talking about dreams we had or planning secret weddings. Then, as if someone hit fast-forward, my mind skipped to the first two years of high school when things had been fun and innocent, then. . . . thoughts of all that had happened and how fast things spiraled out of control the last two years of high school still made me grimace. *So much regret, Father.*

For so many people high school holds some of the best memories of their lives. While part of my time there is fondly remembered, the majority of my thoughts are inseparable from my time with "him." Whenever high school is brought up, by default my mind returns to that place where I surrendered to him—emotionally and physically. It was impossible to *not* think about him now that both feet were returning to yesteryear, and to wonder how he was and what he was doing so many years later. Did he think about us? *Did he think about Matt?* I wondered. *Can a man have three children and only think about two of them?*

My silent reflections carried me almost to the threshold of my former city. As highway markers began to increase in familiarity, so too did my mental reenactments of my life so long ago. I saw the sign for Bailey Road and was instantly transported to the night my car broke down in a torrential thunderstorm as I drove all over the city looking for him. *What was wrong with me?* I wondered. The thought of my less than dignified self sent shivers up my spine. I closed my eyes and gently rolled my head back on the headrest and tried to make thoughts of my life with Randy replace my mental meanderings. For brief moments it worked, until my eyes opened and the next highway marker or familiar location triggered another memory.

I began to feel like a boxer desperately trying to get out of the corner of the ring, but every time I nearly escaped, the mental assault would throw me like a rag doll back against the ropes, trapping me like a wild animal. I couldn't escape this place and its memories; they were too vivid and years later stirred up raw, undealt-with emotions that I was able to suppress in Indiana. Here, I couldn't find my way out.

As usual, my mother's perceptiveness reappeared in the car and she asked me, "Kelly, are you okay? You're awfully quiet."

I should tell her . . . but she hates him. She always has, flew through my mind causing me to dismiss my immediate urge. *Silence is the only one who understands the torment.* I quickly glanced over and grinned, simultaneously nodding my head, "Yeah, Mom, I'm fine . . . just thinking."

She quizzically looked at me and in a drawn out manner said, "Aaabout. . . ?" with her eyebrows raised.

"I don't know . . . just a lot of memories surface when I come back here."

"It's hard to take back our hearts from our first loves, Kelly," she responded, then continued as she shared her own account of being sixteen and giving her heart and the subsequent hurt that came from lost love. I listened intently, glad for the distraction and the opportunity to focus on something besides him. I watched her animation and, despite the forty-some years that had passed, my mother's emotions still expressed themselves on her face as she spoke. Her memories were still so vivid even after all this time that I couldn't help but wonder if there would be a day when Matthew and I would have this very conversation about my relationship with his birth father. "I hope and pray, Lord, that I can be objective about things that happened," I silently uttered. "I don't want him to walk in judgment."

By the time we pulled into my grandmother's driveway, our conversation seemed to wrap up and I paused to just look at my mom. There was so much I could have said but the only words I was able to muster were, "Thank you."

"For what?" she asked.

I wanted to say for understanding, for asking, for not judging me, but instead I kept it simple and answered, "For sharing and for your wisdom. I appreciate it."

And with that, we unpacked the car as my grandmother met us on the sidewalk.

CHAPTER FOUR

LOSING GROUND

*Therefore to him who knows to do good but does not do it,
to him it is sin.*
James 4:17

There was still a spring chill in the air as my mom and I drove back to my grandmother's from the Cleveland Clinic. As usual, I was lost in my own head, looking forward to seeing my friends from high school that evening. It was the one night over the weekend that I would have the freedom to drive myself where I wanted, when I wanted, for my mother had made her own evening's plans. Selfishly I looked forward to reminiscing without interruption as I drove across town for dinner. I wanted the opportunity to see how I would do when left to my own devices.

For all the numerous trips I had made back home over the years, Randy had always been with me guarding and sheltering me from the potential emotional onslaught brought on by past memories—the subtle as well as the big reminders of the years spent with Matthew's biological father, stolen moments when something inside knew I should have known better but instead, I chose differently. This time, however, I was home and on my own, fully aware that I would be coming face to face with some old demons, or at best, packed away skeletons that had taken up residence in some of my well-constructed closets.

Those thoughts danced around my mind throughout the afternoon as I mentally rehearsed various scenarios and conversations I could only wish I had the courage to have with him. In my mental role-play, a false sense of bravado always caused my inner man to stand a little taller or walk a little surer, fully prepared to ask him the hard questions. But somehow the reality of the situation always interrupted, bringing with it the ability to drive me right back into my fearful state. Although Silence was the only one who was actually privy to my innermost thoughts, he never said much about them. It was Shame who welcomed and encouraged my imagination to have its free-for-all.

With every winnowing thought of what I would say to him if given the chance, Shame was right there to encourage me: "You know you want to call him. Just do it . . . you'll feel better and no one will ever know," slithered the gravelly voice in my head.

Then Shame's proddings would go quiet as if he recognized just how much he could say before risking overexposure—the luring so subtle it was almost indistinguishable. And into his trap I would descend until logic would clear a momentary path and I would mentally retort: I'm married . . . *I love Randy. . . God would not be pleased*, etc., which would have worked had I been fighting an intellectual war.

Clearly, I wasn't.

It's interesting now to recognize in retrospect that the battle I was engaged in was not just with the intellect. Which explains why, with every fleeting logical thought that arose in response to Shame's voice, another round of "Yes, but it's just a phone call" would flood my soul, followed by strategic, cunning ways to circumvent my own exposure, thereby weakening my resolve to stay committed to *all* I had back in Indiana.

This was a battle of much darker, unseen forces. As the apostle Paul says in Ephesians 6, *"For we do not wrestle against flesh and blood, but against principalities, against powers, against the rulers of the darkness of this age, against spiritual hosts of wickedness in the heavenly places* (10-12).

Those types of wars are not won by intellectual thought; they're won only by employing Kingdom truths partnered with the authority that comes from the blood of Christ. But the concept of that authority and its appropriation was foreign to me at the time, so instead I continued wrestling with Shame's persuasiveness using the only tool I knew—intellectually arguing it away.

    I desperately fought against Shame's suggestions by trying to focus on how Randy would feel if I followed through with what I was considering. But the more I tried to silence Shame's voice the louder he became and my need "to know" sounded so justifiable that by the time I left my grandmother's for dinner, I was so weakened and vulnerable by the internal battle waging in my soul, I was already a wounded warrior. There was little chance of standing my ground. I had bought the enemy's lie, and my determination to get some answers to some paramount unanswered questions gradually became the sole reason for my evening's plans.

CHAPTER FIVE

THE WILL TO SAY NO

*Was this a betrayal, or was it an act of courage? Perhaps both.
Neither one involves forethought: such things take place in an
instant, in an eyeblink. This can only be because they have been
rehearsed by us already, over and over, in silence and darkness;
in such silence, such darkness, that we are ignorant of them
ourselves. Blind but sure-footed,
we step forward as if into a remembered dance.*
—Margaret Atwood
The Blind Assassin

For as many times as I had driven across town, I could have put the car on autopilot and arrived at my destination without any effort of my own, so I spent my driving time mindlessly navigating while planning out "the conversation." There were pricks of conviction that sporadically pierced my spirit, but Shame's reassurance of secrecy always seemed to make them subside. I was discovering a great sense of freedom in my newfound anonymity—no Randy, no mom, no kids—no one to remind me who I was or what I should do. For the first time in a long time I was free from all accountability, and I had convinced myself that there was little harm in a simple phone call. *After*

all, I thought, *I'm only seeking answers, and regardless, how could people get hurt if they never know?*

Scanning the horizon, the green exit sign loomed overhead as if declaring the soon approaching point of no return. Instantly, my stomach began to twist and knot itself with nervousness, the moisture on my hands increasing. I tried rubbing them up and down my thighs, then resorted to letting the air vent blow them dry. "What is wrong with me?" I whispered, but of course there was no response.

Silence had, at some point, joined me in the car because I could sense his presence hovering next to me as if he now sat in the passenger seat. I knew if I could actually see him, the look in his eye would convey his caution and send me a silent reminder of all that had transpired the last time I threw caution to the wind and acted on impulse. *I know, I know, but it's only a phone call. I'm not going to see him, and I just need to know . . . Why? Why did he leave? What about Matt?* Then I fell silent as memories of what used to be replayed in my mind. *I thought he loved me.*

Regret and shame slowly washed over me once again as subtle voices in my head whispered, "You should have known better," stirring the need for someone to finally answer my questions. Silence sat quietly conveying only his unspoken concern for caution. As I drove down the exit ramp, I offered up one last bartering lightning bolt prayer: "Okay, if You don't want me to do this then don't let me find his number."

Minutes later I pulled into the nearest gas station and parked next to the pay phone waiting for the thunderous sound of my heartbeat to subside. A single moment of hesitation allowed me to listen once more for a split second warning, but the only thing I heard was the subtle purr of the engine accompanied by the sound of blood coursing through my veins. I gasped for one quick lungful of air before I picked up the receiver, dialed Information, then gave the operator his name.

In the few seconds it took for the operator to look up his number then ask if I wanted her to connect me, the surrounding area seemed to warp in waves of slow motion as my heart's beat reverberated in my ears with the same force that it had years ago. Glimpses of standing in the back stock room with the phone to my ear listening to my mother's broken words stammer out "The doctor thinks you're pregnant" instantly flashed through me.

Suddenly I was seventeen all over again. Terrified to hear what the person on the other end of the phone had to say but too emotionally paralyzed to hang up. All I could feel was the slow numbing sensation that crept up my forearm as I squeezed the phone tighter.

I closed my eyes in a futile effort to block out all the chaos and like a voice crying out in the wilderness I could hear His familiar voice from the far recesses of my spirit whisper, almost pleading with me, "Please don't do this, Kelly." Then suddenly, as if they were coming from an altogether different direction, louder and with a much stronger urgency and insistent shout came the clamor of multiple voices shouting, "DO IT!! YOU DESERVE TO KNOW!! YOU HAVE EVERY RIGHT!"

And therein lay my choice: I could either submit and surrender to the still small voice that was so gentle in nature and entrust *Him* with my questions or I could continue to keep the matter in my own hands and rely on my natural circumstances to resolve what had been for so long irresolvable. It would simply boil down to whether I told the operator yes or no. I hesitated, instinctively knowing somewhere deep inside that the better choice was to decline and just hang up.

But instead, with a reckless abandon and complete disregard for everything God had redeemed in my life as well as a trite dismissal of how Randy would feel, I blurted out a careless, "Yes," then closed my eyes, gripped the phone even tighter and waited for him to say hello.

CHAPTER SIX

IRRESOLVABLE ISSUES

I am not bound to please thee with my answers.
—William Shakespeare

One.... two..... three. By the start of the fourth ring my heart was beating so loudly and I was straining so hard to hear that by the time he said hello, my nerve to speak seemed to instantly dissolve in a pool on the ground around my feet. "Uhhum" was the only thing I could utter, but at least it was loud enough to reveal that someone was on the line.

"Hello," he said again, more like a question than his original greeting.

Frantically my mind scoured for words, but all was blank—no words, no questions, no grand accusations—just an ever growing awareness of how compromised I felt and the subsequent growing pit in my stomach. Again the fleeting thought to just hang up flew through my mind, but he was this close, closer than he'd been in years, and suddenly out of nowhere, "Hey, it's Kelly," rolled off my tongue.

An awkward silence filled the distance between the phone lines, an empty space defined by all that had occurred between us, and for me, all that had been lost—interrupted only by the intermittent crackle that came from a bad connection. My mind trampled back through the years of questions and confusion and then I remembered why I called. I wanted vindication. I wanted him to know how much damage he had caused, and I wanted him to finally take some responsibility. But most of all I wanted him to once and for all answer all my whys. *Why didn't you just leave me alone when you met me? Why did you lead me to believe you really cared? Why did you leave us? WHY?* I needed him to make rational sense out of so much pain.

Standing there in the now lightly falling rain, my heart burned more than ever for the truth. Never once did it occur to me that perhaps I should question his answers, that perhaps he or they shouldn't be believed. The simple reality was that something inside me still longed to believe him. I hadn't yet come to the place where I could fully admit or accept that everything I had sold myself out for twelve-plus years ago was really all a lie. *Could I have really been that stupid?*

With an apprehensive "Well, how are you?" he broke the silence and I was back in present time, fumbling for an answer to his very simple question. *If I'm good then why did I call him?* I asked myself.

"Kelly?" he asked.

Stammering, I blurted out, "I'm okay," and from there the small talk slowly took over. Still unable to take the offensive, I answered each of his questions with minimal words as I explained what I was doing back in town, how long I would be there and how life was in general. It wasn't until he asked me if Randy was with me that I heard Shame immediately lure me back into hiding. I closed my eyes, only to see an image of a long wrinkled finger sinisterly curling, summoning me back into the cave. "Answer him, Randy won't ever know," slithered in my ears.

I clenched my eyes closed in hopes of blocking out the insidious image, then took a deep breath before quietly answering, "No, he's home."

Remorse consumed me as soon as I said it, as if my verbal response had somehow propelled me into an agreement with Betrayal. My stomach began to churn as Awareness hovered in the air, my admission of Randy's whereabouts ushering me into the realization that I had just voluntarily stepped out from behind the shield of defense his covering had always given me. By choosing to cooperate with Shame's seduction, I had in essence offered our emotional and spiritual unity as a sacrifice on the altar of selfish desire.

Once again I found myself caught in a quagmire of deception, unable to find my way out. *Why does the exit door always feel so far away when I need it to be the closest?* I wondered. I couldn't make sense of anything other than feeling trapped between my choices. Calling him suddenly didn't feel as justifiable as it had minutes ago. And though I sensed the growing unsettledness that was permeating my spirit, I still couldn't bring myself to deny the feeling that I was entitled to some answers.

Standing there in the dimly lit parking lot, the mist in the air illuminated by the fluorescent street lamps that hung like giant arms overhead, the realization that this was going to end up being a watershed moment began to dawn on me—one of those moments when plowing forward doesn't feel quite right yet you know you can't really turn back either, so you try to rationalize or justify your decision by telling yourself, "I'm already in it this far so what the heck." Only to discover that the real force of change in the moment doesn't lie in what we decide to do, but rather in the choice itself. It's what we learn about ourselves in that one solitary moment of having to decide that we can't do anything but help chart out the course of our lives.

It took a fleeting second to confront the peril that comes with the crossfire of choice, just as it took a fleeting second for me to believe there was no gracious way to undo what I had already set in motion. And it took a fleeting second to decide it was easier to delve deeper into the abyss that was right in front of me rather than realign myself with Randy who seemed so distant and far from reach.

So headfirst I plunged, believing that the precision-point questions I had always imagined I would use as bullets would finally strike the desired target, but instead they merely sputtered out like misfires as his vague responses and glossed-over excuses successfully out-maneuvered my interrogation. Mentally I reloaded, working up enough courage to follow up my initial round of the basic "what happened" questions with round two, asking how or why he could have done such things, until finally either my recklessness or my courage took over and I heard myself blurt out the one unanswered question that had plagued my soul and tormented me since everything had transpired:.

"Why?" came out in a faint whisper followed by a stronger, "Why did you leave and never once look back? Not even for Matthew?"

A torrent of memories flooded my soul as images of shamefully fleeing Ohio amid broken promises then living a shattered life in a lifeless cave washed over me one right after the other. I paused, waiting for the vice-like constraint around my throat to go away, then swallowed before uttering in lingering disbelief, "How could you?"

His response was sudden and blunt—abrupt and to the point. So much so that when he said, "Kelly, I knew you and Matthew were in better hands with your mother," his trite dismissal struck me as impersonal and rehearsed just like the twelve years he'd had to prepare it.

References of whitewashed tombs and decaying bags of bones from Matthew 23 flooded through me as I thought about how much sense his answers seemed to make to all my tormenting questions: He went back to his wife, she didn't want him to have anything to do with us, and since I was with my mother what else could he do? His rationale contained all the necessary elements it needed to appear pristine and justifiable, except . . . something about his answers, something far below their surface didn't feel right.

I wanted to believe him. I fought with myself to believe him. I had spent years convincing myself that what we had shared was real and that I could believe and trust what he said, especially when he talked about how often he thought about Matt. "How can I not think about Matthew, Kelly, especially when there's only three months separating him from my other son?"

With one hand I held the phone while the other traced the curl of the cord up and down, uncertainty tormenting me. I didn't know what to say. His answers were everything I had ever wanted to hear and his words sounded so right. Yet I couldn't escape feeling trapped—caught between what he was saying and the reality his absence declared. Deep inside I couldn't make sense of it. Somehow, somewhere it all felt so disconnected.

Silence engulfed me as I mentally assessed the worth behind the weight of his words. I had always wanted to believe the best about him—that he truly was who I always believed him to be. But listening to him now, for the first time I was no longer certain. *I've always given him the benefit of the doubt; I've never been willing to see him for anything but who and what I remembered. Perhaps because it was the only way to keep from walking in judgment toward him . . .* I pondered. But now . . . now that I had come face to face or phone to phone with my phantom tormentor, I felt my adolescent gullibility start to finally fall off.

For the first time I could remember, I realized that seeing someone for who and what they really are doesn't necessarily mean I haven't forgiven them or that I'm walking in judgment toward them. On the contrary, forgiveness most often begins with acceptance and acceptance is always rooted in authenticity. Nothing can truly happen apart from seeing things as they really are.

So there I stood in the dank air of northeast Ohio, confronted with the reality that despite all of his well-planned reasons and explanations of why he hadn't been there the past twelve years, once I hung up the phone and returned to Indianapolis, Randy was the one who would be waiting for me to come home. And Randy was the one who would be there every day without excuse or reason as to why he couldn't do this or who was preventing him from doing that. And, most important was the newly rediscovered truth that despite all of my inner reluctance, Randy was the one who had been and would continue to set the standard for Matthew, just as he would be there to enforce it. Then as if the proverbial light bulb got turned on I realized, *It always has been Randy.*

Closing my eyes, I chuckled at the simplicity of the revelation. *Is it really that easy, Lord? That all I ever needed to do was look at the fruit of each man's life?* I silently inquired as my inner man began the slow ascent back toward where I belonged. My mind continued to roam as I wondered if I would ever find a valid answer or explanation for what had happened twelve years ago. *Perhaps no matter how many different excuses he gives me, some things will always be left unanswerable and unjustifiable,* I considered as Control slowly loosened its grip.

Silence soothed me as I lost myself in these new discoveries while the voice on the other end of the phone rambled on. A new wave of courage washed over me and I found myself not only resistant but unwilling to be intimidated by the sound of his voice, "I am not seventeen years old anymore," my inner man whispered. Suddenly my more recent self began to reemerge as the darkness of the past twenty-four hours finally began to dissipate.

The revelation of Randy's faithfulness had somehow broken through the deception that had for so long shrouded my perception of things. For the first time I was seeing things as they really were, and I instinctively knew the time had come to hang up the phone. I *wanted* to hang up. The yellow ribbon was flanked across the finish line; I could see it and the sight of being so close to the end and finally putting all this behind me caused adrenaline to course through my veins, surging Courage to the surface. "I need to go," I blurted out, interrupting him mid-sentence.

"What? Why?" he asked. "I was hoping I could see you."

"No, I don't think so," I said, almost snickering. "It's been good . . . so good to talk to you, but it's time for me to go," I said definitively. *Funny, for the first time since I met him, I finally have control,* I thought. Standing there in the damp drizzle listening to him say the same things he used to say, I waved goodbye to the gullible seventeen-year-old teenage girl I used to be, realizing that I wasn't her any more than I was the impressionable woman who had placed the call just minutes ago. Revelation of truth had changed all that.

The person who existed in their place now was a woman who had, on whatever level, just experienced a new type of freedom—a freedom comprised of truth, dignity and honor. And one that included going home, being candid with my husband and praying that even this God in His mercy would be willing to work it all together for our good.

CHAPTER SEVEN

THE ACHE OF REGRET

*Or do you despise the riches of His goodness, forbearance,
and longsuffering, not knowing that
the goodness of God leads you to repentance?*
—Romans 2:4

With a fair amount of ease I placed last night's compromise on the shelf as my mother and I drove back to Indianapolis the next morning. Despite a shared track record of rehashing the weekend's events and discussing the various people we saw, I embraced the distraction that just listening to my mother's voice brought me. I wasn't emotionally prepared to actually hear myself articulate what I had done, at least not to her. I was still trying to find the words to tell Randy.

Not an hour into the drive I had already mentally scripted and rescripted my confession a hundred different ways. Blurting out things like "Hey, by the way, I made a phone call when I was home for the weekend" didn't exactly sound like the best approach. Just as "Thought I'd let you know I talked to him" seemed trite and heartless. Then back to listening to my mother until inevitably an infrequent vacuum of conversation space would invite my mind to wander anew, and like opening different doors, I would mentally rehearse any one of Randy's possible reactions. *If he says this then I'll say this or if he says this, I'll say this. But what do I say if he says this?*

Like a vicious cycle the mental wheels turned and spun until my brain hurt. Yet somehow after all the imaginary flips and turns subsided and the scenarios faded, the ride always brought me back to standing beneath the gaze of his eyes—eyes that have always emitted the deepest pools of compassion and grace. "How am I going to do this, Lord?" I silently asked, "How do I hurt him?"

New "whys?" began to taunt my soul: *Why did I fall so easily? . . . Why didn't I consider Randy more? . . . Why didn't I think this through?* Then as only my mind can do, its mental gears switched—rather than finding answers to those questions, I knew if I had any hope of overcoming this stronghold I had to get to its root, and that would only come from understanding the "why" behind my action. I looked over at my mom who seemed quite content driving in silence, then laid my head back on the headrest, closed my eyes and began asking the Lord, "What makes me still so vulnerable to him when I go back to Ohio, Lord? It's been over twelve years and still . . . Why does deception get me every time?"

Silence resounded in my spirit. No matter how long I rode in that passenger seat or how many questions I asked, silence was all I heard. I tried looking at things from every angle as if my circumstance was a prism of light with all of its different facets trying to get my attention. I didn't know what to look at first.

The only thing I did know was to start with what I had, so I focused on the most obvious facet—the unmistakable warnings of the past twenty-four hours. Even now I could feel the effect of dismissing the faint whisper of His still small voice pleading, *"Don't do this, Kelly."*

Regret immediately washed over me as I questioned, "Why didn't I listen, Lord? Things would have been so different." Then as if time was being rolled back even further, the hiddenness and the secretive strategy I had so cunningly mapped out in my head before I drove to dinner resurfaced as a deep well of nausea pooled in my stomach.

The depravity of my soul and its subsequent bent toward destruction gripped me. *I thought I had changed, Lord.* Reminders of the desperate seventeen-year-old I once was flashed through my mind—my gullibility, my blatant disregard, my complete lack of dignity—all of it just as real today as it was twelve years ago. Maybe not on the same level, but sitting in that car with nothing to do but contemplate the past twenty-four hours, I realized that when left to my own will and agenda, my actions still held catastrophic possibilities.

Like a slow fog lifting off a valley, my internal vision began to recognize the form and shape my hidden self took, which produced a guttural cry, "Why didn't I just tell someone?" I asked myself.

Miles away from all the turmoil, the thought sounded so simple. *But then, Lord . . . then I thought . . . I thought it was what I needed and I could justify it, especially if no one knew.* My heart sank even deeper, and as I remembered how unrelenting I had been to talk to him, my stomach convulsed. *Will I ever be rid of him? Will his grip ever go away?* An unexpected groan escaped.

"You okay?" my mom asked.

It took a split second for me to answer her with an indistinguishable "Mmhmm" rather than pretend like I was asleep. I sat up, took a deep inhale, and stretched my arms overhead before blowing the air out through my mouth. The passing green highway marker on the side of the road declared: INDIANAPOLIS 42 MILES.

"Almost home," I said.

"I know Matt has a baseball game today. Where am I taking you? Home or the ball diamond?" she asked.

"What time is it?"

"Just after 2 p.m." she answered.

I wonder if this is how astronauts feel during reentry. I glanced out the window and watched as the berm of the road sped by, thinking about the shift in my spirit that always occurred whenever I crossed the Ohio/Indiana state line—*Will I ever completely reconcile my life in Ohio with life in Indiana?* I wondered, the sheer thought exhausting.

I pictured Randy and the kids playing at the park as they waited for Matt's baseball game to begin, and once again wondered how I was ever going to tell him the truth.

"Are you sleeping again?" Mom asked, interrupting my mental meanderings.

Shaking my head no, I replied, "No, Mom, sorry. The park would be great. We can just transfer my stuff to Randy's car."

"And you're sure you're okay?" she continued, glancing at me with one eye up and her brow wrinkled.

I quickly shut my eyes, nodded my head yes and said, "Yeah, I'm just tired. Long weekend, ya know?"

She smiled a knowing smile then went on to talk about her time with my grandmother and how her health was still good even though she was beginning to show signs of slowing down. I quietly listened, glad to offer the appropriately timed "mmhmms" when necessary to keep the conversation flowing. It wasn't until my mother flipped her blinker on to indicate she would be pulling off the exit that I felt my heart beat faster and my stomach flip in its cavity.

"Stay calm, Kelly. Just stay calm," I repeatedly told myself as I wrapped my arms around my mid-section in a useless attempt to hold things together. I tried losing myself in the mindless chatter that filled the car as my mom drove the five minutes or so from the interstate exit to the park but it was useless. Somewhere along the way my heart had grown a will of its own and insisted on being heard while my stomach refused to quit its wrenching.

As we made our final approach back into reality, my eyes frantically skimmed the park searching for Randy. Maybe it was nerves, but after two or three quick scans across the horizon I still couldn't find him. Sitting up a bit straighter, I shifted my weight forward and watched as my mom turned the car into the last open spot, then waited before drumming up enough courage to lift my head and look out the windshield.

Seeing Randy leaning on the fence that stood in right field with Anna and Aaron playing nearby was all it took for the familiar sting of regret to once again invade my eyes. "Breaking his heart is the last thing I wanted to do," I told the Lord in hushed tones.

"What?" my mom asked.

"Nothing," I replied, shaking my head. "Do you mind getting my suitcase out of the trunk while I go get Randy's keys?"

I didn't wait for her answer. Instead, I choked down the torrent of emotions that were threatening to drown me, then reluctantly walked over to where Randy stood, laid my hand open and abruptly asked him, "Hey, can I have your keys?"

"Well, hello," he said as he turned and leaned down to kiss me.

I couldn't look at him; Shame forbade it. So I offered him my cheek instead, then wiggled my fingers, revealing my nervous hurried guard.

"I can get your things, Kel," he willingly offered.

"NO!" blurted out sharper than I intended, "I can get it."

As if my words had smacked him, he took a small step backward as his eyes grew involuntarily big with bewilderment. I immediately wanted to scream, "I'm sorry!! It's not you," but I didn't. Instead, I just stood there. And the next thing I heard was a tender but questioning utterance of, "Okay . . . ," as he reached into his pocket to grab his keys.

With a clenched hand, I spun around and started toward the car when suddenly Anna and Aaron came bounding around a tree, jumping and squealing, "Mommy! Mommy!"

I resisted the need to stop—the need to hold my children and draw strength from their presence—but I knew if I did I would never control the expanse of emotion that was currently contained inside. Settling for a tousle of their hair I chose to keep walking, dismissing them with, "Just a minute, I'll be right there."

My desperate desire for more time was suffocating me . . . *I need more time . . . I'm not ready.* I wasn't ready or able to return to life the way I had left it. How could I? I was still trying to come to terms with my recklessness. "How can I embrace what I left when that's the very thing I chose to disregard?" I asked myself.

Trembling, I sorted through the keys before finding the one that would unlock the trunk. With shaking fingers I inserted the key... *Breathe, Kelly,* I mentally reminded myself. Then in one fluid motion I took my suitcase from my mom, laid it next to everything else I had brought, slammed the trunk closed, then drew in a lungful of air.

Seconds passed before I had enough in me to turn and acknowledge my mother. Looking at her was in many ways like facing Randy for she always seemed to know when I was trying to hide something, despite my useless attempts to disguise my turmoil. Yet I couldn't escape what time demanded so when she looked at me and said, "Thank you for going home with me. I really appreciate it," all I could do was avert my eyes and nod in hopes that she wouldn't press me.

Hugging her, I replied, "You're welcome. I enjoyed the time with you."

"Kelly, there's one more thing," she continued. "I don't know what's going on but I'll trust you'll tell me when the time is right. Just know I'm here if you need to talk."

Standing with her arms wrapped around me, Regret consumed me for the third time that day. Everything in me wanted to vomit out all I had done so that I could be clean with someone. I would have given anything to shed my guilt and stand right there, enveloped in the warmth of my mother's security, and avoid the pain that was waiting to be inflicted. But I knew I couldn't; the awareness of life, the honor of commitment and the unyielding cry for wholeness had already invaded the moment.

I held on for a minute longer before finally letting go of my mother and all she represented to me, and after a fleeting glance offered her a quick thank you, walked her back to her car then watched her pull away.

I stood in my mother's former parking space for a long time, the shade of the elm tree dancing overhead, as I searched for the words for what I was about to do. *How does one show herself unfaithful to the one person who has never been anything but faithful?* I wondered.

I tried one final time to entertain the thought of not telling him, but realized that even if I didn't speak it, he would still sense something was amiss. *It's Randy, it's just how he is,* I thought. Besides, if I had learned anything through all this it was that hiddenness never serves any purpose other than granting the enemy access to our souls.

Once again, my mind reviewed all that had happened in the recent hours and I snickered as the irony of it all washed over me. *Isn't that something?* I reflected. It had been less than twenty-four hours since I had grasped the concept that there are just certain things in life that can't be justified or rationalized away—regardless of how good the reasoning sounded. Yet, there I stood, trying to do the exact same thing. Underneath the shade of that elm tree, my heart ached to find the one perfect explanation that would justify my decision to Randy; in the end, though, neither my decision nor the subsequent phone call was justifiable at all. Nothing I could say or offer Randy was going to make him feel better about what I had done. The reality was my heart had betrayed him. I had chosen me over us, and although the betrayal didn't last as long as the conversation, the truth was that in the midst of those few minutes my heart no longer belonged to Randy. I had stolen it back from him and made it mine only so I could lay it on the altar like a sacrifice being offered to the god of my past.

My knees buckled under the weight of the raw awareness that now poured over me—the wretchedness of self, completely revolting. For the second time in my life, I heard the voice from somewhere deep inside me cry out, "What have I done!?!" Then like a rolling fog I felt brokenness envelope me until all I could do was choke out, "Forgive me, Father, for I have sinned."

Weeping, I stood in the stark open space of the parking lot no longer able to hear the sounds of wooden bats striking their targets or the roars of beaming parents and grandparents as they cheered on their young men. Instead, amidst the noise and clamor, Silence had suddenly found me and all I could feel was the warmth of his presence saturate my spirit. "I'm so sorry," I told Him, letting Silence absorb the moment with me.

The Spirit of Repentance consumed every fiber of my soul as I stood and wept for what I had done and all that was to occur. I wept for losing sight of what really mattered and for believing Shame's deception.

But most of all I wept for the separation I caused in the spirit between Randy and me, and for the heartache I knew I had to inflict on him.

"I'm so sorry," I repeated over and over, and like a clog letting loose from a drain I embraced the familiar flow of the Spirit as the warmth of His presence settled all around me.

I'm not sure how long it took before I became aware of my surroundings again or for the rawness of emotions to subside. I do know that my return felt like a gentle let-down, as if someone had taken me airborne and was slowly putting my feet back on the ground. Life began to slowly reemerge in my soul and the awareness of my external circumstances gradually heightened, letting me know the time had come do what needed to be done. I wavered at the thought for just a moment before I pulled my sleeve out from my jacket, wiped my eyes clean, then took a few deep breaths before slowly turning to make my way back to Randy.

CHAPTER EIGHT

DISCLOSURE

Confess your trespasses to one another, and pray for one another, that you may be healed.
—James 5:16

It was the bottom of the fourth inning as I cautiously returned to my husband's side. With a subtle grin I quickly glanced up at him, then turned my eyes back toward the diamond. "How's it going?" I asked.

"Good," he said, "they're up 2-0. Matt got a single, then Eric knocked him in."

Mutual silence lingered in the air. Although I knew the source of the distance, I assumed he attributed it to my earlier behavior. I looked around for Anna and Aaron, ready to finally hold them when he said, "They're at the playground, on the swings."

"Oh," I mumbled, "Okay."

Shifting my weight from one leg to the other, I tried to find a comfortable stance but couldn't so I resorted to picking at a rust spot on the fence. I didn't know if Matt's team was at bat or had taken the field; I couldn't pay attention. I closed my eyes and silently willed for Randy to ask what was wrong, something to jumpstart me. I needed him to take the lead. Blood pulsed through me, being driven by the pounding of my heart as an awkward shiver ran up my spine.

Mindlessly I continued picking at the rust spot until nothing else seemed to loosen and lift, so I rubbed my fingers up and down on my jacket in an effort to not only brush them clean but rid myself of the strange chill that had seeped in.

"Cold, Kel?" he asked.

"Sort of," I replied, putting my hands in my pockets. I looked up at him, wanting to see his eyes. I needed to see if he could still penetrate the barrier I was stuck behind. He finally looked down at me and locked eyes, "What's going on?" he asked.

Where silence once lingered because of uncertainty, I now embraced it so I could prepare and strategize my approach. I looked down, unable to watch the pain my confession was going to inflict, and said, "Randy, I need to talk to you."

"Okay . . . " he responded half question-like and half bracing himself for something he sensed he wasn't going to like hearing.

"I wish I could tell you this weekend went great . . . but it didn't." I opened my mouth, hoping to force out my pent-up confession but closed it after a second thought. Turning back to the ball diamond, I ached to get lost in the joy of watching Matt, in its simplicity and innocence, but there was no silencing what needed to be said.

My body shifted, turning slightly to face him, "I really struggled this weekend, and I know I should have called you . . . but I didn't, and . . . I'm sorry" came tumbling out.

Compassion filled his voice, "It's okay, Kelly. I know being in Ohio isn't easy for you."

Dismissing his kindness I backed up and started again, "Thank you, but there's more."

The seriousness of my tone must have grabbed his attention because he immediately stepped back from leaning on the fence and stood straight up, looking at me with a shielded cast of confusion. "What do you mean?" he asked.

Silence surrounded us as I fought to find the gentlest words I could speak so they would fall on him as softly as possible.

"Did you see him?" Randy inquired with a tone I wasn't sure I had ever heard.

"NO! Oh, my God, no," I responded, shaking my head. *At least I didn't do that* flew through me. I watched the air leave his lungs and his head turn back to the distraction of the game. "But, I called him," I blurted out before losing my courage.

It wasn't the look on Randy's face that seared through my soul or the disappointment I knew was wrenching his heart. It was the depth of pain I saw in his eyes when he looked at me—the pain that only betrayal can inflict and the pain that feels like it will take a lifetime to forget.

He said nothing. He didn't have to; his eyes said it all.

I watched as a well of tears filled his eyes, then felt the sting of my own. "I'm sorry, Randy."

"Why?" he whispered, "Why did you have to?"

"A hundred reasons," I said as I shrugged my shoulders, "and they all felt so valid . . . until now."

His cheeks puffed out as the sound of his exhale wafted over the diamond. "I didn't see this one coming," he said as he rubbed the back of his neck.

"I know." I stepped closer to him, "I'm sorry," I said, leaning my forehead to rest on the outside of his shoulder.

For the first time since I had met him, Randy offered no physical or verbal response—no reassuring touch, not even a glance. He just stood there with his forearms leaning on the fence, eyes fixed straight ahead, seemingly watching the game. *What I would do to take it all back, Lord.* I closed my eyes and prayed. I prayed for Randy's heart and for the wound I had just caused, then told the Lord once again, "I'm so sorry."

Minutes passed before I lifted my head and took a similar stance next to Randy, and before long neither of us had any words. We may have been standing next to each other physically, but in the most important ways—emotionally and spiritually—there was a vast expanse of distance now separating us. The ease in which we had always functioned was gone, and I didn't know what to say or what to do other than give Time space to do its work.

The awkward silence that had joined us on the ball diamond proceeded to follow us to our post-game stint on the playground, but thankfully none of our children were either old enough or perceptive enough to sense the discord that now existed between their parents. Any more than they noticed the fleeting glances and repeated silent visual apologies that somehow helped to numb some of the ache in Randy's heart. And though we were both acutely aware of how absent our usual hand holding and light-hearted laughter were, the chatter of our three children continually reminded us how very much was at stake.

Leaving the playground that day there was little I could do to make right everything I had done wrong. Randy's pain was exactly that—Randy's—and the only thing I could do now was give him the space he needed and pray that despite my betrayal and subsequent crushing blow to our unity, he would ultimately find his way back to me and that not all had been lost.

CHAPTER NINE

WRESTLING MATCHES

*Therefore, my beloved, as you have always obeyed,
not as in my presence only, but now much more in my absence,
work out your own salvation with fear and trembling;
for it is God who works in you
both to will and to do for His good pleasure.*
—Philippians 2:12-14

The emotional damage inflicted by my recent compromise made the following days and weeks crawl by. My heart ached for the days when the ground Randy and I had walked on as a couple was smooth—with no cracks or fissures in the foundation. Even though I understood the reasoning behind the fractured trust in our relationship and tried to be as gracious with him as he had been with me throughout the years, the truth was I frequently battled growing impatient for healing to come and for things to be restored.

Giving Randy whatever room he needed to heal was initially relatively easy, perhaps because my willingness to give him space was proportional to my level of guilt, like equal weights on an invisible scale. A guilty conscience has a way of making me willing to do or give anything to make things right again—as if whatever I could offer would somehow make atonement for my sin. But as the hands of time circled the clock and the days turned into countless weeks, distance continued to define our relationship and frustration added to my guilt, effectively chipping away at any hope that things would ever be as easy or light as they used to be.

I struggled to bridge the emotional expanse that now existed between the two of us. I believed him when he said he forgave me and trusted that forgiveness wasn't at the root of our issue—at least not from Randy's perspective. He had gone above and beyond to reassure me of that, and he certainly never demonstrated any anger toward me. Rather, it was as if ever since that weekend, my compromise had somehow served to isolate me from any and all reassurance I had previously been able to draw from him.

From the beginning of our relationship Randy was the one who, no matter what, had always been able to stabilize my ground with one reassuring look or a silent squeeze of my hand. And when chaos and confusion threatened to pummel my soul, I knew all I had to do was find those piercing eyes and his silent reassurance would wash over me again, bringing with it an unmistakable peace. Yet ever since returning from Ohio it seemed like no matter how often I looked *at* him or *to* him, I was somehow immediately thrust back to that day at the ball diamond, looking into those eyes overflowing with hurt, confusion and disappointment.

His hurt I knew would heal—some through my repentance and some by his forgiveness. The confusion—that would dissipate over time through conversation and hearing each other's hearts. But it was the look of devastating disappointment that had flashed across Randy's face that I couldn't overcome no matter how much time had passed or how many apologies I uttered.

I knew I couldn't overcome it because it was the same look I saw etched on my mother's face when she returned to Ohio with my early pregnancy test so many years ago, and it was the same look reflected on my aunt and uncle's faces a weekend later when I told them my news. Those looks still haunted me years later. The only difference between their looks and Randy's was the amount of time that had transpired since experiencing them. Time alone was all Disappointment needed to imprint himself on my soul and make me constantly aware that I was nothing but a "sheer and total disappointment."

Disappointment is a defining look to someone who desperately craves man's approval. When you spend your whole life trying to make people happy or impress them with who you are or your ability to do things right, then their disappointment can have devastating ramifications. The least of which perpetually reminds you of exactly how far you have fallen, or worse yet, that you never measured up in the first place regardless of how hard you have tried.

The spiritual cloud of disappointment that had clung to me for years was now thicker and heavier than ever before. A whole new whirlwind of spiritual confusion swirled around me and no matter where I turned the cloud followed. Only this time it seemed like the people I had always been able to look to, my mother and Randy, were incapable of reaching into its darkness and pulling me from its engulfing vortex.

The whirlwind was maddening as its winds insisted on playing and replaying that weekend in Ohio, reminding me of my failure to win my battle against Shame and Fear. In the face of such defeat, I once again found myself resorting to my intellect to effectively recite all the right answers, but my spirit man couldn't get there. No matter what I knew to be right, the more I fought against the current's force the deeper I sank, creating an ever-increasing funnel of frustration—not only with myself but with God and His apparent unwillingness to heal me. Repeatedly I cried out to Him, "Lord, I don't want to feel this way anymore," or "Lord, search me and know me. You know how sorry I am."

Then when those prayers didn't heal my soul, I found myself on a spiritual treasure hunt reading everything that had to do with breaking soul ties and what the apostle Paul really meant when he said, *"Flee sexual immorality. Every sin that a man does is outside the body, but he who commits sexual immorality sins against his own body,"* (1 Corinthians 6:18).

I pursued and I fought, then I cried and I begged. I yearned for freedom from that which had entangled me for years, and while my quest taught me an immeasurable amount with regard to God's heart toward purity and wholeness, I still had yet to experience the life-changing freedom I had heard and believed was available in Christ.

The reality was twelve years later I was still walking around scarred from choices I had made as a young woman, and no matter how readily I acknowledged that "wounded people wound people," I was at a complete loss as to how to actually be healed. Only God Himself knows how often I had thrown myself at His feet begging Him to deliver me, to bind my broken heart and to make me whole, but in the end I remained fractured. With each uttered prayer that went unanswered, I saw with more clarity than ever before that not only were my wounds infected, they were now contaminating those closest to me.

Urgency became the motivator at hand. The more time that passed, the more intense my pursuit became. I would love to say it was done with the purest of hearts . . . it wasn't. Each day that ended with my plea left unanswered was like a can of gasoline fueling a fire; I grew increasingly antagonistic. Wondering if the blockage was on my end, I found myself in a similar position as the provisional moment in my kitchen years ago when we were waiting on God to "show up." Routinely I went through my mental checklist of spiritual so-called requirements: Self-reflection. . . check, repentance . . . check, request for restoration. . . check. "I've done everything I can . . . WHAT do You want, Lord?" I demanded. "What else must I do?" I was exasperated.

Again, silence was the only response.

In those moments I was frequently left wondering if my prayers had just merely clung to the ceiling. "He either isn't listening or He's just not going to answer," I told Silence. I wasn't sure which was worse. All I knew was that with everything in me I wanted freedom. Freedom from the sound of Shame's voice that replayed in my mind about what a disappointment I was, and freedom from the condemning voice that repeated, "I should have known better." I was tired—tired of remembering, tired of wondering and tired of wishing I were different. I was worn out.

Frankly, I didn't want to think about him anymore. Or Ohio. Or all the things that came along with all of that. All I really wanted was to live the life I had with Randy and to live it without guilt or condemnation.

Time marched on but failed to allow change to join the parade. Nearly six months separated Randy and me from the weekend that came to be known as *"That Weekend,"* and before I knew it we were approaching our second Christmas in the house God gave us.

My battle with Guilt and Shame became the impetus behind devouring anything I could get my hands on regarding Kingdom principles, restoration and God's redemption. Traces of healing became more apparent as the fractures in the ground that Randy and I walked on slowly became filled. Deeper accountability and transparency began to take root in our relationship, and the faith-based relationships we maintained in our community helped restore our sense of unity.

Thankfully the ongoing restoration of our relationship helped ease the weight of responsibility I felt with regard to hurting Randy, but nothing excavated the root of Shame that had established itself on the heels of my teenage decisions and grown as a result of my recent collective failures while in Ohio. There were days I wondered if I would ever be free from the stigma of it all. Similar to when the Lord brought me to terms with my teenage pregnancy, I found myself identifying once again with the woman in Mark 5:25-34—pressing against my own crowds, growing increasingly desperate to grab a hold of the hem of His garment—if only I could find it.

Shortly after the New Year, Lori, one of the two women I had become incredibly close to, asked me if I would be interested in attending a women's conference in Columbus, Ohio, with her. *"Humph, like that will do any good,"* Discouragement quickly countered. Stunned by my own disheartening response, my head shook as if to knock loose the unwanted voice.

"Is that a no?" she asked.

Confusion etched itself on my brow, effectively betraying what should have been a private emotion. It was as if I was having two different conversations—an internal one that was determined to keep me from considering the external.

"Focus, Kelly" I commanded myself.

My eyes shifted back and forth before fixing themselves on her mouth as if reading her lips would help silence the competing voices bouncing around in my head. A quick, involuntary, "Sure, I'll go," escaped before I could even formulate another thought. No foresight, no thought, and certainly no planning—just a blurted out consent to go. Lori's eyes lit up and a smile stretched across her face as I resisted listening to Discouragement's subtle retort, *"Great, now you've really done it."*

CHAPTER TEN

FIGHTING FOR FREEDOM

Faith is the gaze of a soul upon a saving God.
—A.W. Tozer

Unsure of what to do with the growing knot in my stomach, I waved goodbye as Lori and I pulled out of the driveway to head toward the conference in Ohio, Randy standing in the doorway with Aaron at his feet. I couldn't remember the last time I had even thought about entering a public place crowded with people whom I didn't know without Randy next to me. Yet here I was committed, buckled in intentionally traveling three hours to do that very thing.

Added to that inner unsettledness was the uncertainty that came with not knowing if Lori really understood exactly what she was dealing with when it came to subjecting me to unknown places with unfamiliar people. I had never shared that tormented side of me with her—I hadn't really shared it with anyone but Randy.

Fumbling for normalcy, I tried disguising my short gasps, evidence of my spiritual unrest, by filling the space with a hundred questions, only to lose focus seconds into Lori's answers. Instead my mental eyes drifted toward the familiar landscape . . . the highway markers . . . the various snippets of memories that always insisted on dancing in my head, like personal escorts whose assignment was to accompany me as I passed beneath the now infamous "Welcome to Ohio" iron blue archway.

How many times have I driven this route? I wondered. For the split second my mind went blank, my ears tuned briefly into Lori's answers, " . . . Judith MacNutt, the conference speaker, you know she's married to Frances MacNutt?" . . . then my usual fade out.

"You're always only halfway a part of something, do you know that?" accused the condemning voice in my head, "You're never fully anywhere."

I sat silent, trapped inside a mental labyrinth, wondering if such tormenting thoughts ran through other peoples' heads—or was I the only crazy one? I glanced over at Lori hoping for a mental reprieve, then as if I had surfaced for air, snapped back to present time and listened as she explained how MacNutt was married to a former Catholic priest and how they were co-laboring in ministry and were on the precipice of a new wave of a Holy Spirit movement.

"Hmmm. . . " I murmured, nodding my head. "This should prove to be interesting then, no?" I questioned.

Lori just smiled and said, "You know the prayer, right?" I quizzically looked at her until she continued, "Lord, I want whatever is of You, but if it isn't then guard my heart."

"Sounds simple enough," I replied, happy that we were on the final leg of the journey.

I found myself acting like human glue over the next two days as I stuck as close to Lori as humanly possible, the sea of countless unfamiliar faces breathing new life into my former awareness of self. It was as if each of their strange faces became some kind of mirror that illuminated everything I had always tried to hide about myself. Looking at them looking at me startled me inward as if I could hide or shield myself from the sudden sense of exposure, accelerating the frequency of my air intake as well as the rate at which my stomach fluttered.

Not that the women and their faces weren't friendly enough—they were, especially those we shared our daily meals with, and their tireless efforts to continually engage me in conversation never went unnoticed.

It was just easier to find peace within myself as I shared space with Silence. He was the only one who really knew how much courage was required to enter the banqueting room with all those strangers, let alone actually talk with someone. Of *that,* I wasn't capable.

So sit there I did, spiritually immobilize and void. Any tangible hope that God had heard my previous cries for help had eroded away over the past months and whatever emotional energy carried me to the conference was all but depleted after days of having to face so many people I didn't know. I had nothing to offer and nowhere to go; all I really wanted to do was drive back home and find refuge in my own home surrounded by people I knew, then flog myself for having committed to actually attend this thing. "What am I doing here?" I asked myself, looking down at my watch. "One more session and we're out of here. Thank God," the inner sarcasm undeniable.

I leaned back in my seat and took a mental account of all the women in the room, *I wonder what brings them here. What are their stories?* My eyes bounced from table to table and like a sponge I couldn't help but access the various women engaged in conversation—some serious, some lighthearted—until my conscious self dropped back in to eavesdrop on the dialogue at my own table. I listened as each woman took turns sharing details about their lives and their individual journeys, quickly realizing that none of them sounded like mine. *They've all done it the right way,* I thought. *Married first then children, and here I am one of the youngest at the table, yet I have the oldest child of all.* Everything in me wanted the women to keep talking so I didn't have to share; I didn't want to have to explain everything. History indicated that as soon as I shared the ages of my children, at least one of the women would look at me and say, "Oh my, you don't look old enough to have a child that age," to which I knew I should just smile and say, "Thank you," but I never could. Something inside always felt the need to either agree and say, "I'm not," or explain—anything to dispel those curious stares people always felt the need to give me.

My heart started racing and my palms instantly grew moist as I willed the clock to tick faster. "Please, please don't make me share, Lord," I whispered to myself, "just let them keep talking."

I looked around for the bathroom but didn't want to be rude and send the unintended message that I wasn't interested. I just wanted out and away from the mounting pressure my insides were feeling. It was as if I was in the cabin of an airplane that had just depressurized, and without warning my survival instincts had gone on high alert. My gasping deepened as I strained to take in air. *I can't do this . . . not now.*

As discreetly as possible I slid my chair back and gathered my things as the women kept talking, then slowly stood up, sure that my wobbly legs would give way beneath me. A bead of sweat rolled down the middle of my back as I forced a smile to those looking at me, then mouthed, "I'm sorry," and silently slunk away, assuming that every set of eyes in the room was watching me.

Just about the time my hand went to push the ladies' room door open, I heard the conference organizer announce that we had fifteen minutes before the next session. I briefly closed my eyes as I entered the restroom and offered a silent thank you that I had gotten out just in time. "From here on it'll be smooth sailing," I told Silence as I patted a cool, damp towel across my forehead. "We're almost done."

Recollected and externally composed, I took my cynical self and sat in the seat next to Lori just as Judith McNutt took the stage for the last time and announced, "Tonight, we're going to be talking about forgiveness." Immediately Sarcasm's mocking voice shouted in my head, "REALLY? Of course, they are. But you already know about God's forgiveness, so you won't have to listen."

Fidgeting with my things, I thought twice about disclosing my inner disrespect before finally sitting back, fully intending on doodling away my disinterest, when just as I started to mentally check out Judith continues, "But not the kind of forgiveness we receive from God. Rather tonight we *are* going to talk about forgiveness, just not His. No, tonight we're going to talk about forgiving ourselves."

A silent exhale preceded my undivided attention.

It's not that I took God's forgiveness lightly; I didn't and I don't. . . not at all. But there was something about the way she said what she said about forgiving ourselves that struck the center of my soul that captured my attention.

Judith MacNutt started her delivery that night by speaking about Rahab, the prostitute who helped save the spies (Joshua 2:1-21), then about Saul who before his conversion to Paul was one of the chief persecutors of the first century church (Acts 8:1-3). I listened intently as she taught about how each of these characters had a life before encountering God and how both of their lives needed to be redeemed and forgiven. But it wasn't until I heard her explain that " . . . for most of us, healing is a process that includes the need to forgive ourselves" that caused me to sit up straight and truly focus.

I marinated on that truth for quite awhile as she went on teaching, adding that principle to all the previous material the Lord had put in my hands over the past year. Like pieces to a puzzle being assembled, His overall revelation was beginning to somehow make sense, as if I was learning how to differentiate the edge pieces from the center ones and put them in their proper position. Leaning back in the chair, I blew out a small puff of air as all those months and months of heart-wrenching moments with the Lord began to interlock and weave together, creating definitive lines and casting out blurred hues of color.

Lost in thought and internally scanning my spiritual state, I wasn't sure how to reconcile everything McNutt had taught with everything He was showing me; I just knew it was truth. *"Now what, Lord?"* I asked, tapping my pen rhythmically on my notepad. The brush of Judith's arm against her microphone swooshed over the P.A. system as she moved to close her Bible, drawing my attention upward.

"So, I need you to understand how this usually works. I'm going to pray and ask the Holy Spirit to come, bringing with Him a spirit of revelation and wisdom. Then I'm going to ask you something and I want you to remember that most often your answer is the first thing you think of—there's no need to go on a spiritual excursion." Then she went silent, allowing those instructions to permeate the atmosphere.

"Bow your heads with me, please," she invited.

Closing my eyes, I did as she asked and instantly recognized the tingling that courses up and down my spine whenever He is near. Then, like immediate aftershocks, doubts of God's faithfulness sent lasers through my soul. *What if You haven't heard my heart? Or worse yet, what if You have heard me and don't answer? Then where am I supposed to go?*

The fear of Him not being there threatened to suffocate me and squelch my resolve when suddenly a story from scripture came to mind. Jesus, having given a hard teaching, watched as most everybody departed, then turned to the twelve and asked, *"You do not want to leave too, do you?"* And Peter replied, *"Lord, to whom would we go? You alone have the words of eternal life"* (John 6:66-68).

Instantly I knew: *This moment is it for me—regardless of what happens tonight. I don't have anywhere else to turn but You, Lord. You're it for me. No one else has what I need. You're the one thing, the only thing that makes sense to me.*

Upon that realization my heart began to still and once again, I breathed in His presence, willing myself to focus on what I knew about God's goodness. For the first time that weekend I didn't hear any other voices—no chaos or confusion—just a sweet silence that had an ethereal peace about it, as if no other voices were allowed to speak. So I breathed even deeper and relaxed in His presence.

Silence remained in the atmosphere until quietly Judith said, "Now, Lord, if anyone here has an area in her life where she hasn't forgiven herself, please show it to her," then a pause, and I knew the answer before she even asked the next question, "What sin haven't you forgiven yourself for?"

Instantly Regret consumed me, and I felt seventeen all over again as waves of shame crashed over me with an unrelenting force. "YOU SHOULD HAVE KNOWN BETTER!!!" resounded in my ears drowning out everything else but Shame screaming "WHAT WAS WRONG WITH YOU?"

The memory of who I had become was contemptible. I hung my head lower than ever before, desperate to melt into my surroundings. I wanted to run—I didn't want anyone to see me. The memories of who I was were too ugly.

Everything in me was screaming, "RUN! GET OUT OF HERE!!" The pain too intense. Yet my limbs couldn't move, paralyzed, I was frozen in place. My shoulders slouched in despair as I whispered, "It's hopeless; I can't go back. I can't fix what I willingly broke, Lord."

A second later I internally saw myself standing in the backyard of our former house—the one I believed I couldn't live without and the one that came to represent our "Egypt"—and felt the gentle breeze of His presence blow across my face.

Afraid of what I might see, my gaze slowly lifted, then landed on Him who stood just on the other side of the mini-creek that bordered the edge of our property. With a deep inhale I tried to steady myself, unsure of what was happening or of what to do. My legs teetering beneath me, my heart began to wildly beat, caught between my desire to look at Him and a keen awareness that I wasn't ready for Him to see me like this—unclean with my brokenness hidden in my hands that were clutched behind my back.

The sense of His presence lingered as I stood there fidgeting, shifting my weight back and forth, willing myself enough courage to lift my gaze toward His. Time lingered but finally my eyes fluttered upward enough to see His hand waving a silent invitation to join Him as He gently beckoned me, *"Come here."*

My first instinct was to run to Him—His gentleness and kindness were like a magnet—and those eyes, they beheld such love it seemed as if Mercy himself swam in them. My weight shifted forward as if without instruction my feet wanted to propel me toward Him, but then I remembered my clenched hands and the brokenness they held that was hidden behind my back, and I retreated, my head violently shaking, answering Him with a silent "NO!"

He took a small step forward, His hand waving me over once again, wooing me with another, *"Come here,"* a bit more insistent but gentle nonetheless. Again my head whipped back and forth as my hands squeezed themselves tighter still in an effort to further hide my brokenness . . . then the tears . . . the countless and endless and uncontrollable sobs of Regret and Remorse that always came whenever and wherever my past was concerned.

Trembling I stood there, exposed and shaken by the rawness of the moment, wanting desperately to find something to cover myself with, but unable to move. The only thing I had power over was the force in which my hands held and hid my brokenness. So I just stood there, my hands clenched tight behind my back, and continued to weep as my head dropped and a cavern of pent-up shame rose to the surface.

Memories of wanting to be a good girl and staying committed to my "No" were the first to appear, followed by the gradual justification of his marital status, which gave way to pushing limits until physical lines were ultimately crossed. *I ignored so many warning signs.* My hands clenched tighter as fragmented glimpses of pointing fingers and hushed whispers filled my head, then came the disapproving looks and the wayward glances of disappointment that I knew everyone felt but no one ever said.

Each of them danced across my mental screen like a well rehearsed and choreographed performance accompanied only by the repeated message, "You really should have known better, Kelly. What did you think would happen?"

My body shuddered as the images tore through my soul.

Silence lingered for just a moment longer as I stood shaken to my core before I heard Love speak with a sound that paralleled the look in His eyes when He said for the third and final time, *"Come here."*

I wish I could say it was obedience that willed me to stand before the Lord . . . it wasn't. Beyond His great love I'm not exactly sure what transported me there; I just know that without a single thought or effort on my part, I was now standing directly in front of Him with a downcast head and my clenched hands securely behind me so He couldn't see what was in them.

I didn't want Him to see what had become of what I had done in Ohio. I didn't want to show Him the endless shame and regret I had carried for so long, any more than I wanted Him to see how stupid I had been or how much of a disappointment I was to everyone. Those things had been so deeply tucked away for so long it hurt to take them back out, so I kept them hidden behind my back like a little girl trying to hide the pieces of what she had broken. I didn't want Him to see what a mess I had really made of things.

But then the ever-so-gentle nudge came. "Show me," He whispered.

I wanted to holler, "NO... NOT YOU—PLEASE DON'T MAKE ME SHOW *YOU*," but no words came, just weeping and a subtle shake of my head. Again, with each repeated request His voice strengthened and His authority increased until I knew this was the moment when I either chose to comply or walk away forever wounded and unhealed. So great is His love, the freedom to choose was mine.

Then it happened. My resolve to hide weakened until effortlessly my hands came forward, and as they did, all the brokenness of my life fell at His feet as I fell onto Him. I felt the weight that I had carried for so very long lift as it shifted onto His shoulders. It was no longer mine to bear—and as His arms enveloped me I heard Him whisper, "Give it to me."

One encounter of His grace brought me to the end of myself, and a new wave of weeping came from places I didn't even know existed. I clung to Him and He to me, and the deeper I moved in repentance the more He repeated, *"I know... I know... I know."*

His voice never held any judgment or condemnation, and despite my assumptions I never heard, "I told you so" or any other corrective comment. Instead, there was just an overwhelming awareness of how intimately aware He was of my sorrow and how willing He was to take it from me. There was no punishment nor correction, just His innate understanding of how completely and totally sorry I was for *everything* I had done.

In that brief moment I discovered that nothing else mattered—not what I had done, not even who I was—just Him and the way He felt about me. He was there, and then gradually His presence lifted and it was over. Like a slow waking up from a dream, things began to slowly fall back in place and I could feel myself return to the auditorium where it had all begun.

Gone was the internal striving and discontent—Peace now resided there. I reveled in the revelation that from this moment forward I would never be the same, if for no other reason than the King of Kings, the One who had every right to condemn me for all I had done, had just done the opposite.

I shifted my way to the edge of my seat and began to gently rock back and forth trying to absorb all I had just experienced, when the next thing I heard Judith say was, "Now, Lord, turn their mourning into dancing. . . their tears into laughter."

That's when joy started to bubble up as I thought about how it felt to stand there with Him, naked and unashamed yet clean. Instantly the reality hit me that it took one encounter . . . one encounter for everything that I had wrestled with for years to be gone.

For the first time in nearly thirteen years I knew I was free. *I'M FREE!!* I thought hesitantly, looking around as if I would find the shackles I had carried in with me. I looked at Lori, swollen eyes and piles of tissues evidence of my repentance, and began to laugh. I laughed because I was free and I laughed because it was over. The enemy had been defeated and I was free to dance, free to love and finally free to discover who I was apart from that seventeen-year-old broken girl.

No longer was Shame a part of my identity. The Son had taken all that, and in Shame's place the healing love of the Father now resided. I was His and He was mine, so after thirteen years and some odd months, I threw my head back and laughed! I laughed for the years I held regret, and I laughed for the endless sorrow that had once accompanied me. I laughed because I knew the Father's joy had permeated my soul. Finally, I laughed because for the first time I didn't just believe, I *knew* what Jesus meant when He said, *"If the Son makes you free, you are free indeed"* (John 8:36).

CHAPTER ELEVEN

WALKING IT OUT

*For godly sorrow produces repentance leading to salvation,
not to be regretted;
but the sorrow of the world produces death.*
—1 Corinthians 7:10

The following morning as Lori and I returned home from the conference, it grew increasingly challenging to keep our feet on the ground. Borderline giddy with excitement over all we had experienced with the Lord, we soon discovered that the more we talked the more we interrupted each other with ecstatic, "Oh, I know then when this happened, it blew my mind!" or "What did you think about this?" We were both so enthralled and awed by everything He had shown us and all that had happened, it was difficult to know or understand how much time it would take before we would actually sort everything out and put things in their rightful place.

I was so engrossed in our conversation and the lingering effects of His healing that for the first time in over fifteen years there were no mental goodbyes uttered as we crossed the state border back into Indiana. My only cognitive thought was figuring out exactly how to explain to Randy all that had happened. *Where do I even begin?* I reflected. *How do I explain what it was like when He lifted the weight of my sin from me and bore it upon Himself,* I wondered. *How do I even give it justice, Lord?*

Three hours after leaving the hotel in Columbus, Lori made the final right-hand turn into my driveway, then let the car idle as we both sat there, neither of us fully ready to step out of what we had just experienced. The atmosphere still felt electrically charged even though we were hours and miles away from the source of the current.

Minutes ticked by on the digital readout before I felt the squeeze of Lori's hand, both cognizant that something fairly substantial had been accomplished spiritually even if we didn't fully understand what it would take to walk it out. Squeezing her hand in return, I cocked my head to the left and grinned. "Thank you," I whispered as Freedom's tears stung my eyes, "Thank you so much . . . " She just smiled as only Lori can, and I knew without a spoken word that she understood what a landmark weekend we had shared. I gave her one last cock-eyed grin, grabbed a quick breath, collected my things then hugged her goodbye.

A split second of hesitation greeted me just before I opened our front door. *Oh, please let him see what You've done . . . let the lightness in my step be visible, let the fruit of our encounter be that evident.* Everything in me yearned to hear Randy say, "You're different," then ask me, "What happened?" giving me the springboard for our conversation. *Maybe then things won't get lost in translation,* I silently wished.

Replays of all the different ways I had mentally rehearsed to effectively capture or relay the inherent sacredness so vital to understanding last night's encounter skipped through my mind as I turned the door handle. Without having been there I wasn't sure if anyone would believe or even relate to the spiritual authenticity of the moment—instinctively I knew that it was so fresh and vivid to me because I was the one who had experienced it. "But how do I convey it, Lord? How do I do it justice?"

Standing there lost in the midst of strategizing what to say or how to say it, I realized how unprepared I really was when I heard Randy's footsteps ascend the basement stairs. Our initial greeting was flawless, his excitement to have me home evident, yet I found myself stammering and stuttering my way through the recounting of the past twenty-four hours. I'm not sure why describing my life-changing encounter sounded so much better in my head than what I heard myself actually saying to Randy, but I began to realize it didn't really matter what words or phrases I used to try to encapsulate both the heart of the moment and the work God had done—everything fell abysmally short.

Then came the inner assaults and mental accusations, initially directed at me, about my ability to articulate or accurately convey what had transpired. These then gave way to questioning whether things were as real as I remembered. That's when the assault reloaded and redirected itself toward Randy as various renditions of why he couldn't grasp what I was saying, until I had to fight the urge to blurt out, "Just forget it!" I was frustrated, unusually tongue-tied and discovering with each uttered word that the more I tried to articulate all that had happened, the more awkward things became.

The weight of Doubt's presence pressed down on my spirit like a rude child wanting to interrupt a conversation. Listening to myself tell Randy about standing in the backyard with clenched hands, then struggling to explain how real it felt when He repeatedly said, *"I know,"* somehow felt awkward and heavy-laden—vastly different than anything I had anticipated. No matter how I tried, my narration of the moment felt lifeless, as if it was all merely a dream, the facts of which I couldn't quite pin down. Finally I began to wonder, *If last night's events don't feel real even to me, then how can I expect Randy to believe them?*

One by one, Doubt's questions, like little heat-seeking missiles crafted with sharply pointed heads, began to pierce through me as if they had locked onto their pre-assigned target with the intent of destroying my newly erected structures of faith. At first the freshness of my memory acted like a barricade against the assault, but then Skepticism joined Doubt in the attack, casting sinister shadows on the clarity of my recollection, making me even more uncertain about what I had *really* experienced.

Battling to continue my conversation with Randy, I tried to deny the inroads Doubt and Skepticism were having on my recall but clearly their doubtful inquiries had done their damage. My former excitement over the weekend's transformation quickly ebbed in the light of such second-guessing, initiating a slow retreat both spiritually and conversationally.

    I don't know if Randy sensed my inner turmoil or not, but as the kids' energy began to consume the house our conversation had no choice but to gradually subside, giving us both the much needed time to process. Too much had transpired in the past twenty-four hours to understand or absorb it all in one brief conversation so I reentered family life choosing to believe that regardless of whether I remembered every fact correctly, *something* had happened. On some level it was obvious that I, like Peter, James and John, had had some type of mountaintop experience (Matthew 17:1-8). What I failed to think of or remember at the time however was that I, like my predecessors, would soon be required to come off the mountain and learn how to live in the demon-possessed valley.

CHAPTER TWELVE

LONGING FOR THE HIGH PLACES

When you continue your journey there may be much mist and cloud. Perhaps it may even seem as though everything you have seen here of the high places was just a dream, or the work of your own imagination . . . But you have seen reality, and the mist which seems to swallow it up is the illusion. Believe steadfastly in what you have seen. Even if the way up to the high places appears to be obscured and you are led to doubt whether you are following the right path, remember the promise, "Thine ears shall hear a word behind thee, saying, 'This is the way, walk ye in it, when ye turn to the right hand and when ye turn to the left.'" Always go forward along the path of obedience as far as you know it until I intervene, even if it seems to be leading you where you fear I could never mean you to go.
—Hannah Hunard
Hinds' Feet on High Places

The valley. A land that sits low, hedged in by hills or mountains that author Hannah Hunard calls the "high places" . . . the places where the Good Shepherd dwells . . . the places that reside above all our circumstances. Yet it's the valley that we're called to live in and it's the valley that can present us with our most difficult days—the days that challenge our faith and make us question if what we believe is really true. So we look back up to the mountains in hopes of remembering what we experienced and when all we see are clouds that shroud their peaks in mist and blur their majesty, we forget how real it all was. Our frailty emerges and what we once believed to be vibrant and true transforms into something now blurry and unclear.

So it was during the days and weeks that followed the conference. Although I desperately tried to hold on to the freedom I experienced while on the mountain, little by little the vibrancy of my encounter began to wane and I grew increasingly aware of how the co-conspirators, Guilt and Shame, were lurking in the shadows of the valley trying to find a way to re-enslave their previous captive.

Everything in me wanted to hold my ground and believe what I had experienced was just as real and true as if I had encountered a tangible person who had actually paid my debts for me. Perhaps I fought so hard because something told me that if my encounter wasn't real, then the freedom that came from the encounter wasn't real either, and I couldn't bear the thought of that possibility.

Despite my reluctance time passed, taking with it the sights and sounds of my encounter with the Lord until it was nothing more than a distant memory. In the absence of its vibrancy, a driving need to understand and hold onto what had happened grew, thrusting me deeper into His word than ever before—something about understanding His ways helped me to better understand *Him*. And even though I couldn't explain it I believed that if I could understand and be able to explain the hows and whys behind what He had taken me through, somehow what He had done at the conference would be validated and secured. If I couldn't make sense of things I knew I would never overcome Doubt and the disbelief he continued to cast over the experience.

Life then was like a spiritual treasure hunt—an altogether different kind of quest than any I had ever been on before. The experience at the conference was a line of demarcation in a sense, and though nothing in my life's natural circumstances had changed, everything deep within my spirit was different. Weeks after the conference I still felt light, as if I was walking underneath an altogether different type of yoke. Even amidst Doubt's persistent shadow of uncertainty, there was a new sense of confidence that *something* had shifted, even if I couldn't articulate what.

Scriptures were the first place I turned until a few weeks later when someone handed me Frances Frangipane's *Holiness, Truth and the Presence of God*, which revolutionized my understanding of what authentic faith looked like and how encounters with God are truly essential to a genuine walk of faith.

Frangipane's insight challenged my previous understanding of who God was, but even more than that it transformed how I related to Him. For the first time I found myself having a conversation with the page, highlighting and writing personal scripted notes throughout the first seventy-plus pages of his book. Then when I read,

> There is a difference between seeking answers and seeking the Lord. There is a difference between second-hand book knowledge and a first-hand encounter with the Living One. God must become as real, as full and as all-consuming to us as the world was when we were sinners. [p. 79]

Immediately Frangipane's words answered and dispelled the first round of Doubt's questions. Encountering the Lord in such a mysterious way was becoming less far-fetched of a memory than I had recently considered so I continued to explore Frangipane's treasure chest of truth until the Lord, fanning my desire to understand spiritual process, moved me toward the next trove of discovery.

While the Lord used Frangipane's writing as a means to create a foundation for understanding the scriptural basis and necessity for encounters, He used Hannah Hurnard's classic allegory, *Hinds' Feet on High Places*, to give me a language and to teach me that whether people recognize it or not, our hearts are created to desire encounter.

Their writings became navigational points in my quest for spiritual understanding. Like markers on a road I returned to them over and over, needing to find the deeper and more profound truths of the Kingdom. I read and reread, constructing my own conversations with their pages as the Father used each of their writings to invite me further into His heart. Slowly I began to understand that although I may have encountered Him at the conference, I didn't truly *know* Him. It wasn't until I spent time in His presence alongside Frangipane and Hurnard's Much-Afraid that I discovered the deepest part of my own healing hadn't really occurred until long after my encounter with the Good Shepherd.

That was the first time I considered the idea that healing—true healing—doesn't come because we read about Him on a page or repeatedly recite the right scriptures. On the contrary, if we truly desire to be transformed then we must become like Much-Afraid—someone who so desperately longs to be in the presence of the Good Shepherd that we'll let go of everything we once deemed valuable so that we can come into His presence with our hands wide open—only then, in the midst of surrender, are we truly healed.

I marinated on that jewel for a long time, trying to absorb the complexity of it all. Then one morning, long before anyone else in our home was awake, I sat down in the warmth of the early summer sun with a cup of coffee in my hand and reached for my Bible. The feel of the room's atmosphere was somehow different than it had been in recent weeks; it was as if when I closed my eyes I could feel the warmth of His presence inviting me in to join Him. I took a deep breath, centering myself on Him, then asked if He would speak to me through His word. I skimmed a couple of different devotionals, silently hoping one of them would draw my attention, then relaxed and decided to just wait on Him.

Considering a reading plan someone had told me about recently, I remembered it was June 21 so I flipped back into the Old Testament and fanned the opaque pages searching for Psalm 21 to match the date. Anticipating the catch in my spirit when He spoke, I read the entire chapter rather quickly, then contemplated what King David really meant when he spoke of the joy that comes from the salvation of the LORD. *Do I know joy, Lord, or am I just happy?* I wondered.

Interpreting His silence to mean this isn't where I was to stop and rest for the day, I quickly added thirty to the previous twenty-one per the reading plan, thus taking me to Psalm 51:

Have mercy upon me, O God,
According to your lovingkindness;
According to the multitude of your tender mercies,
Blot out my transgressions.
Wash me thoroughly from my iniquity,
And cleanse me from my sin.
For I acknowledge my transgressions,
And my sin is always before me.
Against you, you only, have I sinned,
And done this evil in your sight—
That you may be found just when you speak,
And blameless when you judge.
Behold, I was brought forth in iniquity,
And in sin my mother conceived me.
Behold, you desire truth in the inward parts,
And in the hidden part you will make me to know wisdom.

Purge me with hyssop, and I shall be clean;
Wash me, and I shall be whiter than snow.
Make me hear joy and gladness,
    That the bones you have broken may rejoice.
Hide your face from my sins,
    And blot out all my iniquities.

Create in me a clean heart, O God,
    And renew a steadfast spirit within me.
Do not cast me away from your presence,
    And do not take your Holy Spirit from me.

Restore to me the joy of your salvation,
  And uphold me by your generous Spirit.
Then I will teach transgressors your ways,
  And sinners shall be converted to you.

Deliver me from the guilt of bloodshed, O God,
  The God of my salvation,
  And my tongue shall sing aloud of your righteousness.
O Lord, open my lips,
  And my mouth shall show forth your praise.
For you do not desire sacrifice, or else I would give it;
  You do not delight in burnt offering.
The sacrifices of God are a broken spirit,
  A broken and a contrite heart—
  These, O God, You will not despise.

The space just up and beneath my rib cage fluttered in response. "This is it, Silence. This is my heart," I whispered, "This—this is how I have felt this whole time." Without reading it twice I knew therein those lines of prose lay everything I ever knew to be true about me and, most important, about Him—from my pleas for mercy to my need to be washed clean to finally the " . . . broken and contrite heart—These, O God, You will not despise."

I could count the years I had spent feeling filthy inside, as if my choices—each one of them—had indelibly tattooed my soul, and no matter what kind of normalcy I tried to create or hide behind within my family life, I couldn't eradicate their stain. They were always there—hidden reminders of what I had done and how far I had fallen.

The image of standing before Him with my sin laid wide open reappeared as the psalmist's words in verse three leapt off the page, "For I acknowledge my transgressions and my sin is always before me." The memory of standing before Him and fighting against the relentless need to run and hide washed over me. Then came the reminder of how I felt when He said, "Give it to me," and sin's weight shifted from me onto Him. Like discovering another jewel in the treasure chest, I realized that if we're to experience healing then we're going to be required to get real with God—gut-wrenchingly real and transparent about what we have done and how we feel, for those are the things the psalmist refers to when he says, "Against you, you only, have I sinned."

Like fresh water on parched ground His truth washed over me all over again. Reminders of my cupped hands filled my mental eye. *I wanted so badly for You not to see, but not letting You see was the very thing that kept me from You*—like an invisible barrier of pride, so long as I tried to appear clean I remained stained. Being cleansed with hyssop only came when I finally opened my hands and became spiritually vulnerable before Him. *You had to have access to every part of me, didn't You?* I silently asked Him. *Only then were You able to clean me, restore me and make me whiter than snow.*

I sat back and reflected on how heavy the burden was that I had carried, then marveled at how entirely different I felt the instant Jesus took it from me. Instinctively I knew I would no longer wrestle with doubt about what He had done that weekend for I now knew He had created in me a clean heart and renewed a steadfast spirit within me, just like His word promised.

Leaning back, I curled my knees underneath me and slowly closed my eyes as I breathed in the intimacy of the moment and wondered what I cherished more—His healing or His word. He had breathed life on Psalm 51 and because of that I now had something tangible to stand on. He had used His word to speak life into me and grant me understanding. "Who are You, God . . . really . . . that You love us so much You would set us free with nothing in return?"

I breathed deep, not really expecting an answer. He was too big to even comprehend. So I laid my head back on the couch, closed my eyes and whispered, "It's good, Silence. Soooo, so good," I whispered. "It feels so good to be clean," then sat in silence as I savored the presence of His peace and basked in His goodness.

CHAPTER THIRTEEN

A Maverick Mentality

It is a terrible thing to see and have no vision.
—Helen Keller

With Guilt and Shame no longer distorting my view, the world appeared more vivid than it had in quite a long time, as if layers of grime and soot had been wiped from a window and the sun's rays were free to dance through the panes, casting things in a whole new light. Empowered with a new perspective, I found life didn't seem quite as hindered as before, and I discovered myself walking in levels of courage and strength I had not previously known.

My shadow didn't frighten me as much as it once had, and although Fear still insisted on occasionally tormenting me, my ongoing incentive and determination was drawn from my children who were growing older at a rate I wasn't fully prepared for and most often didn't even want.

The most obvious surge of growth occurred in Matthew, who at nearly thirteen was now taller than I and excited about starting the eighth grade. For a hundred reasons I was proud of him, but never far from my pride was the ever-growing awareness that we had already spent the majority of our time together. The fleeting days were more than recognizable, and now that I had less time with him than what had already been shared, time seemed to pass by even faster despite my futile efforts to slow it down.

But time has a will and mind of its own and the only thing I had any control over was the choice to embrace the moments of my children's self-discovery. It blessed me to watch Matthew explore who he was apart from Randy and me, especially when it came to seeing his faith mature and become his own. As an athlete, he immersed himself in the huddles sponsored by the Fellowship of Christian Athletes (FCA) and had developed a sweet mentoring/accountability relationship with one of his junior high teachers and huddle leader.

True to how he was as a little boy, Matthew's heart for God remained a driving force in his life. Packed away papers from his elementary years with Jesus' name doodled across the top or Calvary's cross sketched on the side had revealed a unique interest for the things of the Kingdom. And though we didn't have full understanding as to exactly what we were dealing with, we knew enough to recognize the responsibility his spiritual passion presented to us; we had the option of either feeding it or letting it die out naturally due to starvation of the soul.

As a family we were avid churchgoers, and although we had never truly ascribed to nightly devotions or any kind of a structured, refined pursuit of the Lord, we undoubtedly had been given some kind of an inexplicable faith. From the onset of God establishing us, our collective pursuit was motivated by the belief that whatever was happening in the natural world is most often a reflection of what is happening in the spiritual one. In other words, our faith flourished because we had been given an unquenchable desire to discover and understand God's heart in the midst of our natural circumstances.

It wasn't that church life or the spiritual discipline that can come from nightly devotionals wasn't appealing or beneficial. It was more that neither Randy nor I had been raised with any consistent form of faith-based training; all we really knew was what it was like to have a predisposition for His presence. In our hearts, most everything else seemed to fall short. Perhaps because so much of our walk of faith had already included experiences that exposed us to encountering His presence, we didn't know how to find His breath or life or hope or joy any other way. And when those attributes were absent, our discernment was sensitive to the heaviness that comes from living life in the flesh with no spiritual empowerment. Work apart from His presence inevitably creates a weariness because when we are the ones trying to do that which only the Holy Spirit is capable of, we end up bearing a weight we were never created to carry.

That said, "tradition" would say that when you have a child with a natural inclination toward the Kingdom, our parental obligation is to feed that desire through traditional avenues. But what happens when that said child, in this case Matthew, isn't drawn toward tradition or youth groups or daily Scripture reading? How exactly does one then feed this unusual appetite?

The intrinsic value of knowing Scripture and having it written on your heart wasn't the question. Matt knew the Bible stories—from the great feats of old to the miracles of Jesus—but at thirteen the basic stories weren't enough anymore. He wanted more, but finding his spiritual food amidst youth-related Bible studies and topical reading plans was highly problematic. In fact, those things, instead of drawing him closer to the Father's heart, inevitably sent Matthew home frustrated, resenting the all too frequent intellectual approach to a gospel that is meant to be shared in spirit and in truth.

Realizing we were in a bit of quandary, Randy and I began a fairly exhaustive search of local youth groups hoping to find somewhere that taught the things we valued or that brought Matthew life, only to discover that no one geographically close to us spoke or taught of the Father's heart or explored the truths of the Kingdom apart from basic morality.

Yet, we had Matt and despite convenience or locale, his desire to know who God *was* and what His character was really like continued to grow. Alas, I did what all good mothers do who have a child like Matt and no one nearby to aid in their child's development—I handed him another Bible in a different translation, hoping and praying that God would, through His word, find a way to answer Matt's questions. But I soon discovered it wasn't an issue of growing Matt's love for the Word;

rather, his questions uniquely focused on what God saved us *for* instead of what God saved us *from*.

His questions took our own perceptions to a whole new level, which required us to stay one step ahead of him; pat responses and regurgitated answers weren't enough anymore. It wasn't enough to know that David played the harp as a shepherd boy long before he was ever a king—Matthew wanted to know what he learned about God on those fields that helped define him later as "a man after God's own heart" (Acts 13:22). And, it wasn't enough to know that Jesus asked Peter three times, "Do you love me, Peter?" (John 21:15-17). Matthew had to know, "Why three, Mom? Why did Jesus ask Peter three times when He knew what Peter's answer would be the first time He asked?" which sounds simple enough until you're the one answering the child who has a sea of never-ending questions about a God who you are still discovering yourself.

The innate responsibility to spiritually feed this child lingered in the back of my mind most days, so without much direction toward anything else I decided to appeal to Matt's love of reading. I figured if his questions weren't going to be answered by picking up the Bible and reading it, I'll inundate him with books—all kinds—from historical novels to biographies to autobiographies to commentaries if need be. It may not have been the "Word" in the traditional sense, but if he would read them then I was happy to provide him with authors ranging from Max Lucado all the way to C.S. Lewis—anything that would help him explore and understand the Father's heart.

Being a witness to his willingness to read whatever I handed him always seemed to stir my wonderment about what Matt's life would look like ten years from now. *What causes a child to be so uniquely inquisitive, Lord?* I silently pondered every time I walked away from a new exchange. But true to His nature, God only illuminated the steps immediately in front of me, allowing my obedience only to propel me further down the road rather than His easy answers.

We spent the latter part of Matthew's eighth grade year exchanging books and talking about what he was learning through the various writings until one day early the following summer he literally bounced into the kitchen, tossed a particular book emphatically onto the table in front of me and declared, "Mom, I've got to go Wheaton College."

"Do you now?" I questioned, smiling. "Aren't you a little young for that yet?"

"Maawwm," he said a bit drawn out and impatient, "you know what I mean."

Turning to look at him, I immediately noted the stern resolve on his face that reflected the seriousness of his statement. "What do you mean you've got to go to Wheaton College? How do you even know about it?"

His eyes darted down to the book, then back at me, then down at the book again as if it could silently answer me.

"Mom, you know Wheaton College . . . the small private Christian school near Chicago . . . Jim Elliott . . . it's all in there," he said as he pointed to the book.

I looked down and recognized the face of the 1950 martyr, then looked back at Matt. "What are you saying, Matt? You want to go to visit? You . . . what?" I wasn't sure what he meant exactly.

He let out a loud exhale that sounded like a bull's snort, indicating either his frustration or his zeal for the battle; I wasn't completely sure. Then in an effort to collect his thoughts, he closed his eyes and said, "No, Mom, I just finished reading Jim Elliott's biography and he knew the Lord had called him to ministry early on; that's why he went to Wheaton. That's when he first started preaching, then years later he went to South America to evangelize the Auca Indians . . . .but they speared him to death in 1958."

Familiar with Jim and Elizabeth Elliott, I tried to understand the connection Matt was making between the story and his proclamation of going to Wheaton, but I wasn't sure I was grasping it. Was he asking to visit . . . was he declaring his future college choice? Hesitant to verbally cast doubt over him, I allowed my body language to convey my bewilderment instead.

"I just feel a connection to his story, Mom, and I'm telling you, I will attend Wheaton someday."

Emphatic . . . confident . . . assured.

I stood dumbfounded as Matt, with his head held high and his stature exuding nobility as if the King's signet ring had just endorsed his declaration, spun around, turned the corner and went outside to play basketball with Anna and Aaron.

"He's like a spiritual giant trapped in an adolescent body," I told the Lord. I didn't know what to make of his assertion. "Can a thirteen-year-old really know Your heart, Father?" I continued. Remnants of my own childhood surfaced: singing with the nuns at the local Catholic church, admiring their habits . . . wishing I was one of them. Then meeting at the Baptist church on the corner so I could attend a Girls Meeting God study with my girlfriends, then back to St. Nick's before the plays so the Father could bless the cast. . . each my own personal moments with the Lord that carried me through what otherwise had been a fairly turbulent childhood. That's when the realization hit me all over again, "I've always felt most at home with You, Lord, haven't I? And that's how he feels, isn't it? It's the only place where he feels he belongs—is in Your presence."

I glanced back down and took in Jim Elliott's face—his eyes danced and that smile—they radiated off the cover. *He was twenty-eight when he died, Lord, but he always knew he was called.* I looked out over the driveway and watched as my children enjoyed each other's company, all the while wondering what He had in store for each of them. Their little personalities were already emerging with each passing birthday, and they each were slowly becoming their own individual persons. I watched as Matt shot from the top of the key and wondered once again where the Lord was going to take him.

Can you give him to Me? asked the still, gentle voice.

Now? was my first thought. *I'm not ready,* was the second.

Unknowingly my hands clenched into tight little fists as if they were desperately trying to keep water from seeping through my fingers. My heart raced. My eyes glued to the scene being played out in my driveway. "I'm not ready, Lord," I whispered as I leaned back on the door jamb. "How is he old enough already—old enough to know the things he knows, to ask the things he asks and to declare something that isn't as though it is?" I whispered, "He's thirteen. How can he be so sure?"

I stood there for a long time hoping for an answer. None ever came. Yet I could no longer deny the sense that somehow our journey, though unlike any other, had somehow unknowingly commenced years ago. Then I thought about how and where it all began: the altar in Ohio, the counselor showing me the way of healing through the story of Tamar, the buying and selling of our homes, then our finances, always our finances. Collectively, they all pointed toward one unified direction; as if we hadn't already, we were about to experience once again what the apostle Paul meant when he said, "We walk by faith and not by sight" (2 Corinthians 5:7).

And undoubtedly, on some level, I was beginning to understand that a child would help lead the way.

CHAPTER FOURTEEN

Padre—A Cry of the Heart

Here is the God I want to believe in: a Father who, from the beginning of creation, has stretched out his arms in merciful blessing, never forcing himself on anyone, but always waiting; never letting his arms drop down in despair, but always hoping that his children will return so he can speak words of love to them and let his tired arms rest on their shoulders.
His only desire is to bless.
—Henri J.M. Nouwen
The Return of the Prodigal Son, p. 95-96

The road of motherhood showed me more things than just how to cooperate with the Lord on how to nurture and feed my children's spiritual life. Motherhood introduced me to the idea that even though my three children were biologically mine, they couldn't be any more different than if I had gathered them from three different families and brought them together underneath one roof and called them brothers and sisters.

Looks aside, the emergence of my children's intrinsic natures and personalities didn't appear until long after their toddler days when saying no tended to be black and white and stoves were hot no matter who touched them and glass could break no matter whose hands reached for it. But as they grew and the essence of who they were on the inside began to manifest, I soon discovered that though similar DNA may course through their veins, their individual personalities were as unique as the pattern of their fingerprints.

By mid-adolescence Matthew was vivacious, passionate about everything he put his hand to, and had such an infectious laugh that it permeated every atmosphere he entered. My Anna, however, now eight, was already showing herself to be vastly opposite from her brothers. More like her father in nature, she is reserved and quiet, the one who I often watched as she like a sponge preferred to absorb her surroundings rather than dictate them. And just as her brother Matt's unique traits had manifested at an early age, her independent spirit found its initial voice when she was just a toddler. The emphatic "I do's," combined with her fierce determination to exert her three-year-old appreciation for fashion were merely foreshadows of an emerging sense of security in who she really was.

Undeterred by the opinions of others, Anna was never easily swayed in what she thought nor exhibited much need to have a lot of people around her, which always struck me as fairly peculiar. My mind hadn't quite found its way around the idea that, unlike me, Anna didn't need people to define who she was or deem her acceptable. Instead, I saw her through my own ill-perceived filters of insecurity, and when confronted with her contentedness to be alone, I often wondered if it was rooted in her not being well liked.

Anna's propensity toward inner peace and assurance never crossed my mind because, for me, being alone spoke volumes about my own likeability or better yet, people's obvious dislike of me. Being alone was terrifying, for that was when my inner voices screamed the loudest, leaving me no viable place to put my daughter's contentment with solitude.

I didn't have eyes to see the emotional healthiness that forms in a child when she grows up in an environment stable enough that she is free to discover who she was created to be. Or that most often there is a direct correlation between the reassurance and identity a father brings to her life and a child's inner contentment.

Those truths didn't become evident until I was asked to speak on behalf of an abstinence ministry to an audience of young adolescents and teenagers—young lives that had been deemed "at risk" because of their home life or socioeconomic status, young victims to a way of life they had had no say in. Only then did I begin to see how, like indelible marks made by a Magic Pen, the impact a father, or lack thereof, makes on his child and how similar they are to the images that appear only when the pen is put on the right kind of surface.

Like a chemical reaction, every time I watched our daughter run toward Randy so she could spin and twirl for him, my heart would soften to the memory of what it felt like to discover that same beauty my father's eyes reflected when I twirled for him back in my childhood so long ago. I instantly became that little girl all over again as if a time warp had occurred. I would close my eyes and instead of watching Anna twirl, I was the one spinning with my arms spread out, free enough to dance and giggle with my head arched back, knowing full well I didn't have to say, "Daddy, watch me," because I knew I was all he saw.

Then the moment would end, most often starkly and without warning, and my eyes would open while the inner part of me fought to remain where I was—in that solitary moment of affirmation. I was invaluable there and significant; nothing else in the world mattered but that moment of him watching me twirl, and it was all I ever wanted for my daughter. That's why every time she came out of her room, dressed in one of her favorite dresses with her hair softly curled so it framed her heart shaped face and announced, "I'm ready, Daddy," it was as if I could see her heart skip when his look of approval enveloped her.

I was well acquainted with that skip. Even though I have no recollection of ever going anywhere with my father, I knew that every time Randy and Anna went on a "Pancake Date" or she danced on the tops of his feet to "My Girl," the Lord was showing me pieces of His own heart for His children—His heart to love genuinely and purely with a love that never leaves, that never forsakes and never defiles. Rather, His love is the purest form and is one that undergirds, supports and gives exquisite value to all who receive it.

Learning to embrace that love and therefore trust it tends to be the most challenging part for most females, especially for those who only know absence and neglect. Since Anna's childhood days I've come to learn that who we are or who we understand ourselves to be is directly correlated to our understanding of our earthly father's heart toward us. If he deems us beautiful then without thought, we are beautiful indeed. Just as if we're raised to feel we don't truly matter or we don't have a place in his eyes, then we spend a lifetime struggling to be significant in a world that cannot make us or teach us the value of our worth.

Undoubtedly my three children were blessed beyond measure with a father whose heart was *for* them, and for the most part they never wavered in their understanding of him. However, for many of those who the Lord sent me out to—the underprivileged, disadvantaged and forsaken—their experiences were vastly different.

In so many ways those young girls were just like Anna whose standards had been set. Throughout all the years I watched her and Randy go out on dates and he would tell her she was beautiful or open the car door for her or bring her flowers, whether she was aware of it or not, he was creating a standard and modeling a certain behavior. So much so that when Anna became old enough to date, those little things that Randy had done for her as a young girl ultimately became the litmus tests for the men who now court her.

The same was alternatively true for Anna's counterparts—many of the young girls I spoke with had been sexually compromised and/or fully violated, oftentimes by a male family member who claimed to "love" them—which always left me wondering if an indelible standard had been set for them just as it had been for Anna. What happens in the heart and mind of a young girl who, regardless of race or socioeconomic status, is repeatedly violated by someone she trusts and who professes to love her?

I would often ponder and ask the Lord that question, thinking that the only difference is that her experience is tainted and impure and often leads to a life of sexual promiscuity simply because she can no longer separate genuine, authentic love from physical interaction. By the time that same young girl reaches puberty and her sexuality is awakened, she's left with no choice but to ascribe value and worth based on her own sexuality—all because a distorted and perverted standard was set without her knowledge and, all too frequently, without her consent.

Which always brought me full circle back to my own life and my own lack of a father, leaving me to wonder: if my father had lived would my own adolescent choices have been different? Would the adoring affirmation I found in his eyes when I was three have sustained me and been emotionally enough to keep me from wandering into camps I didn't belong when I was an adolescence? On so many levels I'll never know, but I do know that I can instantly recognize the vacant look in a girl's eyes when she's wandering around looking for someone to love her, and I know the look of brokenness when a heart has been shattered and regret is overwhelming. I know it because I lived it.

I have also gradually learned to recognize the eyes that aren't marked by cheap imitations or flawed by twisted acts of seduction. I've learned to recognize them because they are my daughter's eyes—bright, shiny and full of hope because she grew up experiencing the safety and security that comes with a father's heart that is authentically genuine and true. And because of that, she is free to explore with reckless abandon all that God has for her—all because she knows a father who loves her, and does so very, very well.

CHAPTER FIFTEEN

A New Revelation

*For My thoughts are not your thoughts,
Nor are your ways My ways," says the Lord.*
—Isaiah 55:8

Experiencing or even understanding the Father's heart isn't something that comes very easily, especially for those who come from backgrounds like mine. As a young girl I spent a fair amount of time looking outward, taking account of the environmental differences that existed between my girlfriends' families and me. Those observations are where I first learned to identify the inner hole my father's absence had created, as if seeing the ease that existed within their relationships with their fathers gave me eyes to see the "something" that was missing in my own life.

Then as I grew and became an adolescent, what had been for so long obvious external differences slowly grew to become internal wrestling matches. Every time I spent time with my girlfriends, all I ever saw was a growing ease and confidence in the young women they were becoming. They laughed easily and never appeared self-conscious or even had to work at their appearance. They just seemed to naturally become thinner and prettier and taller while I remained acutely aware of how awkward, pudgy and pimply I was—standing in front of my bedroom mirror always made me wish I were anyone but me.

Scanning my reflection, my eyes would inevitably fall downward then rise back up again as I silently wondered what boys thought when they looked at me. Then I'd strike a different pose and wonder what my dad would say if he was here. *Would he still think I was beautiful like he did when I was three?* Eventually I'd cock my head, momentarily take account of each facial feature, determined to find him in my own image—but I never could. Nothing ever seemed to fill the gaping hole so it grew, and over the course of my middle school years I found myself intermittently having idyllic conversations with the paternal figment of my imagination and I would ask him, "Was I not enough for you? . . . Was I not reason enough to say no?"

Silence, of course, was the only one to respond with a hushed, *"Is that what you think?"*

I closed my eyes, wishing with everything inside of me that I would look different when my eyes reopened. I so desperately wanted life to be different. I longed to be like my friends: prettier . . . skinnier . . . clear skinned . . . but more than anything I wanted my father here. "I don't want to be fatherless anymore," whispered my reflection.

My insides ached to be considered beautiful, and I somehow knew without anyone ever saying it that if he were here, if he had been healthy and could have chosen not to drink then he would have known a different existence. Thereby, so too would I. I would have held a different identity, most likely one that would have included the security of believing I was enough.

Therein lay the catch-22—was he absent because I wasn't enough for him or did my inadequacies stem from him not being here? At thirteen I didn't know the answer, then again at seventeen it was too late for me to worry about it. But now at thirty, my need for answers was surfacing all over again, as if the unanswered questions that were such an intricate part of who I was as a young girl could no longer be separated from the truth. Somehow over the years they had morphed from questions into lies that looked so much like the truth that somewhere along the way I chose to believe them. Then once I bought into the lies or made agreement with them they festered, taking root far below the surface, growing and spreading until they ultimately became so entrenched in my way of thinking that they influenced how I perceived everything around me—the way people viewed me, whether I was acceptable or not to others—and ultimately convincing me that I was always the one on the outside looking in, as if I never really belonged anywhere.

Soon enough Isolation and Loneliness became my archnemeses—their voices too painful for me to hear. That's why seating me at the end of the table during any kind of a social gathering would invariably throw me into a panic attack because in those moments their voices screamed at me, reminding me that I was never as desirable as those who got to sit in the middle of the gathering.

Intellectually I knew the crux of the problem lay deep within me, but my mental acknowledgement of such didn't silence my Tormentors. Instead the voices in my head continued to paint a stark contrast to what I continually witnessed in Anna and Randy's relationship. With each passing moment I watched my daughter as she flourished beneath the gaze of Randy's adoration, and each time I witnessed him bring her flowers or pick her up and twirl her, my heart ached all the more for what I had always dreamt of experiencing.

I suppose those were the prevailing moments of revelation when I realized that even though the calendar said I was thirty, my inner self, the little girl who was alive and well within me, still yearned to be found at my father's feet, sitting beneath his gaze, acutely aware that his look only existed in my memory.

It was then, through my daughter, that I began to wonder if the whispered inadequacies that had always plagued me had some correlation to growing up without my father. Otherwise why would the Lord have been so specific about what He was showing me through Anna and Randy or through the young girls I was ministering to downtown?

Yet somehow He wasn't just showing me what I was lacking. For the first time I was beginning to understand and even desire to get beyond where I had always emotionally lived. The concept that there has to be something more—something redemptive—something beyond the natural outcome of my inherited circumstances carried an inexplicable force that propelled me toward Him.

It was as if He had chartered out a course of territory I would need to explore, then prepared me to land on shores I had merely drifted by long ago. This time, entertaining unanswerable questions wouldn't be enough; I somehow knew if I wanted to be made whole I couldn't be satisfied with just perusing the shores. On the contrary, this time I knew He was calling me to actually step off my vessel and delve far deeper into the fractures of my heart and into the land of unfamiliar. I had to be willing to see things the way He saw them so that I could come out the other side with my heart intact and fused together with His.

The cries of Redemption and Restoration began to summon me like never before, like homing beacons wooing me back to Him, encouraging me to press in to discover who the Father really was, regardless of what my natural paternal circumstances may have inferred about Him. I didn't know how to reconcile this Father of today—this Being who seemed to be relentless in His pursuit of my healthiness—and the One the depths of my heart always wanted to question, "Why? . . . Why *my* dad? . . . How has not having my dad worked together for the good? I don't understand."

My heart's intent was never to question *Him*. Rather He and I had a history, and that history had taught me that I could trust Him with my questions. So I approached Him believing that He understood how deeply I needed and ached for the redemptive part of His character to touch this situation. It had plagued me my whole life and I was tired of being held victim to my circumstance. I didn't want to hurt anymore because I couldn't see what aspects of my father were most evident in me, and I had grown weary from my nagging curiosity that always wondered how he would have felt when he saw me or what kind of a grandfather he would he have been to my children.

I found a whole new voice during the ensuing months when my cries became the loudest and my pleas the most desperate. It was then that the apostle Paul's writing in Romans became the most applicable to me: *"Yet in all these things we are more than conquerors through Him who loved us"* (8:37). That solitary verse became my own personal battle cry as God continually breathed life anew on it as a means to empower and equip me to overcome and conquer the orphan spirit rather than allow it to reign over me one more day.

I battled and contended with the Lord in that season in ways I had never previously known. Gone was most of my former timidity with Him for He was using my need for redemption to teach me what it means to *"... come boldly to the throne of grace, that we may obtain mercy and find grace to help in time of need"* (Hebrews 4:16).

Then before I knew what was upon me it was summer and suddenly we were weeks away from sending Matthew to high school, and since every moment with him was becoming more rare than the last, when he asked if I would take him to get new school clothes, I seized the moment.

Pacing the front porch, I scanned the streets waiting for the traffic to dissipate before Matthew and I headed to the south side of the city in an effort to avoid the crowds in for the NASCAR Brickyard 400. "Three-hundred-thousand is a lot of people trying to find parking spaces, isn't it?" Randy said as he came out the front door.

"I know, right?"

Randy's hand extended as he said, "Here's the clothing money; it's not much but hopefully it'll help."

I wanted to thank him. I wanted to tell him how much I appreciated the way he provided for our family. I wanted to especially thank him for providing for Matt, but the sudden squeak of the storm door announcing Matthew was ready interrupted all of it, so I settled for a message-filled grin and a quick goodbye kiss on the cheek instead.

Carrying on a conversation with Matthew has never posed a problem, not even then when he was nearly fifteen. In fact, there was little Matthew *didn't* talk about. I used to credit his persistent "Why, Mommy?" to being an overly inquisitive toddler, but as he's grown older and matured I've discovered that in large part it's one of the ways the Lord uses him. Matthew isn't created to be satisfied with surface answers, and when he probes he's not meaning to pry or be rude; rather his inherent need to understand just always prevails, causing the one he's talking with to look deeper and probe further than ever expected.

So it was at dinner as we sat and discussed his heading to high school and my feeling the need to teach him about the "firsts" in life. "What do you mean, Mom?" he asked.

I tried dancing around things, searching for just the right words. I had always desired two things for each of my children: first, that they would each love God with all their heart, soul and mind. And second? They wouldn't make the same mistakes I did. I didn't want their souls to bear those scars; instead I wanted them intact, free to live carefree and whole. I didn't want them to know regret, at least not the kind of regret I carried, so before I lost my nerve I started, "You know, Matthew, high school is going to open up a whole new world for you."

I locked eyes with his, hoping to sense where he was at but he just looked back at me, expectantly waiting for me to continue. "It'll be a world of firsts, but there are three firsts that you will always remember. Always."

Another pause—another round of locked eyes. I could see piqued curiosity as it toyed with him. Long-lost images of the emotional young woman in the abstinence video saying, "No one ever told me," compelled me to continue.

"Your first kiss . . . your first date, and . . . " I took a deep breath then looked at him and said, " . . . your first sexual experience. Make sure, Matt, God blesses all three. It's the only way to live a life of no regret."

He sat silent with his gaze cast downward for just a while before looking back up at me. "Well, Mom, I've already had my first kiss," he admitted as the softest hint of pink faded up his cheeks, "but I don't regret it. And the other two things . . . I hear you. I've already given those to Him."

Suddenly the front door of the restaurant flew open, casting a loud BANG as it slammed against the exterior wall. I jumped at the disruption while, one by one, five very loud, very intoxicated middle-aged men, all of whom were clothed in Brickyard 400 attire, stumbled into the restaurant and sat at the table just five feet from where Matthew and I were sitting.

With our conversation interrupted and the moment having fled out the open door, Matthew and I looked at each other with raised eyebrows, not exactly sure what to make of the unfolding situation. In comparison to our relatively hushed conversation, they were noisy, crass and apparently under the impression that everyone nearby longed to share in their raucous recap of the day's events.

Matthew and I tried navigating our way through the boisterous atmosphere but their increasingly unruly behavior declared our efforts hopeless. Silence gradually seeped in where our conversation had once flourished as Matthew's attention shifted back and forth from the television to the ongoing disturbance at the nearby table.

I watched my fork as I mindlessly scooted the food around on the plate in front of me in an effort to occupy my wandering thoughts. Stories of my dad replayed in my head as I became certain that if my elder sister were here our conversation would immediately default to a time when my dad was still good and she would share stories about who he was before he became what she called "really bad."

Closing my eyes, I focused on the reassurance she offered when she would say, "He was a good man, Kelly," then she would make sure I knew how kind he was and how she never doubted he loved her. But I also knew that just as real as all that was to her, so too were her other memories—the ones in which my dad started drinking and his decline began then grew worse until life as she knew it plummeted into a constant state of turmoil and unrest. Pain's voice was so recognizable when she spoke, it felt as if I could recall her memories myself—the good and the bad—but more than anything I sympathized with how deeply she wished things had been different.

I don't know how long I sat there playing with my food, lost on Memory Lane before I came back to myself, but when I resurfaced I came up with keen awareness that there was something the Lord wanted me to see about these men. *"What, Lord? What is it?"* I silently inquired.

It took just a few seconds for Peace, like a soft mist, to fall all around as if His assignment was to help prepare me to hear, *"Look at them, Kelly."*

The idea went around my head in circles a few times before I questioned, *Who, Lord? Them? But I don't want to . . . they make me . . . uncomfortable.*

"Just look," came in a soft hushed whisper.

I closed my eyes and let the image of my father sitting slumped on the couch fill my mind before I invited Courage to join me. I breathed deep, taking in the unavoidable stench of stale alcohol that wafted over their table in an eerie haze. A sudden eruption of laughter exploded, creating a plausible reason for me to glance over. Two of the men turned to watch TV while another took a drink from his mug, then wiped the dribble from his mouth with his sleeve. I stared for just a moment longer, taking in the slanted, blood shot eyes, the stubbled chins—some of the things I remembered most about my father.

"You see, Kelly, this is who you would have known—not the father your memory has wanted to create."

What do you mean, Lord?

"Your father was a good man, Kelly, but he was sick. He couldn't be who you needed him to be, no matter how much his heart wanted to. Had he lived, this is more what you would have known."

Reactionary tears filled my eyes as shivers tingled down my spine. *All my conjured up images, Father, that's who I want.* My thoughts slowly drifted toward the men sitting so near. *I don't want him to be like them, Father.*

"In his heart he was always the man you wanted, Kelly. That's why he could look at you the way you remember. That's who he was but not who he would have become."

The tightening in my chest felt like it was going to explode under the pressure. A lifetime of grieving what had always just been a paternal concept finally gave way as I discovered how to grieve its human form.

And all I could do was weep.

"Mom . . . you okay?" Matt asked suddenly, his voice shrouded in hesitancy and concern.

I quickly glanced up, offering a reassuring grin and a nod of the head, knowing that until the constriction in my throat lessened its grip I couldn't verbally respond. Then, like the surf's wave that deposits new shells every time it hits the shore, He returned once more carrying with Him one of the largest and most paramount Truths of His character that He wanted to impart.

Quietly as if not to interrupt He gently asked, *"My grace, Kelly . . . It doesn't always look like grace, does it?"*

The question circled around my mind countless times as my spirit, like Job's, struggled to find the words to answer Him. I wasn't even sure I should.

"Look at the cross, Kelly. It doesn't look very gracious, does it? Yet it is the single largest display of grace known to man."

Stunned, I sat lost in the moment . . . absorbed in His perfection, rendered speechless by the magnitude and enormity of all He had just shown me. I was on spiritual overload, raw from the lies He had uprooted yet tender from the Truth that had just been deposited.

I leaned back in the booth dazed, the table growing increasingly blurry again as my eyes suddenly filled with new pools of water fighting to be released. I didn't want to think anymore; all I really wanted to do was picture my father as I had seen him when I was three—sitting on the couch with kindness in his eyes—but in that instant I knew that the totality of my father would no longer be conveyed in that one memory, for one cannot constitute the whole. There was more to him than that.

Quickly I glanced over one last time, needing to absorb the other part of who I realized my father to be, then grieved as the invisible pedestal I had placed him on years ago slowly and methodically tipped over. Instantly Silence's reassuring presence was next to me, comforting me as if he knew how deep of a struggle it was to keep everything together.

"You're sure you're okay, Mom?" Matt asked me one more time.

Briefly glancing at him, I gave him another quick nod of the head, never fully losing my awareness of the five men God had used to show me so much. I knew in time God would supply the necessary words I needed to explain and speak life to all who listened, but there in that moment, the time had not yet come.

Instead for now or for however long He deemed necessary, I needed to be found like Mary who, after hearing the prophecies regarding Jesus, "... kept all these things and pondered them in her heart" (Luke 2:19).

CHAPTER SIXTEEN

ENTER THE YA YA'S

Ya Ya's: a group of three or more women whose hearts and souls are joined together by laughter and tears shared through the glorious journey of life.

Learning to see things from the Kingdom's perspective doesn't necessarily come naturally or very easily to most people. As a matter of fact it's one of the most challenging things about living a life of faith because all too often our own human rationale and logic are the things we employ to define our landscape, and subsequently what we perceive in the natural world becomes the driving force behind our decisions. It takes a letting go of what we know and a willingness to step into what we don't in order for our faith to take hold and become strengthened.

So it was for me that day in the restaurant when the Lord recalibrated the way I perceived my childhood and growing up without a father. I left that day with no idea exactly where to put what He had shown me, yet somehow empowered by hope—hope that comes when things fall into their rightful place, therefore we're able to set our eyes on our future rather than continually looking at our past. And hope because in the midst of having to accept some hard truths associated with my dad, I also walked away with an assurance that somewhere deep inside of him was the man the three-year-old little girl inside of me always knew him to be—healthy, vibrant and at some point in his life had been able to deny that which seemed to seduce him.

Somehow since the day of seeing those men in the restaurant, Hope had demanded Torment to release his grip, then began to teach me how to finally make peace with being fatherless. Oh, there were still occasions when I would see something occur between Randy and Anna that caused my heart to stir, but those moments no longer carried their former sting. Much like my encounter at the conference, I was learning that the more intentional I became about transferring the ache I felt about my father onto the shoulders of my heavenly Father, the less I hurt.

Instead of being tormented by wondering what my earthly father would have thought of me, I was slowly discovering how to ask Him, "What do *You* think of me?" In response, His answers became the foundation of my deepest restoration. And instead of imagining how my father would have responded to a given situation, I began redirecting my questions to my heavenly Father, asking Him, "How do You feel about this?" or "What breaks Your heart?"

Those were the times and places I experienced Him the most because instead of giving me understanding about my earthly father, He gave me Himself instead. That's when I learned that whenever we find the more of Him, inevitably we understand more about who we are and just exactly who He has created us to be.

Like a trickle effect, the more He gave of Himself the healthier I became. It wasn't that He was just healing my father wounds like the tenth leper in Luke 17, He was in the process of making me completely whole—body, soul and spirit. But wholeness for me usually comes through process and having to walk things out, and this particular portion of wholeness included expanding my relational ground.

With the age span of our three children now ranging from five to almost fourteen, it seemed at times as if Randy and I had our relational feet in two or three different camps. We had the lighthearted friendships we enjoyed with the parents we had met through Matthew's involvement in sports, but we also had our cross-section of friends with whom we walked out our faith, or what we called "doing life deeply" together.

And now it was Aaron's turn. Five years old and on the verge of starting kindergarten at the same school Anna attended, Aaron was known to us as "little man," or by most in our circle, "A-man." Kind and tenderhearted, he is exactly like his father, but his eyes mirrored those in my own father's pictures—deep brown, full and perfectly round in shape. Yet the most striking thing about them is they seemed to dance whenever you looked at him, as if they were capable of hearing the Irish lilts of long ago.

In my heart he's always been *my Aaron*, and just as God used Matthew to introduce me to Kerri, or Anna to introduce me to Lori, so too He would use Aaron to introduce me to Pam.

Standing on the sidelines of Aaron's Under 6 (U6) soccer game, I was completely absorbed in watching him race down the field when suddenly her unprecedented gift for laughter rolled across the sidelines. Not that she or her laugh was loud—just infectious. She stood talking with a mutual friend a few feet away while I admired how humor seemed to define the atmosphere all around her. There was an ease and a comfort or warmth in the way she held herself, despite the noticeable physical limitation that appeared when she walked up and down the sidelines.

Something about her was magnetic as if after so much emotional healing God knew I would be drawn toward laughter. Unable to not eavesdrop I silently giggled at her one-liners while overheard conversation taught me that her son, like mine, not only played for the same team but would also be attending the same kindergarten as Aaron.

Standing there listening, perhaps I should have foreseen the instantaneous friendship that would form between our two families. Frankly I didn't, any more than I could have predicted what a beautiful friendship would take root in a simple cross necklace that had draped Kerri's neck the day I met her, or begin to understand the rock and source of friendship that would ensue after the first day Lori and I had prayed together at Mom's in Touch. It wasn't until after years of doing life together that I would come to understand how each of those women—Kerri, Lori and Pam—embodied certain facets of God's character.

Kerri's faithfulness testified to the nature of God while Lori had an inner silent strength about her that I now recognize is a safe haven or refuge in times of the worst kind of trouble. And Pam? She had a joy that exuded from her in boundless measure. Even in the worst of moods, you can't help but laugh when you're with her. It's what I learned to call my "Pam fix." She gives it as a gift unlike any other.

It didn't take long for our four families to interconnect or for them to become indispensable to me. They quickly became people I latched onto—anchors of stability in a world that for so long felt wind-tossed and unstable. Life with those families was something I never wanted to go without. With them I belonged and in retrospect I now know that's because in so many ways I saw aspects of who God was in each of them, and I couldn't help but discover more of who I was because of the way they reflected Him.

Everything in me cherished them, perhaps in some measure because it had been nearly fifteen years since I had left Ohio and the sense of belonging that comes when you have friends. Loneliness was the one residual place in my heart that God had yet to redeem. Yet for the first time in fifteen years here I was in central Indiana and I had friends—friends who made me feel like I finally belonged somewhere again, and people who made me feel like I mattered. Those women and their families loved me and mine. I knew it because of the way they walked with us through our trials and by the way we enjoyed doing life together. And it was evident by their shared transparency—few things happened in our individual lives that we didn't share as a group or pray together as a spiritual family. Being in relationship with them, for me, was the personification of Proverbs 27:17, *"As iron sharpens iron so a man sharpens the countenance of his friend."*

I don't believe any of us were consciously aware that we were in the midst of something uniquely special just as none of us could have predicted what God had in store the first time we met one another. Individually we were moms who had children who wanted to play together. Then life went on and circumstances melded things together, and what was one or two individual friendships became candid moments as couples or the families joined together. Because we lived within a quarter-mile of one another, it was easy, as if being together was just one of the many benefits that came from living in a small town. But somehow along the way and unbeknownst to us, God began to breathe life on those relationships. Instead of fusing us together in general commonalities, our foundation became established and rooted because of our shared faith in the blood of Jesus and the power that comes from collectively pursuing Him.

We believed in the same things, raised our children with the same values, and when one struggled, another came in to encourage and offer support. We shared our lives, our resources and our love—for God first and our families second.

It was a season of life like none I had ever experienced and I spent most of it, for the first time since moving to Indiana, not looking back. I was finally able to put things in their rightful place. I had friends who loved me. I belonged.

But more than anything, I finally mattered. I was finding my significance in the Father's love, and from that place the overflow of His goodness was evident in every aspect of my life. Redemption had truly drawn nigh, and for the first time in a very long time, I could breath.

CHAPTER SEVENTEEN

WHO AM I?

The best mirror is an old friend.
—George Herbert

Being a part of something, surrounded by people who were doing life right next to me, felt like I always imagined it would have: fulfilling... rewarding... complete. Life was no longer defined by my need to fill the vast cavern that had once existed deep within—the hole was finally being filled. In so many ways I felt new and undefiled.

Even the restraints and limitations that naturally come with having young children were loosening. It was nearly an altogether new existence for me—one that I had not experienced since I was seventeen. And though I had days when I yearned to slow the clock down, more often than not I enjoyed the newfound freedom my semi-independent state was bringing with it.

Contentment was becoming an easier thing to learn as He taught me to enjoy the present and what life was offering, and instead of looking back I learned that hope compels us to look forward. It was a moment of epiphany when I realized, *There really is a reason God doesn't put our eyes in the back of our head.*

Gone were the days when I believed what I had done determined who I was, and in its place was an ongoing discovery of who God created me to be. There were still areas of my past that needed reconciled, but the individual stages of life each of my children were in presented new moments of joy.

High school sports had developed Matthew into a successful tri-sport athlete who was also one of the top in his class academically, while Anna was quickly carving out her own definition of success as she finished her last year in elementary school and was quickly approaching adolescence, donning braces and a junior high cheerleading outfit. Then there was Aaron, always my Aaron, who loved life and overflowed with energy from the moment his feet hit the floor each morning. Unlike the other two, Aaron fought to do his own thing his own way and has always refused to conform to the examples established by his older brother and sister. Even as a little boy, his free spirit presented us with the unique challenge of figuring out exactly how to corral him. In so many ways he bore the same love of God as his siblings, yet his drive and sheer determination to do things independently caused him a fair amount of conflict within himself and, at times, with those around him.

Despite Aaron's intermittent bumps in the road, my children fared quite well, and knowing that they were consistently making better choices than I ever had allowed me to breathe a bit easier and much deeper. Their stability remained my primary concern, and I was fully aware of how much our simple way of life impacted them. School seasons remained filled with not only Matt's sporting events but now Anna's as well, and the hot days of summer were spent at Pam's pool watching our children swim while the rest of us attempted to solve the world's problems, especially our own.

Life was predictable and routine, but most of all it was stable, and that was invaluable to me. Both as a family and a close group of friends, we grew to know what to expect from one another and there was an unspoken reliance that came to define the Ya Ya's—we had each other's backs, if you will. Like fabric in a tapestry, time and spiritual unity had woven us all together and for the most part we were seamless. Yet at the same time we had space and grace to weave in those who God brought along, like Kerri's sister Kelli and her family.

Grafted in through her daughter who was Anna's age, the connection, like all the others, was instant. Kelli, beautiful and soft-spoken, personified the servant's heart. Tireless in her efforts to make others comfortable, she was a modern day Martha (Luke 10)—the first one willing to give or do more than anyone could ask or imagine in order to ease another's load.

Her family's insertion into the mix was as seamless as the relationships that had taken seasons to foster, and before long they joined us as we did life together. We all were experiencing the "summer" of our lives, and although we spoke often of seizing every moment and never wanting things to change, the conscious couldn't dictate the natural order of things. Even though there was an inherent lightness to those days, something inside me sensed that nothing good ever stays the same. If it did it wouldn't remain good.

Consequently, despite the joy of frequently gathering for dinner parties and going on spring break together or spending every hot summer day of the past three years at Pam's pool, an unexplainable unsettledness began to grow within me.

As a young thirty-something, the realization that I had been raising children since I was eighteen was never far from me. While I had found my children's accomplishments rewarding, ignoring the inner rumbling that would bubble up when no one else was around and whispering "There's got to be something more" was becoming increasingly difficult. "But what?" I would frequently ask Silence.

Now that all of my children were attending school I recognized how quickly they were aging and becoming more of their own persons, enmeshed in their own lives, and as a result lessening their practical need for Mom. In the short five years since having Aaron, my life had already drastically changed, teaching me that by account of their ages alone, change was imminent and soon enough my days would no longer be filled with their presence. *Then what?* I wondered. *What will I do then?*

At first those moments of discontent didn't come very often, suppressed by the simplicity that appeared on the horizon when I thought about Matthew going to college in a few years and Anna and Aaron becoming increasingly independent. On the other side of the life I was currently living was the part of me that looked forward to being an adult without the responsibility of raising children. It was a life I had never known, and although the realization that Randy and I now had less time with Matthew than before saddened me, it also made me aware of the fact that I had never really been an adult without him.

Truth was I had been with Matthew longer than I had been with Randy, and in numerous ways it felt like I had done a fair amount of growing up *with* him. Somehow without ever really speaking it, Randy and I both knew that Matthew's impending adulthood wasn't going to affect just him—it was going to transition me as well. I suppose that's when I realized that my growing children were going to launch me, like a catapult, into an altogether different stratosphere of existence. Until now, I had only been a mother; apart from them I wasn't exactly sure who I was anymore—as if no other part of my adult identity had had a chance to really form or develop.

It was in those moments when I was lost in quiet introspection that Randy would suddenly ask me, "So, Kel, where do you see us in ten years?"

My first response was to always say, "I have no idea." My second was to add ten years to whatever age Aaron was at the time, then reply, "Wow, Aaron will be ____ by then," then my mind would go blank because I didn't have vision for much after that. I couldn't see anything on the other side of my children's horizon.

"That's true. But where do you see *us*?" he would ask again. "What do you think God has in store?"

For the longest time I could never really answer him. I'm not sure I even understood who or what constituted the *"us"* beyond our current family unit. Up until recently I had never looked much beyond finding ways to help my children become more than who I believed I was, but now . . . now I had this incessant rumbling and Randy's questions and all I could think to say was, "Long-term plans aren't really my thing."

Thankfully, I always thought better of it.

Randy had no way of knowing the reasons behind my recent inner wrestling matches; I never told him. Nor had I shared with him that until recently I had never seriously considered what life beyond motherhood would look like—not for me or for us. Yet God must have been using Randy's question to invite me to do just that because for the first time since high school I began to entertain questions like, *If not this, then what will I do?* Or, *Apart from being "so and so's" mom or Randy's wife, who am I . . . really?*

Episodic flashbacks from high school swirled through my mind as I reflected on what I had once aspired to be when life was carefree and limitless. Memories of being on stage and pursuing a career in theatre caused an inner chuckle to erupt, *That seems like a lifetime ago.* I thought about how much my life had changed since I had to decline The American Academy of Dramatic Arts' invitation, then remembered an earlier time when I felt as I did now—uncertain of who I was apart from what I did. It was as if two people had somehow learned to coexist inside of me: the one who no longer needed the stage because time and healing had taught me how to accept myself, whose alter ego no longer needing to emerge through a fictional character. Then there was the little girl who still existed in the far reaches of my self. The one who recognized that Fear still had enough of a grip on me that the only time I felt the safest and most secure was when I kept relatively to myself and away from unwanted or unsolicited attention.

Okay, life on stage is out, so now what? I asked Silence. After so many years of being a full-time mother, life's infamous question had finally found its way back to me. "What do I want to be when I grow up?" I asked myself.

"I have no idea," Myself responded.

I sat in silence, unsure of exactly where to go or how to get there. "Ten years," I whispered, "Ten years is a long time." It was quiet in the room and though I physically couldn't see anyone, I sensed the lightness of His presence fill the atmosphere as He joined me.

"Ten years, Father. By then Matthew will be out of college, Anna will be almost through and Aaron will be just about done with high school," I continued. *Funny how a mother's life is often defined primarily by the status of her children,* I thought. So long as my children were home, they needed me. But fixing my eyes on ten years from now required me to consider what my life would look like in the reflection of their adult-like state. "They won't need me like they do now, so what will I do then, Father?" I asked. "Motherhood has been my primary identity; without it what am I supposed to be about?"

That was the integral question for me, for if motherhood wasn't the primary identifier of my life, then what was? Silence hung in the air, bringing with it more Peace than answers, and even though I wasn't sure where to go from here, I couldn't help but sense something was shifting deep inside. Reflecting back, I thought about how far He had brought me, and all that He had shown me about myself, but more important, all He had shown me about Him. "But what do I do with it, Lord?" I asked, "All I see is my need for something more and nothing else." *What is it?* I wondered.

I left that encounter that particular morning a bit undone—feeling as if my questions had penetrated the surface but there were no answers to provide any air. Still submerged in thought, it felt as if I was swimming around, a bit disoriented, looking for how to get back to the surface when Pam called asking if I would help with decorating her dining room.

Returning the phone to its cradle, my eyebrows raised at the timing of her call. As simple as her request was I knew it held something more —as if His fingerprints were all over it because whether she knew it or not, Pam's lighthearted approach to life draws people in as if she's inviting them to do life right alongside of her. She can effortlessly bring things into proper perspective, and without even being consciously aware of what's happening, the weight that felt so unbearable and heavy when you walked in somehow dissipates in the presence of the joy she carries.

The uncertainty of my morning's time with the Lord was all but forgotten later that afternoon as I stood talking with Pam in the middle of her ten-by-ten dining room now crowded with ladders and paint trays. An early June breeze blew through the window while ribbons of paint raced to be the first to gather at the rim of our formerly see-through gloves. The space was tight, the room nearly complete while the conversation remained free flowing, interrupted only by the outbreaks of sudden laughter because of some one-liner Pam had just dropped. Then suddenly, as if her silence should have been the indicator of all seriousness, her arm stopped mid roll as she turned to look at me, then said, "Kel," she paused, "can I ask you something?"

Mindlessly I responded, "Of course."

"Do you ever think about what you'll do after Matt leaves for college and your kids are older?"

A puffed exhale followed by a subtle shake of my head preceded, *Are You serious right now, Lord?*

I wasn't emotionally ready to disclose everything I had been pondering, at least not yet, so I deflected, "I don't know yet, but I do know I want to be doing something more than redoing someone's dining room."

She laughed, knowing full well that although I loved every minute of helping her, the heart behind my response conveyed that I needed more to sustain me. In fact, I was becoming increasingly aware of how deeply my heart ached for it.

Turning back toward her wall she continued, "Have you ever thought about going to school?"

"You mean college?"

"Yeah, have you ever wanted to go?"

Fear immediately presented himself. Images of countless students walking on campus flashed . . . *All those people, I wouldn't know anyone.* My instincts told me to cower in the corner, to find someplace safe, "Oh, I don't know . . . I don't think I could."

"Really?" she asked rhetorically, glancing back at me with confusion. "I've watched you since you started leading the FCA junior high huddle; you're really good with kids, Kel. Have you ever thought about teaching?"

I let my thoughts wander down the wall right alongside the paint. Something about what she said resonated as Truth. I felt it grab hold. Looking back at her I watched for a moment as she meticulously rolled the brush across her wall, wishing I was more like her—fearless and sure of herself.

I turned back toward my own area and thought about what she had said and the power of her suggestion. *Can I see myself on campus? Would I fit with all those people?* Somewhere in the midst of entertaining my thoughts, Silence became interested and joined me. "Maybe it's not a bad idea," I found myself whispering to him. The warmth of his smile comforted me as if to say, "No, not bad at all."

A slight step to the left and a new area to roll was all I needed to marinate on the idea just a little while longer. "Maybe . . . " I finally told Pam. Then seconds later continued, "I'll have to really think about it," understanding all too well that if I was ever going to gain that kind of ground it would require me to face Fear head-on . . . once and for all.

CHAPTER EIGHTEEN

CROSSING OVER

Any time we open ourselves up to fear, we fall prey to his deceptions and intimidations . . . As we yield to God we can master our reactions to fear and the enemy will soon flee.
—Francis Frangipane

Ground worth gaining never comes without a fight, in large part because our fiercest enemies often already inhabit the very land we've been called to subdue or conquer. When God established His covenant with Abram, He told him upon the promise of land, "*. . . to your descendants I have given this land, from the river of Egypt to the great river, the River Euphrates—the Kenites, the Kenezzites, the Kadmonites, the Hittites, the Perizzites, the Rephaim, the Amorites, the Canaanites, the Girgashites, and the Jebusites*" (Genesis 15:18-21). There may have been land promised to God's people, but that didn't mean the enemy didn't first need evicted.

The same rings true when Moses was instructed to lead the Israelites into the promised land. God said, "*. . . depart and go up from here, you and the people whom you have brought out of the land of Egypt, to the land of which I swore to Abraham, Isaac, and Jacob, saying, 'To your descendants I will give it.' And I will send My Angel before you, and I will drive out the*

Canaanite and the Amorite and the Hittite and the Perizzite and the Hivite and the Jebusite" (Exodus 33:1-3).

God may order the angels to go before us, but just as Joshua and the Israelites had to battle to conquer the Promised Land, so we too must learn to co-labor with the Lord and His angels so that we can lay hold and stake claim of the ground He's called us to inherit.

I wish I had understood these concepts at the onset of Pam's question; it would have made cooperating with the Spirit of God a bit easier. But the truth was it took time to learn that each opportunity He extends is really an invitation to become healthier and thereby inhabit more ground. Similar to when He was wooing me from the cave, I didn't understand that the area of ground I was willing and able to walk on actually reflected the current level of my spiritual and emotional healthiness. I couldn't possess ground I hadn't yet subdued and I couldn't subdue that which hadn't been healed.

Since then, however, I've come to understand that the essence of spiritual development and authority actually occurs in the midst of the battle. Our reaction to the foes we confront as we encroach on the land He's inviting us to dwell on is what determines whether or not we'll be victorious in our advance. We can choose to either be like the ten spies and focus solely on the "giants in the land" (Numbers 13:31-33) or we can be found like Joshua and Caleb and lift our eyes upward in faith, trusting that if He has called us to enlarge our territory then He will be faithful to help us defeat the very things that threaten to stand in our way.

For as far back as I can remember Fear has been the resident giant standing on whatever land God has called me to spy out—crouching in every corner, waiting to pounce at the first sign of any possible expansion. Always one step ahead of me, it seems as if he has walked with me for nearly as long as Silence has, making it difficult at times for me to differentiate between the two.

Fear's ability to cloak his presence in silence makes it nearly impossible for me to distinguish him apart from Silence, especially when I am feeling threatened or insecure. Vulnerability involuntarily engages my instinct for survival and inevitably my ability or will to speak becomes surrendered. Instead, out of a feeble effort to keep my head above water, I burrow down deep within, never fully understanding if I've retreated because I'm afraid or if I have become afraid because words, which have always been so faithful to me, vacate themselves in Fear's presence, leaving me speechless, or worse yet, voiceless.

Perhaps it's all rooted in an inner quest to understand exactly what or who it is I am battling before I ever speak . . . that still remains a bit unclear. But I do know my initial reaction to Pam's question about returning to school was seared in me; even considering the mere possibility brought with it the dreaded sensation that Fear was waiting to pounce just on the other side of my life's current boundary lines.

Still something about the idea wouldn't let go. In the places where God's truth reigned and Fear's lies dared not enter, His quiet whisper compelled me onward—toward something more than what I currently knew—as if He was using my growing discontent as an impetus for inviting me into somewhere undeniably appealing.

Therein lay the crux of the matter. Mornings spent with the Father were now centered on choosing whether or not I would take this new ground laid before me, despite the fact that I knew Fear was standing on it. Or would I allow the thought of Fear's presence to bully me into staying in the wilderness and away from the possibility of inheriting what God had for me? Countless moments were spent in Numbers 3 reading about when Moses sent out the twelve spies, and all I could sense was the Father giving me the same choice: I could either be found like Joshua and Caleb, two of the ten who had the faith to believe, or I could choose to be one of the ten who rather than seeing a land overflowing with milk and honey chose only to see the giants. It was if He was asking me, *"Which one will you be, Kelly?"*

Most days my commitment and determination felt like a Ping-Pong ball being bounced from one side of the table to the other; one day I believed I would go, the next I tried to be content with where I was as I wrestled with His question until I couldn't wrestle any more. So much of me wanted to find a way to be content like most everyone else who surrounded me, until my imagination role-played what it would be like to actually walk into a college classroom, causing an unexpected flutter to flit across my heart. It was as if those images were my own private way of spying out the land.

Months after Pam's initial question I had finally found enough courage to actually ask Silence, "Do I have what it takes to do this? Really?"

I never heard much in response. Rather, in place of an answer was just the gentle reminder that the choice to stay in the wilderness or go would always be mine. Beyond that God had already spoken on the matter. I knew He was already standing on the land wooing me over to Him—waiting as only He could do until I would be ready to cross.

I sat for a long time one fall morning knowing the time had come to finally make a decision—the crossroads had come, the watershed moment had arrived. This would forever be a turning point for me, not because of college for the sake of college but rather because if I chose to go then I would in essence be telling Fear, "Get off my ground." But if I conceded solely as a means of evading Fear's presence then he would win and I would forever remain exactly where I was, and that defeat was unacceptable to me. *I can't do that, Lord. Not when I know this is what You're calling me to; how do I say no to You?* And with that I realized that with free will aside, I had no choice. To do anything less but gain the ground He called me to was something I couldn't fathom.

"I can't *not* go can I, Lord?" I whispered as I slowly exhaled. I knew before He even answered that with my fear intact, I had little choice but to cross over; I couldn't let Fear have that ground. My internal had already expanded enough for me to want it, as if the Father had been whetting my appetite this whole time. So, with that I bowed my head and prayed for courage enough to cross over, despite Fear and despite hesitation I knew the time had come to cross and cross I would do.

CHAPTER NINETEEN

GIVING WAY

*Defeat may serve as well as victory to shake the soul
and let the glory out.*
—Edwin Markham

I tossed and turned all night as a hundred scenarios played in my head. Convinced that several hours had passed since I had gone to bed, I looked at the clock that read 12:30. *It's only been an hour,* I thought, agitated. Eyes glued to the ceiling, I mapped out the route Randy had given me, trying to picture each street sign so I wouldn't get lost. "You've driven it with him a hundred times," I reminded myself, "you'll be fine."

I closed my eyes hoping to draw on the assurance that I felt the past few weeks. Mentally placing myself back in front of our computer, I reminded myself what it felt like to decide on which classes to schedule, then in the midst of wondering how to pay the Bursar's office, how surprised and relieved we were when an unexpected check came in the mail that was just enough to pay the tuition. *I know this is what I'm supposed to do, Father, but I'm scared,* my inner man confessed.

Rolling on my side, memories of Christmas morning played in my head as I thought about Randy's gift to me—the brown leather backpack. I breathed deep and reminded myself that I could do this because

Randy thought I could, then tried to calm my nerves as I reflected on the sensitivity of his gift and the care we took to protect and condition it before filling it with school supplies.

Another exhale . . . another flip . . . another exhale.

Nervous energy carried my mind to the classroom doorway as anxiety about my "non-traditional student" status urged me to quietly beg the Lord, "Please let me blend in, Father," I pleaded. "I don't want to stand out."

Eyes closed . . . inhale . . . exhale . . . peace.

By the time the next morning rolled around, I was armed and ready. The brown leather backpack Randy had bought me was leaning on the wall by the front door, silently beckoning me as if it had bore a life of its own over the past weeks. Once again the memory of the afternoon we filled it with the three different notebooks flashed before me—one for each class I was taking as well as an assortment of new and used books I would need for my respective classes.

Turning to pour my coffee, I checked my registration form for the umpteenth time. "Nine o'clock," I whispered before walking to gather all my things. I turned to hold the door open with my backside, then looked around the front room once more as I reviewed my mental checklist: *Keys, check . . . backpack, check . . . coffee, check. Good. Then, a final breath, a step down and a slam of the door,* I thought, *is all that's keeping me from being on my way to inheriting new ground.*

Tossing the backpack on the back seat, I sat behind the wheel and looked up at the house that had always represented so much of the Father's heart to me. "This is it, Lord," I told Him as I backed the car out of the driveway and drove east toward the downtown campus.

Once the initial flutter of nervousness started to subside, thoughts of high school graduation and going to school the traditional way occupied my mind as I stopped at each red light along the route. "This is the ground You want me to take back isn't it, Father?" I asked Him. "This is partly what was relinquished so long ago."

Peace filled the car as if He was giving me a silent but affirmative nod of His head. I drove a little farther thinking about how much I had changed since those first days of moving to Indiana and trying to accept life in the city rather than a simple existence in a steel mill valley. *How far we've come,* I thought, not sure exactly who I was talking to, Him or Silence.

Per Randy's instructions I made the left-hand turn onto New York Street and within seconds noticed the brownish colored tops of some of the limestone buildings amidst the tree line. With a quick visual dart to the right, I registered the 7:55 digital readout, *Good, more than enough time to find a parking space and get settled,* I reassured myself. *Class doesn't start till 9.*

Tapping my foot lightly on the brake, I waited for the light to turn green as I scanned the parking lot for a space. Green rectangular signs designated certain sections as "A" lots or "B" lots, but none of it really meant anything to me. "I just want to find a parking space," I muttered.

HONK!! Not a friendly *toot,* but a frustrated HONK jolted me from my visual expedition, reminding me the light turned green. With two quick left-hand turns, I entered the lot and began my journey into what seemed like car lot haven. Narrow passageways between the aisles served as unintentional road maps among the cars that were parked everywhere, in every direction—in the legal spaces and in the not so legal spaces, on the grass, as well as on the curbs. But for the few feet between the lanes, there wasn't an open space to be found.

A slow gurgle formed in my stomach as the muscle began to clench and wrench in what felt like every direction but outward. I could feel Chaos' presence trying to unravel me as he pressed himself into the car and I wanted to pray in Peace but I couldn't focus . . . traffic wouldn't allow. Horns were blaring and I wasn't sure where I was going or even how to get there, and the only thing that seemed real besides the angry traffic was the thunder of my heartbeat accelerating my already shortened breath.

"Breathe, Kelly," I instructed as Anxiety, like a slow moving spider, started creeping its way from the bottom of my toes upward toward my throat. The feeling was all too familiar—as if something was working its way toward my stomach and gripping it so tightly that soon there would be no room for air to enter and, slowly, breath by breath, life as I knew it would become fuzzy until it was all but choked right out of me.

Fear was making himself known.

I tried holding or warding him off, but with each passed lane and each occupied parking spot Anxiety, Fear's cohort, only crept higher. Thoughts of being the last one to walk into class terrified me, "Lord, I can't be late," I admitted, "They'll all look at me."

Another quick glance to the right, 8:17—time was ticking and I still had no idea where to go.

It's only been 20 minutes; go back to where you started and try again, I instructed myself hoping that someone may have left, creating an open space. What I didn't account for, however, was that time had also brought with it an increased number of students who had just arrived on campus, all of whom were fighting to find the one coveted available spot.

Hopelessness began to wash over me as I broadened my circle of exploration. No matter how many of the campus lots I drove to, the experience was all the same—countless drivers and no parking spaces. I reluctantly looked at the clock once more and shuddered at the 8:45 time. "There's no way, Lord . . . There's no way I can find a place to park, walk across campus and be in class on time." Desperation surged, and that's when Fear rose up to his full height—bigger than I've ever known him—taunting me with memories of how I felt the day I stood in my high school hallway late for the nth time, staring at the doorknob, not wanting to turn it because of the feeling that came when everyone looked up and stared at me.

My eyes began to sting at the memory. "I hate this, Father," I said as I steered the car toward the right side of the lane and shifted the transmission into "park." Leaning back on the seat, my neck relaxed, allowing my head to land on the headrest before I closed my eyes. *All these years later I can still see myself standing there, feeling so embarrassed and ashamed—it's as if it was just yesterday.*

"And that's how they'll look at you today if you go . . . just like they did then," his voice hissed.

A sinister chill covered me as soon as I heard him. I knew full well Fear had just spoken for I would recognize his voice anywhere—his presence just as real as if he was visibly sitting in the seat next to me.

"But it's right there," I argued, pointing to the buildings that stood just across the street. Instantly I saw myself standing on the bank of the Jordan looking into the Promised Land—but this time I couldn't get across. "All I need is one parking space . . . just one," I pleaded with Him as my eyes scanned the lot.

Fear's response slithered through the car, "But you'll never make it in time. You're not even sure exactly where you're going. What will people think if you walk in late the first day?"

I sat there as tears of frustration blurred my vision. I didn't want to listen to him. I knew better, yet I also knew there was truth in what he said. They *would* look at me and I hated that idea more than anything. *I don't want to be seen,* You know that Lord, stumbled out. "But I really want to do this," I cried out.

Glancing around once more, 8:55 caught my eye and I could see the window of opportunity rapidly closing. Defeat was setting in; I couldn't endure the thought of all those faces staring at me when I walked in late. That thought alone was enough to make me cower back in my shell. "I don't think I can do this, Father. I just can't be seen like that again."

This time neither Silence nor Peace responded, just Fear and his crippling power of suggestion that said, "Go home . . . no one ever needs to know *why*."

I sat in the car unaware of anything except the extinguishment of Hope's final ray, and cognitive only of the intimidation and terror that came from walking on land that doesn't yet belong to me. The months of exploring, strategizing and pursuing the possibilities that come with gaining new ground no longer mattered; all I could see now was the effect of the past hour and what it took for me to become completely undone.

I pulled away from the campus that day wholly dismayed and defeated—so much so that not only did I refuse to attend the first day of classes, I went home and immediately withdrew from the entire semester. The thought of Fear prowling around was more than I could face at the time.

But just because Fear may have won that battle, it didn't mean he won the war. Yes, I retreated from gaining any ground that day then ran for cover in the one place I felt the safest—home and in the land of familiar. And yes, it would take a full six months before I could even begin to address just how deeply embedded my fear of people was and how quickly, without any cognitive awareness, Fear could and would be able to use it against me. However, it would be God's faithfulness that would reorchestrate my circumstances so that the next time His child engaged in the battle, she couldn't do anything *but* win the war.

CHAPTER TWENTY

REDEFINED BATTLEGROUNDS

*There is no fear in love;
but perfect love casts out fear because fear involves torment.
But he who fears has not been made perfect in love.*
—1 Timothy 4:18

On the days and weeks following my withdrawal from school, Fear remained so tightly wrapped around me there was little to no room left for logical thought, nor did I feel the need to rationalize my decision. Silence had found me. Fear's claws had sunk in so deeply that day that whenever I even considered the remote possibility of trying again, his presence towered over me, making me feel like a crazed, wild animal reacting to the enormity of the giant who possessed the land.

I had to get away from him. The innocent exuberance that had once compelled me to register and prepare for classes had been sacrificed in the battle, and what little confidence I had initially found to even approach that particular Jordan and take dominion over the new ground the Lord had been beckoning me toward was long gone.

I felt myself slipping downward, retreating inside myself, searching for solace in my daily routine. *I just want to be left alone,* my inner voice cried whenever someone proposed the idea of trying again in the fall semester. It was a constant fight to suppress the overwhelming panic that I now associated with branching out. Just like after Matthew was born I was finding great security in staying home and protecting myself from the external threat that comes from stepping too far over your boundary lines. I was no longer zealous for a heart of courage or insistent on getting the "something more" out of life. Instead, I heard the inner murmurings quietly beg, "Please, please don't require me do this. Make me content in staying home—I'll learn to let it be enough for me, I promise."

Every time I'd close my eyes, the parking lot scene would play in my head and the familiar sense of dread would again form and begin to take hold, "I'll stay where I'm at so long as I don't have to go through that again," I'd tell Silence, the only one privy to my inner turmoil—walking with him was like walking in pools of grace. Pressure never comes with his presence, as if he's quite content to just comfort me and give me space to contemplate while everyone else wants to prod and encourage me forward.

Not that they didn't mean well; they did. But I also knew that none of the people in my circle had ever experienced or battled the same things I did. Their history was different, people weren't terrifying to them any more than new experiences were intimidating. In the face of their courage, the reality became clear—it took every ounce of courage I had on a good day to walk into a room of strangers with Randy by my side let alone into a classroom full of them completely by myself. The sheer thought of such a thing is paralyzing, especially if I'm the last to arrive and late. Those three things combined: strangers, being alone and late was like the trifecta of spoons when it came to stirring up the memory of being stared at and the shame that I felt for being 'that girl'.

The idea of it all evoked a gut-wrenching paralysis that overwhelmed my soul. Similar to the paralyzed man lying next to the pool of Bethesda in John 5 who, unable to immerse himself in the water, lay there a "long time" (John 5:6), waiting for someone to come along and help him so that he would be healed. It wasn't that he didn't know what he needed to do to be healed; he just didn't believe he had what it took to get himself there. "I understand him . . . completely," I told the Lord one day, "I'm just like him except it isn't a physical paralysis that keeps me from immersing myself in the healing waters; it's an unseen one."

Visions of driving around campus circled my mind as I sat in that truth, wondering what really kept me lying next to my pool. *What am I so afraid of, Lord? Is it fear of man? Fear of being looked upon?* I wondered. *Is that what keeps me from stepping out—because I don't want to be seen? Or is it being seen through the lenses of disapproval?* Then I remembered what someone had once told me, "We tend to exert the most control in the areas we have the greatest fear."

"So, if stepping into the unknown, into a sea of unfamiliar people is currently my greatest fear, then am I controlling it by living in the land of familiar? In the land where I know what to expect and I can control?" I silently asked Him.

The air was steeped in a peaceful silence, which I interpreted as a silent "Yes."

"So not only am I like the man at the Pool of Bethesda, stuck in my current circumstance, I'm also one of the Israelite spies who after spying out the land chose to focus on how big the giants were rather than what You had for them? And, like them I'm fighting my way to stay in Egypt?"

Another quiet, assured silence filled the room confirming I was beginning to see things through the lenses of the Kingdom rather than my own personal experience.

Churnings from the previous growing discontent began to swirl once again as I thought about life as I knew it continuing for as far in the future as I could see, exactly as it looked at that moment. Then I thought about school and how excited I had been before

Fear stomped his heavy foot all over my unexplored ground. *That's the land, isn't it? It's not just about school—school itself doesn't scare me. It's about having the courage to step out . . . out of the only adult life I've known and not being afraid to be seen.*

Affirmation filled the room as I sensed Him say, *"This is the way, walk ye in it."*

Taking comfort in His assurance, I pressed in a bit further. *And it's about taking back land that was surrendered years ago—relationally and academically.* I leaned back and focused on that revelation then minutes later concluded, *That's why You didn't answer during the drive down there . . . from the beginning, You knew there was so much more ground to reclaim than what would come from just returning to school.*

I sat back realizing that Truth was working toward unearthing a huge chunk of Fear's root, and now that it was exposed it would no longer be enough for me to stay hidden. The Father was wooing me into something through discontentedness, but that didn't mean I wouldn't have to face Fear's Goliath-like tauntings. On the contrary, "I have to go. I must take this ground," I whispered knowing full well that it was said with more confidence than I actually felt.

"Grant me confidence, Lord," sure that that was all I would come to need. Yet as fall approached and the memory of Fear's intimidation loomed in the imminent future, my recently found courage slowly began to diminish. My sense of security strong and intact in the face of far-off battles became an altogether different story when the conflict approached and turned out to be up close and personal.

As fall registration neared, so did the memories of the spring semester's debacle. Visions of lapping the various parking lots tormented me, conjuring up scenarios in my head of every eye turned on me because I walked in late. Convinced anew that I was still the paralyzed man by the pool, I read the first five verses of John 5 over and over, scouring the story for some kind of encouragement. "I need You to talk to me," I declared but all was quiet until early one morning when for the first time I could remember Jesus's words to the paralytic in verse six leapt out, *"Do you want to be made well?"*

In the lull of the moment the weight of Jesus' question immediately closed in on me as if He was standing there asking me, "Kelly, do you *want* to be made well?"

His tone, the articulation of how my inner man heard Him speak, I *knew* it was Him for only He can ask a question in such a way that it cuts right through the heart of all the confusion and clamor.

"Yes, Lord, You know I do," was the first thing I wanted to shout. I longed to be well, to be free of all that tormented me but admittedly I was hesitant to say yes. My history with the Lord lent credence to the fact that my own inner healing has most often required a willingness to cooperate. More than once, I've had to go back to my personal Jordan, cross the river and take the land He had already marked out as mine. My sense told me this time would be no different. In fact, it was the only way I would ever be able to "Rise, pick up my mat and walk," (John 5:8).

"I'm scared, Lord. The people frighten me . . . and I'm scared of being looked at . . . . but most of all, I'm afraid of being by myself and having to do this alone."

I listened as my own confession rolled off my tongue, instantly recognizing Fear's fingerprints, and knew at that moment the choice was mine. *Whose voice would I listen to? Whose lead would I follow?*

Consumed with my own assessment of the fruit each decision bore, remnants of a sermon I recently heard came back to life, "If you want to undo the works of the enemy, then do the works of the Kingdom," our pastor instructed. Then, like illuminated lights that line the aisle in a movie theatre, each of these things made way for the next: the paralytic . . . Jesus' question . . . our pastor's quote. As individual lights they only showed part of the whole, but collectively assembled, they were all pointing me in one unified direction—toward the door to healthiness and freedom.

Jesus' previous question stirred in me once again, *"Kelly, do you want to be made well?"*

My physical body didn't move even though I could feel my inner man sigh in response. Clearly the time had come to decide. Weighing my options, the haze began to lift, revealing that when things were all said and done, the heart of the matter wasn't really whether or not I would stay where I was—at home, secure, inhabiting the ground I had known for most of my married adult life. God didn't have any issue with that; in fact, He would more than bless it if that were truly my heart.

No, the real issue lay in the *why* I would stay home. Was it because that was my heart or because I was too afraid to do anything else? Was I willing to continue to give Fear that kind of power over me?

Memories of being a little girl flashed through me as I heard my mom say, "We don't quit, Kelly. We never quit," her words sending me back to the beginning of the semester and the overwhelming panic I felt in Fear's presence. *Do I have what it takes to overcome such anxiety?* I wondered. Then thoughts of what lie on the other side of his intimidation sparked a flicker of hope as images of walking across campus played in my mind. "I want that, Lord," I whispered, "I want to be free enough to walk on that ground."

Those spoken words were all God needed to then teach me that the most effective key we have when it comes to winning a battle is first learning how to identify our adversary. Cloaked in disguise, he often lies in cover, whispering the subtlest of lies in hopes of thwarting God's plans by destroying us in the process. It's taken a fair amount of time for me to learn that victory is almost always connected to our ability to discern the fruit of the one who so vehemently opposes us. In other words, the battle is never truly rooted in our circumstances but rather what rises to the surface in the midst of that which longs to oppose us—that alone reveals who and what we're coming up against. It's in the undoing of that opposition that we discover what lies we've chosen to believe.

In my case, intimidation and insecurity became the key weapons in Fear's arsenal that kept me bound and confined to my current location. However, it was my agreement with his tactics that empowered him and ultimately limited and restricted the Godly fruit being produced in my life. It wasn't until I set my eyes on the ground that lay beyond the battle that my desire for freedom and wholeness finally overrode my willingness to be defeated.

It took six months before I allowed Courage to grab a stronger hold of me than Fear, and it took six months of circling the mountain many times before I actually allowed Him to have His perfect way in me. It was at the end of those six months just weeks before the fall semester started when, like the closing paragraph of a chapter, the Father led me to 2 Timothy 1:7, *"For God has not given us a spirit of fear, but of power and of love and of a sound mind,"* then immediately followed it up with 1 John 4:18, *"There is no fear in love; but perfect love casts out fear, because fear involves torment. But he who fears has not been made perfect in love."*

I took those scriptures and read them and reread them until their truth was seared on my heart. Then, as if they were my own personal weapons, I carried them with me the first day of class, reciting them over and over as Fear taunted and mocked me, then carried them with me like arrows in a quiver every day I walked on campus.

Admittedly it took a long time before Fear's voice wasn't the loudest one I heard, and it took even longer to be made perfect or whole enough that I would walk more with Courage than Fear when entering class a few minutes late. But the hardest steps to take were the first ones. And though my nerves still flutter when I'm without a seat in a crowd, and I remain a bit vulnerable to the voice of Intimidation that still wants to taunt me in hopes of pulling me back toward captivity, I am learning how to use those voices as invitations to experience more of Him.

It's *because* of what they have tried to do to me that not only have I come to experience the Father's perfect love, I now *know* the voice of my Shepherd. I *know* His voice because He alone has laid me down in green pastures and He alone has led me beside the still waters. He has been the One who has restored my soul, and He is the One who speaks peace in the midst of my most turbulent chaos. I *know* because He has and will be faithful to do it all again and again.

But more than anything, because of that season in my life, I know that my most ardent enemy is sure to be defeated by the Father's goodness and mercy for they continually pursue me. They first found me as a young girl making her First Communion then met me again at the altar nearly ten years later. All the days of my life He's been chasing me—not because of who I am, but rather because that is who He is, those attributes are the very essence of His personhood.

He can't help but be altogether good, all of the time. From the beginning to the end, He is fathering me into His goodness, and I am thankful.

CHAPTER TWENTY-ONE

An Expanse of Possibilities

A man's heart plans his way, but the Lord directs his steps.
—Proverbs 16:9

*E*ach step of new ground I took required Fear to retreat just a bit farther. Frequent encounters with various circumstances gave me new insight into who God said I was as well as opportunities to walk that insight out. My boundaries were expanding until the victories I was experiencing began to overflow into my family. I was discovering a subtle release on how tightly I held everyone, as if my recent discoveries were unwinding a tightly woven spring.

Excelling in subjects like math or learning how to systematically break down major assignments like a twenty-plus page thesis paper allowed me to walk on the land called "Excellent" rather than "Average" or "Failed". Little by little I was becoming more of who I was created to be rather than who or what my circumstances declared me to be.

Those moments were the first of several times when I identified the invisible line that seemed to run parallel between Matthew and me. In many ways it felt as if we were running alongside each other, having different experiences but each producing similar results. We were, despite what others may think of us, in our own individual seasons of becoming more comfortable in our own skin. Striving for man's approval was for both of us starting to wane.

Just as I was starting my third semester of college Matthew's senior year was also beginning, which included another season of football, but this time letters of interest from various small colleges in central Indiana began arriving as well. Impressed with his statistics and athletic records they invited him to showcases and recruitment camps, which, for a moment or two, would naturally pique his curiosity. Then Randy and I would watch as Matt's inner resolve would reemerge and a look would come over his face and instinctively we knew even three years later his spiritual eyes were still set like a flint on Wheaton College.

Randy and I on the other hand weren't quite so quick to dismiss the incoming attention. Much like trying on clothes before buying them, we believed there was value in knocking on the various collegiate doors and that, frankly, no harm could come from visiting their campuses and exploring prospective scholarships. It was something Randy simply called "fact finding missions."

Most Saturday afternoons were spent "knocking" on the doors of numerous college campuses, exploring their options and taking in their individual climates or atmospheres. Our visits didn't mean that we didn't share or even believe in Matt's conviction regarding Wheaton; it was just that Wheaton felt so beyond us—so much more than what people like us ever aspired to or achieved—therefore, we needed to be somewhat realistic.

We especially didn't want to put God into any box so in the name of open mindedness we required Matt to visit, talk with and explore the offerings of each college that had contacted him, and because of his congenial nature, he willingly went along with it. But always, despite their academic packages, their newly renovated campuses and their stellar football programs, he always came back to the same conclusion: "I just can't let go of the thought of Wheaton," he would say with a mixed amount of certainty.

The more campuses we visited, the more predictable Matthew's reaction became, bringing with it a resurgence of his eighth grade/Jim Elliott/Wheaton declaration. It was as if each campus visit somehow added to his resolve to stay committed to what he believed God had spoken to him years ago. Regardless of how often we tried to redirect his attention, he stood with the same surety of faith he had demonstrated when he was just thirteen.

In the years that followed Matthew's initial introduction to Wheaton College I had done a fair amount of research, and though Randy and I were duly impressed and enamored by the spiritual reputation of the small, suburban Christian campus, its price tag as well as its elite academic requirements always served as a reminder that it was far greater and better than anything our family had ever achieved to date—simply put, it was out of our league. *People like us just don't go to places like that,* was a reoccurring thought that I kept to myself.

Obviously, I never actually put voice to those words, yet it remained a silent consideration that subconsciously played a role as Randy and I helped chart out Matthew's course in life. Undoubtedly Wheaton had always been Matthew's unspoken standard, but it wasn't until we drove home from visiting a small impressive school in southern Indiana that we gained an understanding as to why.

Hours after listening to academic presentations and touring various aspects of the campus, all three of us were glad to be heading home. We had spent the past few Saturdays doing what Randy called "windshield time" with one another, so I was glad to finally sit quietly in the passenger seat and listen as Randy asked, "What are your thoughts, Matt? They're offering a great financial package. You'd get to play football *and* they've got an amazing academic reputation."

I looked out the window watching the golden silk of the fall corn dance across the wind-tossed field waiting to hear Matthew's response. Yet only a silence consumed the car—one that lasted long enough to make me wonder if Matt had fallen asleep. Glancing over at Randy I considered twisting around to see, when suddenly Matthew cleared his throat and hesitantly replied, "I don't know, Dad. I just don't think it's what I'm looking for."

His tone was unusually tentative—a subtle betrayal that seemed to disclose the inner turmoil he was apparently trying to contain. I wondered if I was right.

"Dad . . . ," and another moment of silence as the uncertainty that apprehension carries added itself to the car. I sensed the expansion of Matthew's lungs as the sound of his inhale worked its way to the front seat, then another pause before he continued, "I don't know . . . it's just that my last three years of high school have been spent explaining why I don't drink or why I won't be with a girl or why I don't go to parties. I really want to go somewhere where I'm not the only one who doesn't do those things . . . I don't know . . . " his voice trailed off before a quiet, "I'm just tired, Dad," the weariness evident in his voice.

Something told both Randy and me to remain quiet and listen because Matthew wasn't quite finished. "I'm tired of explaining . . . and I'm tired of defending. I want to be with people who are like me—people who don't do those things because their faith offersthem something more. I'm tired of being lonely." He paused then finished with, "Dad . . . I don't want to have to explain anything anymore."

The articulation of Matthew's heart captured my attention. It was as if someone had finally unplugged whatever had been damming him up and he was able to release all that had been behind his insistence on Wheaton. Through the course of reading about Jim Elliott, Matthew had come to strongly identify with the spiritual DNA that defined Wheaton's atmosphere, and because of that he now recognized the weariness that comes from trying to live righteously in an unrighteous world.

For the first time since Matthew was a little boy I recognized that although he had countless friends and was loved by many, he felt relatively alone. Never really feeling *known* . . . not in the depths of who he was, where his love of God existed. Although his magnetic, life of the party personality was an incredible blessing for those around him, the reality was few, if any, had ever tapped into the inner part of who he was, not really.

A hundred scenarios ran through me as I thought about who he was becoming, and the fight for faith he had been willing to wage. *He's always been this way, Lord, from the very beginning. In fact, I think he was born this way and he doesn't want to work at fitting in anymore. But, Father, Wheaton? I don't know that we can do that...* My heart so badly wanted to say yes but I couldn't get my head around the numbers. I quickly glanced over at Randy, hoping to anchor myself in his stability, but all that was written on his face was the depth of compassion he felt for Matthew's solitary spiritual life of conviction.

The reality of Matthew's call escorted us home as glimpses of his childhood danced across my memory . . . those early days when he was just learning to talk and the first thing he would say to anyone he met was, "Hi! I'm Matt, do you love God and Jesus? Because if you do I can be your friend" . . . and within minutes he had an entire store evangelized. I smiled at the memory as the solid white line on the road scrolled by.

Fast-forward to a few years later when, as a first grader, he responds to a "I'm special because . . . " assignment by drawing a picture depicting the Father's hands forming him in the womb and writes a caption above that says, "I'm special because I am fearfully and wonderfully made by my Father."

What seven-year-old does that, Lord?

Minutes later and miles closer to home . . . memories of Matthew in the sixth grade, seemingly cool in his aviator glasses running in the front door, a school paper waving in the air above his head as he announces, "Mom! I got an A!" And what do I notice? Not the A, though proud of him as I was, but the doodling of Jesus' name all along the border of the paper and the three crosses of Calvary sketched across the top right-hand corner. That was the first time I thought, *There is something on this child, Lord. I don't know what, but You've marked him for something.*

And now here he is, still entrusted to us, not only as his parents but as his spiritual guardians. And though we may only have him for a little while longer, You have given him to us to form and to fashion him for Your use. What do I do, Lord? How do we direct him? I can't afford to do what You have spoken to him.

"But can you afford not to?" came His gentle response.

The car ride remained relatively silent for the most part for the remainder of the ride home. I suppose we each became lost in our own memories . . . college bound children can do that to families. It wasn't until hours later when Randy and I were getting ready for bed that he asked, "Kel, how are we supposed to do this?"

"Do what?"

"Require Matt to go to a state school or a secular college when he has the reasoning he has? How am I supposed to argue with that heart?"

I sat down on the bed as perplexed as he was and just looked at him.

"Kel, I don't know how we can afford Wheaton," then he paused before continuing, "for that matter, how can we afford anywhere?"

A flashback of God's earlier question surged through me as I shrugged my left shoulder upward then grinned at him. "God has always been faithful, Randy. If He's called him there, He'll show us the way to pay for it. We've always walked by faith . . . this is no different."

Taking a slight step toward me, he looked down at me, sending me a silent but hesitant "My head says you're right, but I'm not completely convinced" look.

I leaned back on the headboard of pillows, knees tucked up under my chin, and thought about Fear, about how it is bred on the grounds of Doubt—two adversaries whose life goal is to win the affection of one's soul. Fear and Doubt are partners in crime when it comes to preventing Faith from taking hold. It never really matters which one of them prevails, so long as Faith doesn't become the bedrock or anchor unto which our souls learn to walk, because only then have they done their job.

The past days' events began to play in my mind: colleges and classes, football and fraternities all seemingly viable options, especially to a girl who has only dreamt about what traditional college life might be like . . . then Wheaton, always Wheaton, like an inexpressible standard that no other school could compete against. "Is this You, Lord? Are you really asking us to take this big of a step of faith, Father?" I whispered. "How does one know when he's 'called'?" I asked Him.

Again Matthew's zeal and passion coursed through me. I couldn't deny his heart or how I believed he would prosper in an environment such as Wheaton. *If he's come this far and few have invested into him spiritually, what could You do if the multitudes chose to pour into him. Is this what You want for him?*

I slid my legs under the covers, knowing full well that if this was really going to happen, it would be an act of His hand for He was the only one who could open the doors and make things happen. "Open the doors that no man can shut and shut the doors that no man can open, Lord," I prayed. "We don't want it if it's not You and won't go if Your presence doesn't go with us. Besides, Father, I can't afford it if You don't provide it."

The weight of uncertainty and doubt began to lift as His presence filled the atmosphere. I closed my eyes and centered myself on His peace.

Then I heard that voice, so recognizable and so distinct: *"I AM the Lord your God, faithful in all my ways. That child is Mine and I know the plans I have for him. Plans to prosper him and not to harm him, plans to give him hope and a future. You must trust me with him and where I am taking him."*

With that I said not a word, merely kept my eyes closed and breathed Him in, knowing that so long as I stayed in the midst of His presence, Fear and Doubt couldn't have access to my soul. His Spirit wouldn't allow it.

CHAPTER TWENTY-TWO

THE LINE OF DEMARCATION

Above all, be the heroine of your life, not the victim.
—Nora Ephron

We pressed in that following year to a life that was clearly changing. Growing increasingly more comfortable with the idea that despite my non-traditional status I was an official college student somehow helped me come to terms with the idea that instead of being at the starting gate of raising children, my race was somehow nearly half over. In the places where Little Tike basketball goals, bicycles, and Barbies had once filled our home, college applications, motorized scooters and braces now took their place. All of which meant life doesn't ever wait for us to be ready; inevitably change comes, often times bringing with it opportunities to make peace with the past.

As Randy and I gained a whole new understanding of what it meant to surrender control, Matthew's completion of Wheaton's college application rose to the top of the priority list over the past year. Somehow God was bringing us to a place where our desire for what He wanted was greater than our fear of what could only be done in the natural. Therefore, we conceded our resistance and joined Matthew as he journeyed down his walk of faith.

Then, as if their varying ages required us to switch gears, there was Anna—the epitome of emerging adolescence with her experimental tries at fashion, innocent crushes and a steadfast resolve to remain fiercely independent. She was stoic and passionate all at once. Her calm waters ran immeasurably deep, and the only ones who truly understood her were those who took the time to stop and listen to her silent way of speaking.

At thirteen and unlike me in nearly every way, she remained a sort of mystery to me, but I was learning—learning how to communicate with her and learning to value the unique nature that she embodied. On one hand Anna was active yet something deep inside her was always still, quiet most days yet boisterous at the most appropriate times like when her cheerleading uniform came out, as if it empowered her to step outside herself even if only for a few hours each week.

Unlike most of her peers, Anna always appeared confident within herself even as a young teenager. She was never one to look to the left or the right for assurance; she just always seemed to move straight ahead, comfortable to do what worked for her regardless of what everyone else was doing. In many regards she was immovable, and when life got hectic and unpredictable she rarely became flustered. Instead a calm resolve would emerge, and when she began experiencing a mysterious pain on the right side of her jaw, it was her resolve that empowered her to remain unshaken, centered only on enduring it until it passed.

Most days, when I had the time, I marveled at not only Anna's tenacity but the character within my boys as well. The other days were spent juggling a full-time academic schedule and the class assignments that came with it. Gone were the days when classes were casually spread out over the week; after three semesters of trial and error I learned to limit my time on campus to two days a week. Doing so helped keep the rest of my life in balance, but it also meant those days were packed full with back-to-back classes, leaving only enough time to rush across campus before the next one began, and certainly no time to make friends, which was fine with me. I was there to reach a goal—one that did not include stepping any further out of my box than absolutely necessary.

With each passing semester, however, as I worked my way up the academic ladder, course assignments increased in difficulty and projects became more and more partner or group based. Sitting in the back of the room then scurrying to the next class unnoticed was becoming less and less of an option. On the contrary, the higher up the academic ladder I climbed the more narrow the field became as classes got smaller and the opportunity to remain invisible winnowed, requiring me to actually speak with people I normally would be too frightened to even look at let alone converse with.

But now, with half the semester behind me, I, still in my fairly covert state, had grown pretty comfortable with my assessment of the students in one of my writing classes. Knowing most of them were young and artsy in nature, and that I wasn't like any of them, I was intent on just getting the job done if you will—do what was required and put all my efforts in the assignments rather than in getting to know people who were nothing like me—*especially that one over there,* rumbled the unexpected thought in my head.

We were polar opposites, unlike each other in every conceivable way. Me, conservative; she, liberal. Me, overtly feminine; she, part of a community who identified themselves as "gender neutral," which I wasn't even sure what that meant. Me, a person of deep abiding faith; she, a self-proclaimed atheist. Over the course of our time together as a class she had made it abundantly clear that she had no place to put "those Christians," always sounding trite in her mocking tone. She considered them, " . . . close-minded and backward . . . not relevant or in touch with the youth of today," she said.

Smiling at her perceptions, or more appropriately her misperceptions, I figured that from her vantage point we did resemble those things. *Little does she know about the road it's taken to get here,* I thought as I listened to her stereotype a group of people she didn't know individually, and wondered what it would take to infiltrate her perception.

"Are there any questions on the assignment?" the professor asked, her voice drawing me from its curious mental interlude as if buoying me back to the surface in search of some much needed air. I glanced around the room noticing the five or six hands extended in response to her question. "So, you want a three to five page paper detailing an organization that meets a specific need in the community, and it has to include an interview with one of its volunteers. Correct?" asked one of the young men sitting next to me.

"Exactly, and it's due next Friday."

I scanned the suggested organizations listed in the packet on the desk in front of me and wondered which one would catch my attention: Habitat for Humanity, Indiana Rape Crisis Center, Indiana Youth Institute, etc. . . . on and on the list continued to the bottom of the page.

Scanning it once again but this time in reverse order, my eyes stopped at the write-up for Indiana Rape Crisis Center. Something about it drew my attention while all the other choices seemed to blur out of view. ". . . Formed by former victims of relationship and/or family violence for the purposes of assisting others to find resources, receive guidance, and enjoy the support and empathy of others who have 'been there, done that.'"

Perhaps it hit the same chord that Tamar's story from 2 Samuel had when my counselor had given it to me years ago, or T.D. Jakes' assurance that being physically accosted isn't the only form of rape—emotional rape is also violating; it just looks different. I wasn't exactly sure why but something about this organization leapt out at me.

I spent the days following the initial assignment researching and dissecting all the various services the Indiana Rape Crisis Center (IRCC) offered, then made feeble attempts to systematically put everything into some kind of cohesive written order, all the while leaving space where the results of the upcoming interview could then be inserted.

The uncertainty that came from not knowing exactly what questions to ask or if I even had the tact to ask such things in a way that was sensitive or honoring made me nervous, which, I've come to learn, is never good. Nerves always seem to get the best of me, resulting in one of two things: they either tie up my tongue completely, rendering me speechless, or the opposite—I lose all social filters and out of nervousness blurt out whatever response comes to mind. Most often I end up being the walking poster child for what could be called "foot in mouth" disease.

I knew from the IRCC write-up that whomever I spoke with would be a "former victim" in some capacity, so I decided to start with what I had. From my own emotional experience I was well aware of how violated and betrayed I felt. *Losing my voice in the process just complicated things,* I thought.

Somewhere in the back of my head the video from the abstinence training from years ago began to replay, and I remembered how real it felt when the young girl said, "No one ever told me I would feel this way." *That was the first time I felt like someone understood how I felt. There's a power that comes from knowing someone understands because they've been there.*

It took seconds for the principle to transfer, then seconds more to realize this interview, this assignment I'm doing could give a girl an opportunity to describe what it feels like to be a victim of rape, to give her voice the chance to be heard. Then I assumed that once she started talking, additional questions would naturally form from her story, thereby creating a strong interview that would highlight the different services the organization offered and how they are constructed around the needs of their clients. *Brilliant,* I thought, *now if just my stomach felt the confidence my head does.*

Entering the building, I reminded myself that I was as prepared as I could be, and since the focus wasn't on me I would be fine. "All you need to do is ask questions and get her talking," I whispered as I waited for the elevator doors to open.

Ding.

Once inside the elevator my weight shifted in antsy response to the frozen white light announcing the fifth floor destination. *This is it.* One last deep breath, then one final silent command for my stomach to stop fluttering before stepping into the hallway as I made my way to the frosted bubbled glass door that had *Indiana Rape Crisis Center* scrolled in black lettering across its middle.

Peopleless desks filled the room, each set of two partnered together to make numerous ninety-degree angles throughout the office space. The décor was seemingly bright, enhanced by the multiple windows that allowed sunshine to roll in and workers to look out over a small downtown park amid the clutter and piles of paperwork. I looked around curious as to where all the desks' inhabitants were, but only heard a small chatter coming from around the corner . . . two, maybe three different voices at the most.

Scanning the room one more time, I wondered which desk belonged to the receptionist. *They all look the same . . . now what?* I waited. I could still hear their chattering, but then slowly their conversation eased, giving off a finality that sent a silent "Just a few more minutes."

When a heavier set woman walked around the corner minutes later profusely apologizing if I had been left waiting, I smiled at her then worked up enough courage to stammer out, "Um . . . Hi . . . I'm Kelly Williams . . . I'm here to conduct an interview with one of your volunteers."

With my gaze still fixed on the woman who greeted me, I hadn't noticed the specific characteristics of the woman who had taken a seat at one of the desks in the far-off corner. I was too zeroed in on maintaining my ground. "Yes, yes," the woman said, "I remember talking to you on the phone. I think Mel is ready to see you, aren't you?" she said, turning her attention to the woman seated in the corner.

My eyes instinctively followed to where she was looking, and I had to immediately fight the urge to chuckle at God's sense of humor. The volunteer I was scheduled to talk with, the "Mel" the woman referred to, was none other than the young woman from my writing class—the one who for the past eight weeks had continually stereotyped people like me, and who, as a result, I had stereotyped as well.

"Of all people, Lord? Really?" I silently asked.

Silence was usually His response in situations like this—those moments He puts you in when everything defies the way you would have ordered it, leaving you with nothing except to laugh and wonder what in the world

He is up to because only He could have orchestrated such a thing. Yep, it was exactly that kind of silence.

The second prayer I muttered was one of requesting He give me a poker face because if I was looking at her with any semblance of the emotion that was evident on her face, it was undoubtedly going to be a long interview . . . a very long one indeed.

Internally bracing myself, I took a deep breath, smiled at the woman who had first greeted me then made my way over to Mel's desk. It didn't take long for either of us to exchange social pleasantries, for we were both at an unusual loss for words. The fact that she was well-acquainted with the assignment certainly helped pave the way for the question/answer portion of the interview.

Mel filled our initial time together explaining the vision and mission of the IRCC, then wrapped up her presentation with the most recent statistics on sexual crimes committed in central Indiana. As she spoke and I listened and asked questions, we somehow unknowingly entered each other's worlds; the invisible wall erected by our mutual misperceptions slowly began to lower.

The information she gave me was crucial to the academic success of the paper I was writing, but what amazed me even more was how we had gone from being complete and total opposites in every regard to two women openly discussing the needs of sexual assault victims and ways to best meet those needs. The common ground had been so easily laid out that I don't believe either one of us ever even noticed we were actually walking on it till it came time for the personal interview and I pulled out the list of questions I had prepared.

I reviewed the first two or three questions, sharing with her that through the course of our conversation she had already answered them. Next, not sensing room for much else, I decided to just jump in—"Okay, Mel, the mission statement says that the Indiana Rape Crisis Center was formed by former victims who have 'been there, done that' in order to assist others." I paused, praying that grace and sensitivity would coat my next words before I asked, "Can you explain what it feels like to be a rape victim?"

Her brows immediately burrowed in confusion and her head cocked to the left, then slightly shook back and forth. "I'm sorry, Kelly, but I am not a rape victim," she said, before pausing.

Confusion jumped to my side of the desk. "But the mission statement says . . ."

Before I could finish my thought Mel continued, "Oh, don't get me wrong. I have been raped, but I am *no* victim," she continued relaxing back in her chair. "I am, however, a rape survivor."

Then, as if Dignity and Grace were her escorts, she went on to describe her understanding of the overcoming life and how she had learned not to be defined by what she termed "that one event." Rather, it wasn't until after the assault that she had to make a choice to either remain victim to it or learn how to stand on top of it and use it as a platform to help other people.

"How? Mel, how did you do it?" I asked for more reasons than to just complete the assignment.

"I had a great counselor from the very beginning."

As her eyes revealed her own internal journey down memory lane, something told me to pause and grant her space so she could formulate her thoughts. I prayed while she travelled, and when she spoke again, she spoke of the many well-intentioned friends who came barging in the night of the attack, telling her what to do because she was shattered and unable to think clearly. One friend told her to do this and another friend told her to do that, but all she could think about was the driving need to shower and to " . . . wash him off of me but no one would let me. They insisted I call the police. That's when I found this place. She came in and instead of telling me what to do, she asked me what *I* wanted to do."

"It's the first step toward giving power back to the victim, Kelly. You see, rape isn't a crime of sex, it's a crime of power and at that moment I had been rendered powerless. So when people, no matter how well-meaning they were, came in and told me what I should do they were, in essence, keeping me powerless. Giving me back my right to decide, my right to choose who to call or what to do was the first step toward reestablishing my sense of power. It was also the first step toward my becoming a survivor rather than staying a victim."

Struck dumbfounded by shock and an unexpected awe I wasn't sure how to respond. The irony that such profound truth had come from such an unlikely source was inescapable. Sitting there I never anticipated anything more than answers to a class-assigned interview, and instead I walked away feeling as if Truth itself had broadsided me with the power of its impact.

Here she was, an overcomer in every sense of the word, not victim at all to the violation and trauma she had experienced, while I in so many ways could be found licking my own wounds that lingered from years ago. To use her words I wasn't "standing on my life in Ohio and using it as a platform"—at least not entirely. Instead I still avoided discussions about the ages of my children because I didn't want to have to explain, just as I evaded people's bewildered stares upon first seeing Matthew and me together; I preferred the "legitimate" feeling that came from people's assumption that we were just one big happy traditional family.

Hours after leaving Mel in the IRCC downtown office, I was still trying to come to terms with all the Father had revealed to me through that interview. Mel's strength and overcoming spirit had made its mark. "She owns that thing, Father, doesn't she? It clearly doesn't own her."

Remnants of Psalm 51 played in my head as I considered what it really means to have truth in the inward parts. "There are still places . . . things I haven't let go, aren't there?" I asked Him as I turned the steering wheel toward the driveway.

Sitting on the front porch bench, my feet swinging back and forth like a pendulum, I watched as the autumn leaves surrendered to the call of the season as past events that could prick my soul at a moment's notice came to mind: sitting in the U-Haul truck the first time my mom and I moved to Indiana . . . standing in the hallway of my high school months later feeling completely and utterly alone . . . permanently leaving Ohio for the last time.

"I didn't ask for that life!" I whispered, the collective pain of it all rising to the surface.

The betrayal . . . the violation . . . the overwhelming feeling that comes when there is absolutely no one there to help shoulder the weight. It all came flooding back, the anguish just as real that day as it was when it all happened. Each moment played and replayed in my head as if I was being allowed to view it for the last time. Then Mel's words, *"Oh, don't get me wrong, I've been raped I'm just no victim. I am a rape survivor,"* began to take hold until a quiet whisper finally arose, "I don't want to feel this way, Father. I don't want to be a victim . . . not anymore."

"Then give them to Me, Kelly. Release them into My care."

I breathed deep, remembering from the Judith McNutt conference how things worked. I knew I would have to lay them down, but it wouldn't be until I was ready. That was how my empowerment would come—by me being the one to decide when I was ready. Until then, I knew He would wait.

Moments like those with the Lord can't be measured or quantified by the hands that circle the face of a clock. Time becomes infinite in His presence. To that end I'll never know how long it took for me to gather those moments one by one and allow the sting and the anger and the frustration to wash over me one last time, any more than I'll ever know how much longer I held them before deciding the time had come to lift each of those memories to the Lord as if they were individual offerings. Then, when I knew I was ready to let them go I asked Him to help me release them into His hands. "I don't want to hold them by the throat anymore, Lord. I want to be free."

It didn't take long for the Peace that comes from open hands to fill the atmosphere, but I do know that once I was done—once I was poured out, void of unforgiveness and washed clean—the only thing my hands held were His. Every grimy ounce of regret, resentment and bitterness had been wiped away, and I became acutely aware on a whole new level what Jesus meant when He said, *"Behold, I make all things new,"* (Rev. 21:5).

Like old war wounds I had worn as a distorted badge of honor, those memories had been with me since the day everything began. I had held them as part of my testimony, the things that made me credible to talk about the goodness of God and how He met me. While there is truth to His goodness, my holding on to them like scars in a battle wasn't honoring anyone. Instead, it was holding me captive to the very things I so desperately wanted to overcome. But in the end, it was my choice. Sitting there with Him that day I learned, it always has been.

For whatever I chose would be the very thing that I empowered. The freedom to choose to let go . . . to trust and believe Him when He says that He *will* work all things together for the good . . . and to know that though there may be times when our freedom to choose becomes limited or even revoked by others, in the end it is the Father who is always there to faithfully restore. He does so through choice and something called free will. It really is a beautiful synchronized, mysterious work of grace. Then after He redeems and shows us the pathway toward restoration, it is the Father who sets our feet firmly on the rock, offers us a platform, then whispers to us, ". . . *tell them what great things the Lord has done for you, and how He has had compassion on you*" (Mark 5:19).

If only we will trust Him.

CHAPTER TWENTY-THREE

THE ONSET OF WAITING

. . . of all the hardships a person had to face none was more punishing than the simple act of waiting.
—Khaled Hosseini
A Thousand Splendid Suns

My spiritual experiences, like the one that resulted from my interview with Mel, have a way of imparting such Truth into my inward parts that inevitably I leave my time with Him with a spirit that's been washed clean, taking nothing away with me except His goodness. I can exist like that for days . . . soaring, never really feeling like my feet need to touch the ground because He's got me. His presence is that good.

Those moments have a way of becoming our personal mountaintop encounters, but then soon enough He calls us, just like He did Peter, James and John, to come off the mountaintop and dwell in the valley where His glory is harder to see because life eventually returns to normal, and normalcy requires us to steward the divine Truth we once received on the mountaintop.

Because of those moments on the mountain I could feel myself becoming completely His, and although there were times where certain places in my heart remained fatherless and were tender to the touch, they were getting harder and harder to find. His adoption was slowly overtaking me.

As a result the inner vacuum that had always yearned to be filled was growing increasingly smaller the more time I spent in His presence. For the first time since I was three and twirled for my natural father, I was experiencing the validation that comes with a father's love. The only difference was, the more I pursued Him the more boundless His love became, whereas my father's love always seemed to stop with my memory—one twirl, one accolade and then it was over. With Him, it's never over . . . there is always more.

The absorption of those truths was still occurring for me as I descended from that mountaintop season. Having spent the majority of my life without the presence of my father, I still had much to learn about the faithfulness of the Father and what He means when He says there is truly no changing or shadow in Him, (James 1:17). In so many ways I already knew that, because my experiences with Him had taught me such. But like a book that's read time and again, while the words always remain the same something about the timing or the season of life you're in allows you to discover something new every time you pick it up to read it.

I found the boundless character of God to be much the same way. On so many levels I had come to understand who He was and how He operated, yet there remained moments when circumstances would cast doubt on what I thought I knew and I struggled to find the words—words that could adequately explain or define the character of God that I had come to know versus the One that seemed to appear in the midst of circumstances, especially those that swirled around the lives of my children.

Holding Truth as I had come to know it was easier during the initial descent from the mountain—my encounters were fresh, as if my faith had been nurtured and its roots were able to deepen within the soul of my heart. Perhaps that's why I could join in Matthew's excitement as he submitted his Wheaton application weeks before the November 1 early registration deadline; it made sense to me that him doing any less would have rendered him disobedient. He had remained so unwavering in his commitment to Wheaton and Wheaton only throughout the past five years that somehow it just felt right for him to walk through the door as soon as it was able to open.

There were other times though when the idea of allowing him to put all of his eggs in one basket, as my mother would say, concerned me. Logic reminded me that's it's unwise to not have a back-up plan. In fact, in most cases it's downright foolish. *What if Wheaton doesn't come to pass?* I often wondered. *Then what will he do? He hasn't applied anywhere else.*

But there was no clarity— just Matthew's persistent conviction that this particular path of faith didn't allow him freedom to consider anywhere else. Wheaton was where he was supposed to walk. I would counter his conviction, concerned by the enormity of the risk that came with throwing himself on the sword of faith, but then reminders of how congenial his nature had always been would wash over me and stand in stark contrast to his tireless determination regarding Wheaton. *It's as if something else compels him, Lord. I've never seen him so determined . . . about anything.*

Then the Lord would remind me of what He said nearly a year ago, "*I AM the Lord your God, faithful in all my ways. That child is Mine and I know the plans I have for him. Plans to prosper him and not to harm him, plans to give him a hope and a future. You must trust Me with him and where I am taking him.*" Then Peace would flow and undergird my steps with rest.

His rest carried me through the remainder of the fall season and early winter as we waited with expectation for Wheaton's decision and filled the rest of our time with Matt's basketball games, as well as Anna and Aaron.

Still active in junior high, Anna's days passed with schoolwork, cheerleading and frequent reoccurring trips to her orthodontist. Months had passed since she initially complained of the pain in the right side of her jaw and still we had no medical reason for her condition.

Simply put, her chronic pain was baffling—to us as well as to her treating orthodontist. No other place on her body was painful except the right side of her jaw yet nothing seemed to help, and no explanation could be given. The best her orthodontist could offer after repeated adjustments and x-rays was a high dosage of ibuprofen to try and keep Anna ahead of the pain as well as the prescription of time. "It's a matter of patience," she said, "we need to let the jaw calm down." And with that she sent us on our way.

A blustery wind blew across the narrow parking lot as Anna and I left the orthodontist's office late that one afternoon. Bewilderment seemed to have silenced both of us as we collectively resigned ourselves to the fact that there was little more that we could do *but* wait. It was the only viable option available—for both of my elder children as well as for Randy and me.

I couldn't expedite Anna's recovery any more than I could make the calendar days pass faster for Matt. Wheaton's decision would come and pain would flee as they both saw fit. It seemed that for both of my children time was the great determiner. All any of us could do in the midst of it was hope that Anna's pain would mysteriously go away just as oddly as it appeared, and that Matthew's faith and obedience would be duly rewarded with an acceptance letter from the college of his spiritual dreams. As a family, we could hope and we could pray, but in the end all we really learned to do was wait.

CHAPTER TWENTY-FOUR

SWORD OF FAITH

*But Moses' hands became heavy; so they took a stone
and put it under him, and he sat on it. And Aaron and Hur
supported his hands, one on one side, and the other
on the other side; and his hands were steady
until the going down of the sun.*
—Exodus 17: 12

Collectively we were sure. Over time we were all but convinced. Since the proclamation of his eighth grade summer, Matt had fixed his eyes on Wheaton College, never once wavering. Randy and I, on the other hand, had taken a bit more persuading, but some five years later we were where we believed God had wanted us: at peace and excited about taking the next step of faith. Perhaps that's why when the letter from Wheaton arrived in the mail days after Christmas explaining that "Regretfully Matthew doesn't meet the necessary requirements for early admission," a collective stun filled the room.

We weren't prepared to watch Matt's heart plummet, not when we had fully expected to see it soar. Wheaton's preliminary decision had invited an invisible weight into the atmosphere and suddenly there wasn't enough air in the room. I gasped, not sure if my lungs would expand, their natural capacity for air severely diminished by his disappointment.

Matt's shoulders slumped even further as he laid Wheaton's letter on the table. With a momentary sideways glance toward Randy I silently pleaded with him, *"Say something."* But what do you say when confronted with the realization that you truly have no answers for the walk of faith that has just rerouted your child? Navigating their hearts seemed so much easier when they were young, and their faith had not yet become their own. Simple answers satisfied their simple questions. *But what answers do we offer him now, Lord?* I pleaded. Intuitively I knew the questions that were waiting to taunt Matthew's soul in the face of such a disappointing setback: "But God, I thought this was You? I thought this was Your heart . . . Your word says, 'With the faith of a mustard seed . . . '"

On and on they would go. Yet unlike when Matthew was younger and our answers guided him through his lands of inquisition, this time what *we* believed and what *we* knew to be true wouldn't be the things that would guide his way. His own faith would have to do that, which meant the answers to his questions were only his to find. *He no longer believes in You just because I do or Randy does,* I silently conversed. *But this, Lord? I didn't see this coming,* I confessed as I watched the effect of Wheaton's decision rest on Matt's shoulders. Standing there, I was completely helpless; there was nothing I could do to ease Disappointment's blow or soften the pain it inflicted. The reality was my child's faith had sustained a crushing blow and there was nothing I could do to fix it.

The awkward silence in the room began to ease as Matthew slowly lifted his head. Still with shoulders slumped and eyes downcast, he reached for the letter, slowly folded it according to its original tri-fold crease and reservedly said, "Well, at least not all hope is gone."

Another fleeting glance passed between Randy and me as we tried to interpret what he meant. "They went on to say that even though I didn't make the early admission requirements, they weren't outright denying me admission. Instead they deferred me to the 'Regular Pool.'" He paused to look at me, half of him still spiritually bleeding, the other part beginning to clot. "We should know by mid-April," he finished.

That moment was the onset of Matthew joining his sister on the team of Difficulty in a game called Waiting. Between the two of them I found myself desperate to find the right words to ease their pain, both physically and spiritually. But none came. Instead, Confusion fought to find a place as specialists began to appear on Anna's horizon and Matthew struggled to rest his eyes on April.

Physical therapy appointments welcomed in the New Year, as did a new level of participation in cheerleading. "We need to limit her involvement in things right now, Mrs. Williams—as a way to let her jaw calm back down. I think if we do this, she'll turn the corner," her treating orthodontist encouraged. Admittedly, this latest piece of medical advice was met with a fair amount of skepticism. Something about it just didn't feel quite right, and for the first time since Anna initially complained of pain, subtle moments of questioning regarding this woman's competency began to prick at me. Somewhere over the past months my confidence had begun to wane.

Despite my gnawing sense of uncertainty over Anna's condition and Matthew's inner turmoil, melting snow gave way to the budding of spring flowers and a flickering sense of hope. The physical therapy appeared to be lessening Anna's headaches but failed to address the chronic throbbing in her right jaw. In that regard her pain was worsening almost daily, despite her daily usage of ibuprofen and reduced physical activity.

As a result, she was referred to an altogether different specialist in lieu of physical therapy—one who asked brief and concise questions and conducted an even briefer exam of my daughter's mouth. Repeated bites on blue paper as well as an abbreviated sanding of the enamel on two of her back molars were the precursor to a fairly disinterested turn of the head and a calloused suggestion that I consider " . . . allowing me to run tests on your daughter for possible Lupus or Juvenile Rheumatoid Arthritis."

Frustration's voice fought to scream out, "ARE YOU KIDDING ME?? The only thing that hurts on this child is her jaw! WHY would I allow you to test her for anything beyond that?" Exasperation longed to be set free, but presence of mind thought better of it—a slow count to five and an intentional deep breath were all that separated me from completely becoming undone with that woman.

Why won't anyone listen, Lord? It seems so obvious, I inquired as I took another deep breath, tried to offer a look of truce before quietly responding, "The only thing that hurts is my daughter's jaw so why would I do that? I guess I don't understand your reasoning"—at which a rapid spreading redness of offense appeared on the specialist's face as my maternal logic fell on her deaf ears. Instead of anyone listening to what seemed to Randy and me to be completely logical, Anna's orthodontic treatment continued along with her daily dose of ibuprofen, and the not-so-subtle suggestion that I consider the possibility that my daughter was psychosomatic.

Exasperated more now than ever and filled with an enormous sense of distrust, Randy and I allowed the orthodontist one last appointment to remove Anna's braces, then left completely unsure of where to go or what else to do—for either of our older children.

As strong and sure as our faith was, neither of us knew how to take our personal convictions and experiences with God, who we *knew* had the power to make all things right for both of our children, and impart *that* faith in a practical way into our children's spiritual health. All we could really do was watch and pray as they each learned how to manage their own unique levels of frustration, confusion and physical pain.

Although months had passed since Matthew had received Wheaton's deferral, it had done little to dampen his resolve when it came to applying to other colleges. Most days it was as if Silence offered some kind of insulation from the difficulty that came with not knowing—one way or the other. Yet the days when his childhood friends would announce not only the colleges they would be attending but also the scholarship offers they received, Matt would come home conflicted. Torn between his excitement for them and the struggle it was to not get angry or frustrated as he continued to wait on the fulfillment of something he believed God had spoken to him—those days were the hardest of all.

For the first time in his young life Matt struggled to see what God was doing in the midst of his circumstances. He couldn't identify exactly what was being brought to the surface in the middle of Wheaton's fire, and after months of waiting all he really wanted was an answer and all I had to offer were spiritual clichés that tend to wound a person more than encourage him. I could tell him that God's timing was perfect or recite again, "God knows the plans He has for you." But despite how truth-bearing those words are, to the person in the midst of a faith crisis they do little to bring salve to the soul.

In my silence, I interceded for the lives of both my children. Using Lamentations, *Pour out your heart like water before the face of the Lord; lift up your hands toward Him for the life of your children* (2:19) as my foundation, I learned how to pour my heart out before the Lord on my children's behalf. I sought Him for insight or wisdom on how to help navigate my children through such murky waters, learning in the process that with regard to nurturing them, it was becoming as much about my own faith walk as it was theirs.

I hadn't yet acquired an understanding for exactly how to empower my children in the midst of their own circumstances. I knew I didn't want them to become victims—yet I didn't know how to make them survivors. I felt inept, and was growing increasingly frustrated and confused. We had completely exhausted all the known options with regard to Anna's jaw pain and still she hurt. And the only thing I could think to do for Matthew was what made intellectual sense—ease his pain by redirecting his eyes toward the April deadline for the general admission students. Focusing on that was like looking at the light at the end of the tunnel; it helped to see more than just the darkness.

But it wasn't an answer, and it certainly didn't have any spiritual power to it. It was just another way for him to hold out hope until April came. And April did come, bringing with it Wheaton's next letter extending their regret that they were unable to offer admission to Matthew at this time. The best thing they could do was put him on their waiting list. That's the moment that taught me intellectual solutions to spiritual challenges are like Band-Aids—they only work for a season but when the Band-Aid comes off it can't help but expose the original wound.

Matthew's faith was completely exposed. "I don't understand, Mom." he said, shoulders slumped for the second time after opening a letter from Wheaton College. "I really believed Wheaton was God's heart for me."

Silence prevailed in the room. I didn't have any words because I didn't have any answers. Few people I knew had walked in the faith Matthew had displayed and now I, like him, couldn't help but question what it was all for. A hundred silent accusations about God's goodness fought to stake claim in my head, and with the waiting list as Matt's only option, the door that once seemed so wide open felt like it had all but closed. The light at the end of the tunnel was dimming as darkness began to settle in.

After months and months of waiting and wishing and holding out hope, Discouragement had finally entered, his lies so seemingly true. This most recent disappointment didn't feel like God—*Where are You? Where do I put everything You told me about this child being Yours and that I have to trust You with where You're taking him? I don't understand, Father,* murmured my silent pleas. I was at a loss as to what to say to this child who sat with the same questions in his heart that lay in mine.

Brrrrring... Brrring...

I thought twice about answering it; the timing seemed completely off. But with one look at Matt who, sitting at the table, just looked at me with a quick but silent "It's okay" glance, I decided to turn and pick up the receiver before another annoying ring blared.

"Hey, girlie... been thinking about you. How are you?" Kerri asked.

I immediately fought the urge to blurt out, "I'm terrible. Matthew's faith is in a wrestling match over Wheaton, Anna's jaw hurts her more than ever and we can't find anyone who knows how to help her, class is crazy, and I don't know what God wants, and the mail is late, and..." Choked back emotions fought to add whatever other frustration I could think of, but I forced them back in their place, drew a deep breath, then responded with a very controlled and contrite, "I'm okay, how are you?" hoping it sounded stoic enough for her to believe me.

Silence lingered in the phone line, and I could sense Kerri's knowing grin looking back at me, conveying the assurance that she knew full well

I was anything but okay. I closed my eyes hoping she wouldn't press, the lump in my throat threatening to unleash itself.

"I'm okay?" she responded hesitantly, the gentleness in her voice like a soft breeze fanning the hot embers in my throat. Everything about her approach disarmed me and I felt the walls of isolation begin to crumble, giving way for the release of all the pent-up frustration and fear of the past weeks.

Everything came pouring out . . . I told her about Anna and how we had exhausted all our options. "We don't know where to turn for help . . . " then I told her about Wheaton's most recent letter and the best they could offer was placement on the waiting list, meaning his admission would depend on another applicant declining.

"He's devastated, Kerri. He really believed the Lord had called him there; I don't know what to tell him," I cried, "I just don't understand."

"But the door isn't completely closed, is it?" she asked, already knowing the answer.

I wanted to rear back and scream, "THAT'S NOT THE POINT!" but I didn't. I wasn't angry with her; I was just angry. Not even angry, I was confused. She was one of the YaYa's; she knew how strongly Matthew believed in what God had shown him, so much so that he never wanted to apply to any other college. "He's not even applied to another college, Kerri. He never wanted to . . . " my voice trailed off. Desperation fought to consume me.

Silence's gentle presence joined me somewhere along the road of hindsight and I could feel some of frustration's ensuing pressure transfer over to him. Tired and weary, all I could utter was a hesitant, "I don't know anymore, Kerri, it's been seven months. Maybe we've missed something somewhere along the way."

"Kelly," the uncharacteristic authority in her tone of voice, more than her personal address, commanded my attention as if it really wanted to say, "Listen to me."

"Do you believe God called Matthew to Wheaton?" she asked.

I hesitated before answering, taking time to scan my spirit to see if I truly believed that or not. Images of Matt's eighth grade declaration surfaced, coupled with, "... *with the faith of a child.*" Then the memory of Matthew's four spiritual guardians: Randy, my mother, John (Randy's brother), and me standing in front of Wheaton's Edman Chapel in the freezing rain as we lifted Matthew up in prayer, declaring God's sovereign will over his life but all believing in one accord that included Wheaton. *We all knew then,* I reminded myself. Then came the prophetic decrees from various places and people, all moments meant to encourage and strengthen us as we walked this road of uncertainty.

I closed my eyes and fought to grasp my resolve once again. "Yes," I said weakly at first, then repeated with more assurance, "Yes, I believe God called Matthew to Wheaton."

"Then you stand, Kelly . . . you stand even though you may not understand and have grown battle weary. Stand even though you may only have enough faith to fill the head of a pin. You must still stand. And when you have done everything else, you stand because only defeated warriors fall, Kel. You stand assured of His faithfulness, and you stand on the truth of His word. But you must stand."

We both fell silent knowing Holy Spirit had just joined our conversation, and we were in the presence of the Father. Silence enveloped us, reassuring us that what my family was going through was about so much more than simply what college Matthew would attend. This was about the depth of faith He was crafting in Matthew and calling the rest of us to walk in. I offered up a silent thank You as my tears finally found their exits.

"One more thing, okay?" she asked.

"Absolutely," I said, laced in gratitude.

"I just feel like we need to read this . . . it's out of Romans: *Therefore, having been justified by faith, we have peace with God through our Lord Jesus Christ, through whom also we have access by faith into this grace in which we stand, and rejoice in hope of the glory of God.*"

She paused, sending me a pregnant sense of expectation, then said, "Now really listen, okay? *And not only that, but we also glory in tribulations, knowing that tribulation produces perseverance; and perseverance, character; and character, hope. Now hope does not disappoint, because the love of God has been poured out in our hearts by the Holy Spirit who was given to us,* (Romans 5:1-5).

"Don't be afraid to hope, Kel," she encouraged. "Don't give Fear that room; we hope because He doesn't disappoint, and what you and Randy and Matt are hoping for is rooted in God's love for you. So stand knowing you have no reason to fall," and with that she went silent, knowing her job was done.

I sat on the top step of my basement stairs for a long time after we hung up the phone, wanting the Truth she had spoken to root deep into my soul. *What is this walk you have called us to, Father?* I silently pondered. *A walk so pervasive, so all-consuming that You desire to have every part of us? How far will this journey take us?*

"As far as you are willing to go," He replied.

A wide expanse of land consumed my thoughts as I considered what He had just said. *Just like Abraham and Joshua*, I thought. He was offering me and my descendants a land that stretched as far as I could see with no boundaries and no border—just a wide-open space that was ours to inherit if we wanted it. But it would come only through faith . . . *and faith comes by hearing and hearing by the word of God* (Romans 10:17).

Silence swirled in the space all around me, making way for His still small voice: *"In these coming days, Kelly, you must adhere yourself to My word. It is and will be the anchor of your soul, the very substance of your faith. Then you must hold fast and know that I AM good and right in all my ways.*

Shivers coursed all through me, followed by an ethereal shudder as I took in what I had just heard. "I want to believe, Father. Would you help me in my unbelief?" I asked, then chuckled at the realization that He already had. He had surrounded me with so great a cloud of witnesses in my little community that not only did they have the faith to believe when I didn't, they willingly helped shoulder my unbelief.

Days later Kerri organized a prayer gathering in the basement of her home, and all four of the Yaya women and their husbands came to fill in the faith gap and intercede for our eldest son. They prayed for God's intervention and called forth His sovereign plan, declaring the entire time that it was Wheaton.

Weeks after our prayer intervention a letter came in the mail postmarked May 23, bearing Wheaton's steeple logo, inviting Matt into the 2002-2003 family of Wheaton College. For the second time in eight months we were stunned, but this time it wasn't because Matthew was deflated. Rather this time it was the goodness of God and His faithfulness that nearly took the air from our lungs, and not just because He said yes. More because of all He had accomplished throughout the eight months of the process—we learned how to rest our hope on the faithfulness of the Father, for He alone is worthy.

Long after my family and I walked through that particular valley, Bill Johnson from Bethel Church in Redding, California, said, "When children get to rest, they dream. And they put on capes and they fly. And they jump off the furniture and they conquer the world. It's just what children do. Children just don't dream of feeling insignificant."

The purity of the Father's heart won't allow it. He alone makes it safe to dream for He alone is the Dream Giver. Because He is good and right in all His ways, our dreams really *do* matter to Him. Why it's taken me multiple trips through various valleys to accept that truth, I don't know. Perhaps it's because my "father chalkboard" had been left blank for the better part of my life; nothing but vacancy had ever really been written on it. But I know now that that is no longer true. I have loads of truths about who He is written all over the chalkboard of my heart, each one of them building on the previously written truth. Maybe that's why the Wheaton season was so profound because that was when He wrote, in the brightest colors of chalk, the deepest truths about Himself; it's what makes His Truth easier to find when the darkness rolls in.

Little did I know how much darkness was waiting to find us.

CHAPTER TWENTY-FIVE

SNAGS IN THE SEAM

*Why do you go away? So that you can come back.
So that you can see the place you came from with new eyes
and extra colors. And the people there see you differently, too.
Coming back to where you started is
not the same as never leaving.*
—Terry Pratchett
A Hat Full of Sky

The upcoming school year would mark the passing of nearly ten years since we reestablished our roots in the small community on the west side of Indianapolis. Ten years of raising children together, and ten years of pursuing faith alongside people who became more like family to me rather than just friends.

Doing life with the YaYa's had become an intricate part of my daily experience, as if something was missing if I didn't talk to one of them. I was completely content when I was with them—their presence had a way of healing the open wounds that had been inflicted when I left Ohio as a young girl.

I loved and adored them, but more importantly, I *knew* they loved me. Those women were my go-tos or what Anna called "my people." We celebrated life and God's faithfulness together, and we reflected on spiritual journeys and how far God had brought each of us on a regular basis. Then as our children grew and approached young adulthood, we breathed a bit easier as each of them made their own decision to love the Lord for themselves.

Life doesn't get much better than this, I often reminded myself. For the first time that I could remember my previous tormentors Shame and Regret no longer walked with me, which allowed me to stand taller and hold my head higher than ever before. Though Fear and Insecurity still occasionally toyed with me at the most unexpected times, my knees didn't rattle and my breath didn't shorten quite so quickly when they appeared. I was learning how to battle them successfully with each encounter.

On some level we all believed that what we were experiencing was truly something greater than us. Spending time together felt as natural as gathering for family dinners on a Sunday afternoon—it was automatic and understood. There was a seamless enjoyment in how we celebrated life together and none of us had ever experienced that kind of cohesive unity before. It was an amazing season that many of us would have frozen in time had we been given the option, but just as children grow up and bicycles somehow become cars, so too was the world around us changing.

Where two-parent families once defined the landscape of our small community, divorce and broken homes were becoming increasingly more common. As parents we found ourselves working our younger children through things at twelve and thirteen that Matthew hadn't confronted until the latter part of high school. The societal tides were turning, and maintaining the Mayberry feel of our small town was becoming increasingly challenging. No longer were families like ours the majority. Instead, I was learning that the bubble I had been raising my children in had slowly begun to burst, and for the first time since leaving "Egypt" the need to protect my children began to simmer and rise to the surface.

Utopia or my perspective of it had begun to decline and, frankly, I wasn't ready. I loved life inside the bubble—it was safe and secure, and I felt whole. *I learned to overcome here, Lord.* Perhaps that's why I was as resistant to the idea of change as I was to the rate at which it was occurring, especially in the midst of my own family.

Wheaton's football program required Matthew's August departure to occur weeks earlier than we originally anticipated and Anna's junior high years had come to an end. Standing at the threshold of high school, her adult-like personality was taking hold and becoming characteristically *hers*.

Unlike her elder brother Matthew, Anna is an introvert, fiercely independent, and is unusually comfortable with being completely different than anyone around her. Spoken words are not really her thing; rather Anna's choices and subsequent actions are her best form of articulation. She speaks a language unto herself and only those closest to her can truly understand the complexity in which she moves and communicates.

My daughter is a silent deliberator and one who is cautious to give voice to her thoughts until she has methodically processed through them, considering every facet of the whole—only then is she able or willing to share her heart. She is quietly pensive and thoroughly thinks the complexity of things, making her ultimately very decisive. She possesses a mind that thoroughly understands why she believes what she believes, making it therefore nearly impossible to sway.

Anna's resolve in any given situation is partly what makes it so challenging to argue with her. There is an assurance or air of confidence that she has always seemed to exude. For the longest time I assumed that was what helped her cope with her ongoing jaw pain; somewhere along the way she had accepted there was little she could really do about it so instead of grumbling, she chose to fix her eyes on the future, and draw from the depths of her internal strength until it took her to the other side.

But, unbeknownst to Randy and me, there was more than finding the other side of jaw pain driving Anna. At thirteen she was in the throes of our evolving community and struggling not to get sucked in by the winds of a changing culture. Caught with her feet in-between two worlds, Anna was intimately aware of the innocence that life in the bubble brought her, but that didn't mean that as an adolescent it was always appealing.

Some of the things that were seeping into the community were alluring to her, piquing her curiosity in ways that made her increasingly uncomfortable, none of which neither Randy or I knew at the time. We simply experienced the consistent, steadfast, never wavering Anna so when she came to us early that summer unable to fully articulate the complexity of her conflict, but simply asked if she could transfer to the private high school five minutes down the street, I not only was taken off guard, but the tiny hole in my perception bubble unexpectedly grew even larger.

Uncertain as to whether the bubble was slowly deflating or if the air had just been instantly sucked out, I knew that either way I was losing all sense of control. I didn't like what was happening and how Change was consistently trying to thrust my family and me into a world in which I wasn't fully prepared to enter. Memories of my last two years of high school and all the instability and change it held for me began to play in my head. All these years later, I had come to understand the role they both played in the choices I had made in my young life. Therefore, nothing in me was very open to the idea of uprooting any one of my children. My own transplant was the impetus of all things irreversible—how could I allow the same for my daughter?

Unlike Randy, it didn't matter to me that Anna's request was to transfer to a school where the focus was Christian-based and Christ-centered, just like it didn't matter that it was the place Randy had always wanted his children to attend. All that truly mattered to me was that my children experienced the stability and security that comes from growing up in one place, in one house surrounded by the same community of people. I was convinced it would have made all the difference in the world in my own life.

For the first time as Anna's mother, I found myself just like her, caught between two worlds—mine and hers. Mine was the one where nothing changed and stability reigned supreme while the other one required me to hear her heart and believe her when she said, "Mom, if I don't break away now I'm not sure I'll be able to withstand what's coming down the pike."

Most importantly however was I *knew* my daughter. I understood her resilience as well as how reticent she was, so when she spoke candidly I innately understood the weight that her words conveyed. Shrewdly aware of her limits, Anna isn't one to complain or be dramatic; her statement was simply spoken as a way to share the primary fact as she saw it. To her it was simple and fact-based, and therein lay my conflict—my own personal dilemma, if you will.

I loved and cherished everything I understood life in the bubble to represent—stability, permanency, and community. Ten years of doing life within those concepts had somehow reinforced the idea that had I gone through my adolescence never being uprooted and able to maintain my friendships, life would have gone much differently for me. As a result, I established a cause-and-effect type of relationship between the two—one that kept me from being willing or excited about introducing change to my children.

Yet change couldn't help but reintroduce itself to me. Undoubtedly the security that came out of the past ten years was giving way to the reality that with Matthew graduating and leaving for college, transition for my family was both imminent and unavoidable. Life as we had known it was on the cusp of forever changing, and now that Anna had made her heart to transfer be known, what had always been a reinforced stronghold now was beginning to sway.

Watching the peer pressure mount on Anna's shoulders didn't help my internal argument. Knowing she was battling to stay above it all was the next thing that challenged what I had always believed as true. Softly, and over time, Wisdom began to whisper that unless I listened, *really* listened to the cry of my daughter's heart, chances were Anna would struggle to weather the storm that was brewing on the horizon.

"She needs time to find herself, Kelly. Her feet need to find solid ground," Randy said one night.

A hundred thoughts ran through my mind . . . *She needs to learn to withstand the pressure . . . How will we pay for it . . . I always saw my children graduating from this high school.* On and on my mind went, thinking everything and anything to resist making this move. "It's not that I have anything against the school . . . I just don't want to leave any aspect of what we have here," I replied. Flashes of the YaYa's and their children ran through me, "I want *her* to be a part of *them*."

Randy sat on the edge of the bed silently inviting me to join him. Sitting down next to him, I sensed Silence's gentle presence come alongside me. A brief but audible exhale was released before I felt the familiar salty sting in my eyes signal the release of my pent-up emotions. I looked down hoping to avoid Randy's gaze and watched as my toe drew clockwise circles in the nap of the carpet.

His fingers gently curled around my hand but he said nothing. Instead he gave Silence time to linger. The kids' distant laughter rolled down the hallway, bringing with it the reminder that the sound of their youth was fleeting.

A soft exhale preceded a hushed, "Kel . . . " Randy muttered then paused, "I know how much you love doing life here and what it means to you, but . . . " he stopped, the tapering of his voice indicative of his hesitancy.

I closed my eyes knowing full well what was coming. *Please God, I don't want to hear this.*

In gentle tones he continued, "But I want you to consider something."

I quickly looked up and glanced over at him, sending him a silent, "What?!" as my heart braced for a slice of pain to rip through it.

"Maybe what this place has been for you and for me and for Matthew isn't what it's been for Anna. Maybe . . . just maybe . . . she needs something different," his voice trailed off.

Taking refuge in Silence's presence, the only thing I could picture was entering the school's circular driveway to drop Anna off at a place we weren't familiar with, filled with people we didn't know.

Stepping out of hiding for just a second I responded, "It just doesn't feel right, Randy. We belong here . . . *this* is where the Lord moved us. Not there. "

"I understand that, but I've been praying for a long time that God would change her heart about going there and now she's asking. So, where do I put that?"

I didn't have an answer for him. The thought of Anna going to a different school, separate from anywhere she had ever known wasn't exactly appealing—not because I didn't hear her heart or because I was worried how we would pay for it, although those were factors to consider.

Something about it felt like we would be disrupting the stability and familiarity my family had come to know—*that's* what wasn't appealing. I wasn't sure I knew how to navigate what I couldn't see coming.

A new school feels like a whole new way of life.

Yet the reality was that with Matthew leaving for Wheaton we were being ushered into that anyway. Sitting on the bed, my heart sank at the thought of additional change. Still, something Randy said resonated as truth. . . that what had worked for me and what worked for Matthew wasn't necessarily going to work for Anna. Something in the cry of her heart, despite my lack of enthusiasm, refused to be ignored.

Unwelcome images of sitting in the U-Haul truck the first time my mom drove us to Indiana flashed across my mind, reminding me once again of how easy it was to feel the ground beneath me shift then nearly give way over the course of the following two years. Then, like a major turn of the page, the next flash leapt into the recent past—the afternoon on the porch after interviewing Mel, and the release of all the pain that Holy Spirit invited me into. The awareness of coming full circle washed over me bringing with it an unwavering sense of reassurance that our life as a family had become incredibly stable over the past ten years. *I'm not a teenager anymore suspectable to the winds of change,* I reminded myself, *that life has been given over.* Then suddenly, as if someone had flipped a switch to turn the lights on, my inner man *saw* it.

I saw how life with Randy, it's routine and stability, had been God's way of teaching me how to relax and let down my internal guard—as if it was a gentle command to one of His soldiers to "Stand down." I realized somewhere along the way, unbeknownst to me, I had stopped living on high alert. For the first time since my own early high school years, before my mom decided to leave Ohio, I was safe—free from being uprooted apart from my own choice.

Without any cognitive awareness life had ceased being lived like a tightly wound spring. Instead, peace had come to fill my days expanding my ability to relax while slowly my lungs learned to breathe deeply once again. Minutes passed as I delved deeper into the last years of growth:

moving into the house, taking pictures of Anna's first day of kindergarten, her courage to attend church camp all by herself when she was ten, her excitement over making the cheerleading squad. All the passing snippets of her life began to paint the broader picture. *She was learning how to become her own person, making her own choices which really means that her desire to change schools isn't about me at all, is it?* I silently inquired.

It was on the heels of that silent question that Truth finally began to emerge—projecting my history onto her future wasn't what I had been called to do as her mother. By keeping her where she was, I wouldn't be giving her what *she* needed; I would be giving her the things *I* had always wanted. *God help me* . . . the thought of holding her back because of me or my past grieved my heart.

Uncertainty filled me as I reviewed both options—breaking open our neatly woven nest or clipping her independent wings on the basis of my own adolescent experience. I vacillated between the two options, asking the Lord to sift through my motives before I lifted my head, turned toward Randy and said, "Can I ask you something?"

"Of course," he quietly responded with an eyebrow raised and a nod of his head.

"I'm not too sure about this; you know that, right?"

Now with both eyebrows raised, he just grinned.

"Do you think it's because it hits a place in me? In other words, because of everything that happened to me in high school, am I able to be objective?"

As soon as the words tumbled out, the realization that sometimes some decisions just aren't up to me suddenly brought me a sense of immense freedom. The power behind that one question led me to discover that even years later, there were areas where I was still not emotionally or spiritually healthy enough to make certain decisions because too much of my own "self" is invested and I struggle to separate the then from the now—like an overlay on an old overhead projector, the past still laid beneath the present marking the landscape and influencing my own internal picture of how I perceived things.

Understanding the limitations of my own healthiness became key in helping me to relinquish even more control, and most often those are the moments when God uses Randy, who somehow simply understands the complexity of my life and its subsequent limitations—he meets me in those moments in gentleness and strength because he just *knows*. I suppose over the course of time I have learned to just simply trust him and where he's taking us.

It was with that knowing that he like a torchbearer led his family to two different locations that fall. With an immense amount of support and love from the YaYas, we left Matthew at Wheaton College the first week of August 2002, then turned around and drove Anna to the driveway that circled the school of her choice two weeks later.

Without question it was a season of choices and changes. One that thrust our family into a new way of life and widened our eyes to new worlds of community that forever changed the dynamics of our family. As that season expanded, it became a year of adjustments and growing up in the midst of trying to hold on. It became a year of triumphantly rejoicing in God's faithfulness and His miraculous provisions once again, as well as learning how to function five less one.

And, it became a year of trips—trips to Wheaton football games and family weekends and trips to Anna's school as we helped her acclimate to a new environment. Then in the midst of it all, there were the endless trips to the doctors with Anna—jaw specialists then more physical therapists and chiropractors. Till finally, through a "chance" meeting we learned about a northside orthodontist who has a national reputation for specializing in TMJ issues.

Most of all it was the year the Lord laid a broader foundation for our understanding of *Him*. For that was the season when I was first introduced to the concept that God doesn't like boxes, no matter how big of one we may try to construct for Him. We cannot tame that which is inherently wild. For it is exactly as C.S. Lewis once said about Aslan in the *Chronicles of Narnia*. "Of course, He isn't safe, but He is good."

CHAPTER TWENTY-SIX

Faith's Twilight

*The seeds of faith are always within us;
sometimes it takes a crisis to nurture
and encourage their growth.*
—Susan Taylor

The arms of the office chair fought to remain still against the jiggle caused by the incessant and mindless bouncing of my left knee as Randy and I watched with nervous curiosity the TMJ specialist examining Anna. His assistant had given us firm instructions to not speak during the forty-five minute exam, "You are only to watch. If you interrupt the doctor, he will ask that you wait outside."

There we sat, idle and helpless in the soft lighting of the examination room, as he called out numbers that made no sense to us and took measurements of Anna's mouth to assess how operable her jaw was. We must have been taking turns breathing because for each inhale I took I could hear Randy's exhale. Without thought our hands would find each other's and the nerves that could only be heard in the sounds of our breathing were felt in the death-like squeeze of our clasp until involuntary clamminess reminded us to let go and try to relax.

It's been an eighteen-month journey to get here, Lord. Please let him find something, I prayed. I watched my daughter who was reclined so far back in the dental chair that I wondered if all of the blood had rushed to her head, and remembered that this wasn't the first time we had been rendered helpless as parents. Suddenly I was transported back to a hospital corridor some ten or so years ago, watching as an orderly wheeled my three-year-old daughter toward her tonsillectomy—that was the first time I experienced, as a parent, what it feels like to be completely and utterly powerless held only by the mercy of those to whom we entrusted her. Watching her lay there now beneath the mindful care of his measuring tools, here we were again.

All other options exhausted, this doctor was our last resort. *If he can't diagnose what's wrong, I don't know what else to do . . . where else to go.* We had been to every doctor, therapist and specialist we could think of most who caused us to merely raise our eyebrows and leave. Yet still our daughter hurt—at fourteen she had omitted from her menu most anything of substance. The first to go was gum, then bagels, then before long pizza crust was added to the "can't eat" list, until with no improvement in sight, her diet consisted of only soft foods or liquids because anything that required force was too painful, even with her daily allotment of ibuprofen.

Being a silent observer to this specialist's forty-five minute exam gave me time to stew over this most recent journey and my frustration over the many times my voice had been dismissed by doctors because I was " . . . only her mother." Logic indicated that prior to her orthodontic treatment that had begun three years ago, Anna was perfectly health and pain free. Therefore, it was easy to surmise that once all of the variables had been isolated, the only remaining common denominator was the orthodontic treatment. Yet no matter how many times I questioned it or how many doctors I asked, we were always rerouted or sent off on an endless bunny trail that left us answerless and in pursuit of another solution.

Until now.

The subtle shift of Randy repositioning himself in the chair drew my attention. Shared tension steeped in the unknown passed silently between the two of us as we momentarily held each other's gaze before I tried releasing a half-hearted grin but neither of our nerves could relax enough to smile.

The "Ahem . . ." coming from across the room drew the attention of both of us, and in one seamless effort the doctor snapped off his gloves, reached toward the one-bulbed swinging arm, turned off the light, then stood up. In one single motion, he turned himself our direction, looked at us and said, "I'll meet you in my office in just a few minutes."

Then he was gone.

Unsettled by what I had just witnessed, my attention rested on the doctor's assistant as she tenderly helped Anna regain her bearings having been inverted for so very long. Then just as quickly, my focus went back toward my husband, who sat as still as I remembered, with his right ankle balanced on his left knee, gaze fixed beyond the immediate while his face was void of any emotion. Statuesque in appearance, control was the only thing that emanated from him.

The sound of scrunched paper drew my attention back toward Anna. Now standing, with one solitary motion her hands smoothed down the wrinkled part of her pants as her legs jiggled back and forth in what I presumed was an effort to get feeling back in her lower extremities. *Is this how people in shock feel . . . numb and void of all feeling?* I wondered.

Minutes passed as we all silently readied ourselves to transfer into the doctor's personal office. Collecting both our personal items as well as our inner thoughts, silent conversations passed amid shared looks and collective wonderment over what we had just witnessed. I think all three of us sensed that what had been rooted in the unknown for nearly two years now was about to reveal itself bringing with it the sobering reality that the answer we had pursued to discover was most likely lurking on the other side of the wall. The unspoken weight in the atmosphere grew palpable even if the strain that comes with discovery remained undetectable on both my husband's and daughter's faces.

With a flip of the switch, the overhead lights in the examination room began to hum as the incandescent bulbs flickered then came back to life. Huddled in a small diamond shape, my eyes absorbed the fluid movement of the assistant's left hand as she mindlessly reached for the doorknob while Anna's file lay upright in the woman's right arm. *Everything they know about my daughter is in there . . .* my mind concluded.

Snippets of unimportant information fought for my attention—what time is it, did her shoes match her outfit, how much longer before we hear what the doctor has to say. I reminded myself to stay focused, but I couldn't stay that way for long. As kind as she was, she sounded like Charlie Brown's teacher to me with her garbled words and elevated protocols. All I could really set my mind on was hearing what the doctor had to say. Yet my external reaction continued to mask my internal ponderings. Instead, like a bobblehead doll on a dashboard with no thoughts of her own, I nodded in mindless agreement to the instructions she gave and acted as if I understood the information she had just doled out.

"Does that all make sense?" she asked.

I looked over at Randy, certain that my eyes looked like those of imminent road kill—full of fear and dread as I waited for him to answer. His face looked as if it had been washed in ash. *He is as overwhelmed as I am,* I thought. *Oh Lord, You've got to help us,* I prayed as I slipped my hand into Randy's.

"Okay then, if you don't have any questions I'll show you to the doctor's office," she said as she opened the door. "Anna will be in the waiting room when the consultation is over."

One step toward the assistant while the other pivoted in place. Anna's eyes locked in on mine as she whispered, "I'm okay Mom, you and Dad go. I'll be right over there." A point and a slight nod of her head was all she gave before I took my next step. The sense of foreboding that had begun just minutes ago had grown in size and stature the nearer we got to the doctor's door. The oxymoron was almost laughable—we had been seeking answers to Anna's woes for months and now here they were, neatly prepared and packaged, lying just beyond the closed office door, and I was no longer certain I was wanted to hear them.

A major part of me, the side that just wanted everything over with, resisted the need to burst through the door and holler, "JUST TELL ME!

Please, please tell me what's wrong with my daughter!" The other part of me, the one that was afraid to hear what the truth might be, fought to stay in the obscurity of the unknown.

I'm a walking conflict, I thought as I squeezed Randy's hand tighter.

We followed his assistant through the door and stood momentarily absorbing the statement his oversized office made: rich in color hues with masculine, deep mahogany furniture . . . medical bookcases lining the wall to the right . . . his work desk on our left, positioned far enough away from the windows so that the table light inlaid in the center of his desk could successfully illuminate his patients' x-rays.

His assistant invited us to take a seat as I scanned the walls, taking note of each degree and each award he had earned: University of Illinois . . . Indiana University . . . Post- Doctoral Orthodontic Program . . . on and on they scrolled, nearly too numerous to count, his national recognition evident yet his credentials, as numerous as they were, brought only minimal comfort to a mother's heart laden with worry.

I looked around the room one last time before sitting in the tweed-covered chair closest to the wall, repeatedly shifting my weight in a futile effort to get comfortable. Wonderment made it difficult to find any ease. *What did he find? Would he come in with answers . . . anything?* His assistant's declaration that the doctor would be right in interrupted my thoughts and before either Randy or I could ask a question, she quickly excused herself as she pulled the door closed behind her.

Silence lingered in the atmosphere as if both Randy and I had been rendered speechless by the intensity of the attention to detail we had just witnessed. What had begun as part of the assistant's instruction to 'remain silent,' had carried over to remaining that way because despite not understanding exactly what had just happened, we had the real sense that he had discovered *something.* That sense brought with it a sobriety to the situation as if on one hand we sat waiting with bated breath to hear what he had to say yet equally we were so deeply anxious about the answer to the questions we had spent the past year asking. My heart raced in anticipation of hearing the door open, its beat growing increasingly louder in my ears interrupted finally by the sound of Randy's voice, "Well, what do you think?" he asked me.

A slow exhale released through puffed cheeks, I looked his way and replied, "I have no idea," nodding my head in sheer confusion. "Just figure that knowing *something* has to be better than living in the land of having no idea."

His gaze shifted downward as he too deeply exhaled, concern etched on his face.

The room fell silent as both of us wandered through our own individual but somehow collective thoughts. As parents we couldn't help but think the same thing, *I'll do anything to make her well.* It didn't need to be spoken. *Anything to remove the pain that seems to emanate from her face.* That alone was enough to place us on the same page. It was the helpless feeling inside that shared our unspoken space. The minutes ticked, the memories flashed as the weight of worry and uncertainty pressed down even further upon us.

Leaning back in the chair, my foot began to shake just as it had in the examination room—the only release for the torrent of emotions that continued to escalate.

"I hate waiting," I whispered as my hands wrapped around my head.

In the middle of Randy's, "I know . . . me too, but he'll be here," the door suddenly swung open with an authoritative force, sending streams of hallway light into the dim office. As quickly as the door opened, he turned to close it. Readjusting once again to the dim lighting of his office, my eyes scanned his shorter frame as he turned his desk chair to sit sliding the tails of his white medical coat off to the side. With Anna's medical file now laid before him, he leaned his crossed forearms on his desk then bellowed, "Well, well . . . we have a bit of a dilemma with our patient, Anna."

The command of his presence effortlessly filled the room, silently conveying that he was a straight-forward, no-nonsense kind of guy and would cut to the chase either because he was busy and didn't have time to waste or because like ripping off a Band-Aid, he knew the information he was about to deliver was going to hurt so he might as well do it quickly.

One immeasurably deep breath and a close of the eyes was all I had time for before he said, "Mr. and Mrs. Williams, your daughter is not in good shape, not in good shape at all," he said as he leaned back in his chair. "I'd like to know who did this to her," he said before falling momentarily silent. Before either of could answer, he continued indicating that his question was more rhetorical than literal.

"The disc on the right side of her jaw, which cushions her TMJ is completely worn out. In essence, Anna's jaw joint is operating bone on bone, and frankly her left side isn't much better."

He paused, looking at us to make sure we understood what he had just explained. Then, leaning forward once again, he reached under his desk, flipped a switch and the lights under the center glass flickered on while he pulled a film from the brown packet of x-rays.

Laying the thick negative on the glass, he circled the area on the skull, explaining, "This is an x-ray of a healthy disc and TMJ. You can see . . . " he went on to describe the function of the TMJ and its correlated disc and that Anna's had unexplainably deteriorated, causing the symptoms she had been consistently complaining about as well as producing what he called an "unstable jaw."

"That's why even though she is only months out of braces, her teeth or what is called her midline—the line between her front top and bottom teeth is already off-center. Her bite is out of alignment because her jaw cannot hold its rightful position," he said as he leaned back in the black leather chair.

My head swam in the sea of medical terminology. *I just want my daughter well. I don't care about midlines and alignments or joints and discs. I just don't want her to hurt anymore.* Unsolicited thoughts ran through my head like a ticker tape, all of them wanting to escape out in tumbling questions but the doctor's demeanor didn't allow for it. Therefore, Silence urged me to wait.

I looked over at Randy who seemingly without thought inched toward the front of his seat, took a quick breath then asked, "Can you please help her?"

This doctor, who had degrees plastered on the wall like most athletes fill a trophy case, rolled his chair close enough to his desk so his elbows could rest on it once again, then proceeded to repeatedly twist his pen open and closed before looking at Randy and saying, "Mr. Williams, that is exactly what I plan on doing."

Again we simultaneously turned to look at each other for reassurance before silently imploring him to please explain how. From that moment forward, we spent every ounce of energy we had focusing on his "overarching plan of attack" as he called it. The first step would be to get Anna pain free, which would require a custom-made splint that he would design and she would need to wear non-stop until he was confident her jaw was stable enough to endure another round of orthodontic treatment.

"You mean braces?!" I blurted out in disbelief. "But she just got out of them months ago."

His attention turned from Randy toward me, his eyes filling with compassion as he spoke, "I understand that, Mrs. Williams . . . and I am sorry. But if you want me to help your daughter and if we're to get her healthy then this is the safest and most conservative course of action we need to take."

My cheeks expanded from my audible exhale. *She's going to hate this,* I thought, holding down the eruption that was brewing inside.

Desperately seeking to ease the burden associated with the news, I so wanted a positive response to my next question: "For how long?"

He looked at me quizzically. "How long will she have to wear them?" He leaned back as if strategizing how best to deliver his next chunk of news while Dread filled the atmosphere. It was now the doctor's turn to deeply inhale, then with pursed lips he began to slowly speak, "The purpose of the braces is not to realign her teeth . . . " I felt confusion scrunch my forehead. He paused for a second longer then said, "Before this is all over your daughter will need surgery, two in fact: the first will occur within a few months. She needs to have all four of her wisdom teeth extracted for our procedure to take full effect."

"And the second?" Randy's question shrouded in both protection and confusion.

"The second will occur sometime over the summer based on how well her jaw responds to the treatment over the next six months. As the time draws closer we will call upon an oral surgeon I trust unequivocally who will be responsible for reconstructing Anna's jaw," he said very matter-of-factly.

"*What?*" Randy and I exclaimed in unison.

Disbelief caused our jaws to gape open while shock held my breath in place. All the countless trips to all the countless doctors—I didn't know how to feel. Instead, all of the maternal emotions began swirling at once as if as if they had been lying in wait. All the frustration, the helplessness, the time we lost as we searched for the needle in the haystack all the while she kept getting worse and yet no one would listen.

I couldn't breathe. My heart felt like it was stuck between beats as I tried to process what he was saying. I wanted to scream but the decorum of his office didn't allow it so instead my I began to implode, my stomach twisting and turning inside out as he continued to explain, " . . . braces are needed so the surgeon can wire her mouth closed for six weeks." Air made a long, slow escape from my lungs with each illumination of the arduous journey she would have to walk. I was sick. My only source of shelter was found in Silence so I said nothing, merely wept at the thought of what she would have to endure because of someone else's negligence.

For the first time that I could remember in my whole thirty-some years of existence, I met Anger—a deep seething, nearly uncontrollable emotion that literally wanted to explode through my skin. The more I listened to the doctor and what he was going to take my daughter through, the more I came to understand exactly how Fury feeds and nurtures Anger's existence.

Sitting back, I closed my eyes, certain that I couldn't absorb any more of what was being discussed. Until I heard Randy ask, "So if we're understanding you correctly, Anna's treatment will be done in four parts, if you will? A splint, braces, removing her wisdom teeth, then the reconstructive surgery?"

"Exactly," responded the doctor, slowly nodding his head.

"Okay . . . and I'm assuming my insurance will cover the majority of the associated costs?"

My head lifted to discern the hesitancy I sensed fill the room.

"That's a fairly interesting thing, Mr. Williams. You see, because there is such a mystery that surrounds issues concerning TMJ, the insurance companies are quite particular about what exactly they are responsible for or willing to pay. In most cases, related costs such as what you are facing are usually paid out of pocket because they are not covered by insurance companies."

"But I have dental coverage as well as major medical," Randy replied.

"I understand that, and it is probably best to speak with my insurance coordinator. I can only speak based on what I have experienced firsthand," he said as he quietly began to organize Anna's records.

I watched Randy as he sat completely upright, indicating the seriousness of how he felt. "Doctor, exactly how much are we talking? The ball park I mean?" he asked with his eyebrows furrowed.

"Exact costs are something you really need to speak to my coordinator about, but a good estimate for my services would be somewhere in the range of $10,000 for everything. Then, of course, you have the surgeon's fees and dependent on whether he will need to reconstruct just the right side of Anna's jaw or both will determine his cost. His minimum fee should be somewhere in the $20,000 range." Then like a final punch before the knockout he said, "But if both sides need reconstructed then it will be more."

Any air that was left in the room vacated when the doctor said his final goodbye then quietly left his office. With shoulders slumped and Defeat lurking in the corner, Randy and I leaned back in our chairs, aware that there were no words to express how overwhelmed we felt or how to react to what we had just been told. We needed time. Like one who is in shock, all I could identify with was the questions that had been racing through my head.

"*Why?*" . . . as if having an explanation of things would make them easier to accept.

"How?" . . . Knowing we had faced the impossible before didn't necessarily make this impossibility any less insurmountable.

"Why?" . . . *Again and again it coursed through me. Hundreds of kids get braces ALL the time and none get their TMJ blown out! WHY, Lord?*

Silence stayed with us like a sole companion unwilling to leave us in our despair, and for a long time we sat completely still, disrupted only by the occasional sniffle caused by the magnitude of the situation and how insurmountable it all seemed.

After what felt like a very long time, I finally turned my gaze toward Randy and asked, "What are we going to do?"

His own eyes filled with tears of compassion before looking down, holding his index finger up as a silent request to give him a minute. A second or two passed by before he lifted his head, gave me a cock-eyed grin of reassurance then said, "We're going to fix her," reaching his right hand over to grab mine. "What choice do we have? I don't care about the cost . . . I want my daughter well."

I pivoted my chair directly toward him, and he followed suit, our knees touching, as our hands clasped together. Bowing our heads forward far enough so they leaned on each other's, Randy quietly began to pray, just as he had prayed years ago on the night our only car was totaled and we were so desperate for God to move. He poured his heart out before the Lord on behalf of his daughter, then when his prayers had reached their end, he slowly and melodically began to sing a song that has been passed down through the ages never fully aware that it would become the cornerstone anthem for the next great season of our lives:

Great is Thy faithfulness! Great is Thy faithfulness!
Morning by morning new mercies I see;
All I have needed Thy hand hath provided—
Great is Thy faithfulness, Lord, unto me!

CHAPTER TWENTY-SEVEN

IF THIS CUP . . .

Love, in its own nature,
demands the perfecting of the beloved.
—C.S. Lewis, *The Problem of Pain*

Sight was the only sense that seemed to be noticeably functioning as we walked out of the doctor's office. I knew I was moving because I could see the floor passing beneath me, but everything else had grown numb . . . mechanical in the face of such news.

Like a little wind-up doll going through the motions, I could move but not a single viable cognitive thought was occurring. Snippets of his language, the words he used, so foreign from my own, played in my head over and over: *Custom-made splints . . . unstable jaw . . . mid-lines . . . reconstructive surgery.* I didn't have a place to put any of it. I suppose that's why it just continued to roll around in my head—those thoughts didn't have anywhere to go until I figured out where to put them.

Hashing through the physical aspect of Anna's treatment was the most difficult part of our unexplored territory. In the days and weeks that passed since our initial appointment with the specialist, large chunks of time were spent deciphering which was the greater cause for upset—the thought of my daughter's jaw being wired shut for six weeks or the reason behind the necessity. "Had someone just listened, Lord . . . things would have been different," I frequently told Him.

But my righteous indignation did little to alter our circumstances or alleviate the physical requirements now being placed on Anna. Unfortunately there was no way of getting around what the doctor had told her would occur over the next eighteen to twenty-four months. "This is the necessary course of action we have to take in order to make you well," he explained as she silently nodded her head, showing little emotion beyond dignified determination.

Sitting there at fourteen years old, her head upright and back straight, Anna's controlled resolve governed everything about her—as if in the face of such news a switch somewhere inside of her had just automatically flipped. Where I fully anticipated an emotional, frightened teenager to show herself, I marveled as she, like her father, allowed Self-Control to hold her completely together. No tears ever fell; her lip never quivered, and the assumed cries of "It's not fair" were never uttered.

Instead, Anna's determination and commitment to endure seemed to draw her inward, escorting her to a place where only she could go. I watched Silence's soft presence blanket her as the doctor's information began to find its place within her.

"She's finding her resolve, Kelly. Let her be," came the familiar quiet voice.

I closed my eyes wishing for the nth time that she could be spared . . . that things could be different and she wouldn't have to go through everything the doctor had just described. But when I opened them again, things remained exactly as they had been, so with little option and a reluctant acceptance I held my daughter's hand as she silently assented to take her first step in what I knew was going to be a very, very long journey.

CHAPTER TWENTY-EIGHT

The Abyss of Injustice

*They say that God is everywhere,
and yet we always think of Him as somewhat of a recluse.*
—Emily Dickinson

Three weeks was all it took for Anna's custom-made splint to show signs of working. After eighteen months of pursuing and going on what felt like wild goose chases, three weeks was all any of us needed to alleviate the majority of what had been Anna's chronic pain.

On one hand we rejoiced for after so much time of watching Anna suffer, she was actually beginning to show signs of becoming her old self again. Yet always looming in the distance was the road she had yet to travel and the unrelenting question of how we were going to pay for everything it would take to make her completely well.

On the worst days when panic rumbled and threatened to cut off my airways, I tried to do what Joshua did at the end of his life (Joshua 24) and remind myself of our history with the Lord and how far He had brought us. I recounted all the times when supernatural provision would unexpectedly arrive at just the right moment—beginning with when we were pregnant with Anna and my mom handed us her jar of coins that held just enough money to pay for a new crib. Then I worked my way to the most recent "unexpected" provision for Matthew's first year at Wheaton.

"But *this*, Lord? I thought to myself whenever I reflected on the surgery, "Twenty thousand dollars? Really?" the size of the number as daunting to me as David's Goliath.

My head swirled amid the figures and the details. Zooming across my thought life, I struggled to grasp just one thing to keep from spiraling out of control. But I couldn't wrap my head around everything fast enough. The vice-like pressure mounting as the cost of Anna's splint came due followed by her second set of braces. Recitation of what I had learned years ago from Mike McIntosh, the morning my children and I prayed for milk—that the Lord supernaturally provided for the Israelites on a daily basis; that they were not to store up nor worry about tomorrow, but rather live in complete reliance and dependency on God and His provision fought to find its place in my internal swirl. I tried to hold ground, I fought to do so yet the looming deadlines felt like choke holds threatening to strangle the life out of me.

We had already jumped through all of the hoops our health insurance company had set before us, then when they denied our claim, pointing their fingers to the dental side, we jumped a little higher praying for favor all throughout the appeals process. By the time we finished exploring every option and exhausting every possibility, the end result was the same—both sides of the same coin denied our claims and subsequent appeals, deciding that any and all costs associated with Anna's treatment must be paid out of pocket.

Each setback added speed to the rate in which things were spinning. I tried again to focus on the principle that since fear and thankfulness cannot coexist and God always starts with what He has, I should be thankful that Anna was finally getting the help she needed—the money shouldn't matter. Yet that grace didn't come immediately; it was something I would have to grow into over time. Until then, my foot often times found itself on the starting line of mockery where bitterness over the insurance companies' decisions loomed and the ever increasing rage I felt toward the entire situation festered.

I felt hemmed in and trapped. But more importantly, I felt voiceless—initially ignored by countless medical personnel only to be dismissed and silenced by boards of bureaucracy who deemed my daughter's condition "our responsibility" when I *knew* it wasn't. According to most everyone involved on Anna's case, including her current specialist, there was only one primary person responsible for Anna's condition—her original orthodontist.

Randy and I weighed our limited available options for some time before we finally settled on returning to where it all began. After collecting all of Anna's numerous medical records and frequently consulting with her current team of doctors, we finally penned a letter to Anna's original orthodontist outlining Anna's current condition as we understood it, the orthodontist's involvement and requested an appointment to meet with her. We strongly believed that because she was treating physician with regard to Anna's condition it was only befitting to ask her for financial help in getting Anna back on her feet. We were not looking for anything more than her to assume rightful responsibility in Anna's physical restoration. However, she saw things a bit differently. Instead of agreeing to help, from the onset of our meeting she made it abundantly clear that she was well within what she called the "Indiana Standard of Care."

For the second time in just a few short months Randy and I left an orthodontist's office feeling as if we had just been sucker punched. Void, and without a viable place to put the doctor's adamant refusal to accept any level of professional or financial responsibility, a slow consuming numbness seeped its way through both of us. *Now* we were optionless. Hemmed in and buckling under the full weight of financing Anna's recovery, the unrelenting pressure gnawed at the growing pit in my stomach.

Silence that had grown its roots in stunned disbelief governed our drive home that early spring day as we once again fought to remain focused on God's faithfulness in the midst of natural circumstances that wanted to testify otherwise. Caught between the heart to fix my daughter at any cost and the bewilderment as to how to fund it, I found myself waffling between wanting to be the spiritual giant who commands provision down and Much-Afraid in *Hinds' Feet in High Places* terrorized by the fear that taunts me whenever we don't have what we need in order to pay for what had to be done.

This cycle is relentless, Lord. I'm so tired of it, I confessed as newly plowed fields scrolled past the window. The all too familiar lump in my throat began to form as the accumulating numbers slowly rose to become mountains and surgical procedures that I knew were necessary seemed impossible to provide. My throat constricted. The frustration of having to do that which we couldn't afford to do burned in my throat. Like a wild bronco anxiety bucked at my resolve. The reoccurring feeling that once again I had been left to hold the proverbial bag washed over me, the ensuing fear relentless in its pursuit of peace.

A subtle slip of Randy's hand over mine was all it took for pent-up tears to fall and the question, "What are we going to do?" to come tumbling out. "We don't have this kind of money," I whispered, desperately wanting more than him to hear me.

Engrossed in the task at hand, I watched as Randy drove down the interstate, his eyes fixated on the road as if he knew if he took one second to glance my way, he would lose his own sense of self-control. Both minutes and miles passed before he quietly responded, "I know, Kel . . . I'm not sure what to do either. I just know we'll figure something out."

I let out a frustrated exhale, feeling my breath as it quickly blew my bangs upward then dropped them back in place just as fast. "Why does it always come down to money, Randy? No one else we know has to live like this . . . ."

His gaze remained on the road as I wrestled to keep every nerve in my body still.

The months of escalating tension and pressure made my skin feel as if it wanted to crawl off my body. Mindlessly I fidgeted and rearranged myself in the passenger seat only to squirm again, convinced that if I didn't get out soon, I would implode.

Closing my eyes, I massaged my forehead in an effort to relieve some of the mounting tension when suddenly memories of being a young girl transported me to Ohio, back when I lived in a pastor's house on a numbered street in a small steel town in the valley.

Instantly various clips of being speculated over and whispered as a teenager replayed on the screen of my imagination. That season of adolescence when unwelcome comments couldn't help but be heard and the murmuring over my circumstance wafted into every crevice of every hallway. Sitting in the car that day I felt the same sense of helplessness and desperation that I had when I was a teenager. Unable to escape the curious stares or unspoken words of judgment over a situation that most knew nothing about, not really. Yet regardless of its source, the outcome felt the same—I was as inept at freeing myself or my daughter from our shared tormentor as I was back then.

Confronting that reality is different than accepting it. That acceptance only began to take hold once I recognized that there was little else I could do, I had exhausted all other options. The reality was we had nowhere else to turn and nothing else that could be done to change the circumstances as we knew them. Therein lie the art of acceptance as we knew it, which ultimately became our precursor to endurance. Not endurance as in grit our teeth and bare our way through it but rather Christlike endurance that is only found and formed through our unrestrained willingness to say yes to a way that we never anticipated He would allow us to go, all the while trusting that *even in this,* whatever the *this* is, God will work all things together for our good.

Sitting in the car that day, all of that wasn't in the forefront of my mind. Fear and anxiety were too blinding at the time and needed to be quelled before I could see that Truth beaming at the end of the tunnel. But He is faithful, and while I may not have started out with that belief system intact, He is pleased that I at least started. For it didn't take long for Him to meet me in the midst of fear and loneliness, then beckon me to surrender my adolescent heart that didn't know quite what to do or really where to turn.

It was in that surrender when the seed of spiritual resolve quietly began to form and take hold. A resolve to believe and agree with the Truth that He has me and will be faithful to never let go. His heart as a father won't allow Him to. I marinated on that Truth daily then like a toe being dipped in the water, I began making agreement with it in hopes that what Paul wrote in Romans would actually begin to occur—*Do not conform to this world, but rather be transformed by the renewing of your mind,* (12:1).

Little did I know how quickly it would be put to the test.

CHAPTER TWENTY-NINE

FINALIZING DETAILS

"In everything, through prayer and supplication, make your requests known to God,"
—Philippians 4:6

Since the initial days of making splints and removing wisdom teeth, I had spent the majority of my time praying and believing that the worst of Anna's days were behind her. Witnessing so much improvement in so little time, I had all but forgotten about the possibility that both of her jaw joints may need repaired.

We were nearly three months into the "Overarching Plan of Attack," and Anna no longer mentioned the chronic pain her jaw held—between the splint and the second set of braces, she was responding favorably to the treatment. Perhaps that's why the surgeon's phone call came as such a shock. My heart wasn't prepared to hear what my eyes had failed to see.

Sitting on the front step, the rhythmic bounce of Aaron's basketball was interrupted by the ring of the phone lying next to me. After a quick press on the 'Talk' button and an equally fast "Hello," the sound of the phone being lifted off its cradle preceded the clearing of his throat. "Good afternoon Mrs. Williams, this is Dr. Buttram, Anna's oral surgeon."

Immediately, I waved my hand catching Aaron's attention then signaled him to hold the ball. Turning my attention back to the phone call, I quickly replied, "Oh hi, how are you?"

With the niceties behind us, Dr. Buttram didn't waste time or mince words. "Mrs. Williams, I've got some difficult news. I want you to know I have looked at the x-rays of Anna's jaw at least a hundred different times and drawn at least as many diagrams in an effort to give her the most optimum outcome with the least amount of invasive treatment."

My eyes closed as the same ominous feeling I experienced in the specialist's office slowly returned. Breathing that had been involuntary just minutes ago became a conscious effort. Seconds of silence passed before my tentative, "Okay . . . " broke through the unspoken tension.

"I'm sorry to tell you this but Anna's jaw is not in very good shape. In fact, her jaws joints no longer have the ability to remain stable in any way. Therefore, I have no other option but to rebuild both her joints—the right *and* the left side of her jaw." A pregnant silence momentarily filled the airspace before he continued, "I'm sorry Mrs. Williams, I'm sure you were wanting to hear something different," and with that, the phone line fell silent once again.

Breathe Kelly was the first thing that went through me. The second was, *But she's doing so well.*

Another momentary pause passed before Silence suddenly fled, disrupted by the new storm surge of details. "Bone grafts . . . screws . . . plates . . . wires," each detail sounding worse than the first. Like a vortex spinning out of control, the sound of his voice reminded me of Charlie Brown's teacher as he garbled out something about her mouth being wired shut for weeks, liquid diets and the need for suctioning apparatus to avoid any choking for the first 24-48 hours after surgery. My stomach rolled at the sound of his description.

Why, Lord?

The familiar sting of tears . . . the sickening feeling in the pit of my stomach . . . the gasping for air. All of them reasons to scream, "STOP

TALKING!" but my tongue didn't move. I struggled to still my mind by telling myself to breathe.

I don't know how much time passed before some level of clarity slowly began to return and the surgeon's voice stopped sounding as if he was talking underwater. I'm not even sure I mentally ever fully returned to the conversation. I just remember sitting on the front step of my porch, fighting to stay focused as I spun strands of hair in a mindless, knotty effort, anxious to hear his response to the one remaining unanswered question.

"I think I understand most everything you've said; there's just one thing I'm not sure of," I quietly began.

"What is that, Mrs. Williams?" he kindly asked.

"Repairing the left side of her jaw . . . " I paused, closing my stinging eyes, not sure I really wanted to hear his next response, "Is that part included in the original fee you quoted us . . . the $20,000? Does that fee cover everything you need to do for her to make her well?" my voice cracked underneath the weight of it all.

The sound of him clearing his throat was the only thing that interrupted the returning pregnant silence that had enveloped the moment. Imminent dread washed over me as I waited, fighting to gulp down the growing Milk Dud that had formed in my throat. *Please God, please . . .* all I wanted to do was go back, go back to before we ever walked into her first orthodontist's office. I would've been glad to go back to the first time she complained— *why didn't I stop the treatment then??* My heart ached over the futility of it all—it ached for Anna, it ached for us, and it ached over the need to brace myself for the next impact.

"Mrs. Williams," he said hesitantly as if he knew I needed time to breathe, "I know this isn't easy." Another orchestrated pause of compassion before he continued, "Unfortunately, because I need to reconstruct both sides of Anna's upper and lower jaws, the cost is more."

Breathlessly I waited, phone pressed to my face, for him to continue.

"Having to do the additional repair will cost approximately nineteen-thousand dollars more than my original estimate," he concluded.

The pressure in my chest tightened as a growing sense of numbness washed over me once again making everything, inside of me and out, strangely quiet. I couldn't think. I could barely breathe. Everything went dim. I had nothing—just a feeling of somersaulting down an endless abyss of injustice. Silence tried giving me a reference point to focus on but it felt like each time I tried saving myself from plummeting farther, the truth gave way beneath my grasp. My stomach convulsed in response to the spinning vortex in my head.

"Nineteen thousand?" I choked out in disbelief. "So thirty-nine thousand total for what you need to do?"

"Roughly, yes, ma'am," he said quietly, "plus room and other miscellaneous fees, like the anesthesiologist."

Air exited in chunks as I heard myself reply, "I see," in a rushed manner, anxious to hang up the phone. I had no other words. *It's not his fault she's in this condition,* I reminded myself as I leaned back on the porch railing. The numbers were so staggering it was as if there was an aloofness to them, like we were exchanging Monopoly money. Numbers of that magnitude were so far beyond our comprehension we had never even entertained them before . . . for anything, let alone having to restore our daughter.

"Whew, Lord, this is a big one," I whispered as I laid the phone down.

The eerie silence was back—no kids playing in the yard, no traffic on the street, no muffled voices in my head—just Silence who now sat next to me. "What are we going to do?" I asked fully aware this wasn't the only mountain we were facing. We had barely been able to pay cash for Matthew's first year at Wheaton and now his second one was right around the corner.

This is all so overwhelming, Father . . .

Every scriptural truth that had even found its way into my spirit resurfaced. . . *Don't look at the giants in the land . . . Your Father knows your need before you even speak of it . . . Your Father owns all the cattle on a thousand fields . . . Do not be anxious in anything but with prayer and supplication make your requests known to God . . .* each of them true in their entirety, if only I knew how to swing them like the sword Paul talks about in

Ephesians 6. But I didn't, not yet. Deep down I knew they were truth but sitting there that day those verses were like the rocks laying in the stream before David picked them up in I Samuel 17—they were no good to me until I learned how to pick them up and fling them at my own giants.

Until then all I could utter was, "We'll never make it, Lord."

My mind floated from family to family as I thought about the ease in which they seemingly did life. No one else in our circle had college-aged children and certainly none of their children had experienced setbacks via orthodontists. *I covet their ease, Father. Forgive me,* I pleaded as I shifted myself on the hard concrete.

My heart hurt. I wanted so badly to be found as a giant of faith but sitting on the porch that day, I wasn't. I was a mess. Scared, frozen and completely undone. All I saw before me was a daughter who needed help and an insurmountable mountain of debt that I had no way of climbing. I cried out, but never heard a response—just a deafening silence in a place that desperately needed Truth to be spoken . . . *something . . . anything that I can hold on to.*

Silence was all that came.

Silence, who for the first time, was accompanied by the sound of a subtle rumbling far off in the distance. A sound that sent shivers down my spine because it wasn't accompanied by victory or the promise to overcome. Instead, this time the sound wave, as muted as it was, was carried closer by Uncertainty and Doubt who unbeknownst to me had found a place to rest deep within a wound that had been inflicted so very long ago.

CHAPTER THIRTY

BLESSINGS AND CURSES

And you shall remember that the Lord your God led you all the way these forty years in the wilderness, to humble you and test you, to know what was in your heart, whether you would keep His commandments or not. So He humbled you, allowed you to hunger, and fed you with manna which you did not know nor did your fathers know, that He might make you know that man shall not live by bread alone; but man lives by every word that proceeds from the mouth of the Lord.
—Deuteronomy 8:2-3

Uncertainty quickly tried to define our existence in the weeks and months that followed the surgeon's phone call. Left with zero negotiating room, Randy and I resigned ourselves to the idea that need necessitated action, and so we began working diligently at coming to peace with second mortgages and 401K loans as a means to pay for the Mount Everest of debt that now lay in front of us.

Wrestling with God's faithfulness came in waves as I fought to keep my eyes fixed on the restoration Anna would experience, knowing that otherwise the bitterness from the injustice of it all had the potential to overwhelm me. There were countless days when the hardest match to win came from choosing between either resenting the position we had all been placed in, or being thankful that we had found the right professionals to help her and at least we had options available to pay for everything. *What would families do that don't have that?* I often wondered.

Merely considering that possibility drove me to the end of myself because nothing, *no thing*, mattered more to me than my daughter. In that regard, gratitude became a sort of weapon of warfare in my battle against frustration, injustice and helplessness. Somehow offering thanks for the smallest of victories helped my spirit stay clean and worked toward shifting my spiritual perspective from demanding justice from a just God to learning how to be still before Him, asking Him to teach me what it means to *"Rejoice always, pray without ceasing, in everything give thanks; for this is the will of God for you in Christ Jesus"* (1 Thessalonians 5:16-18).

Those are incredibly difficult words to receive when you are hurting and having to reconcile life's unjust circumstances with the concept of a good and faithful God. I was discovering the first part of the verse was much easier to accept than the latter. "In *everything*, Lord? I'm to give thanks in everything?" I asked Him bewilderedly. Anna's medical history mentally replayed as I questioned, "*This*—all that she's facing—*this* is Your will? If so, then I don't understand—how does what she is going through, what we're all facing align with your nature? It feels so unjust, Father."

Those moments of ongoing questions lingered—all without answers, therefore irreconcilable—always redirecting me back toward the same root issue: Did I believe He was altogether good or didn't I? The chasm between the circumstances and the truth seemed too wide to cross whenever I tried to reconcile what was happening in the natural with the mystery that the sovereignty of God inherently contains.

Never before had I swam in such unexplored waters. Never had I wrestled so deeply with the Lord as I had in that season. Even when I partnered with Him at the altar as a teenager, I never questioned His goodness, primarily because I knew that it was my own choice that had predicated my encounter. But *this*, this "Plan of Attack" we were facing seemed so unwarranted. One round of braces had turned my daughter's life upside down, leaving all three of us albeit for different reasons feeling violated and without recourse due to something simply called the "Indiana Standard of Care."

I desperately longed to find the Lord's protection, hoping it would appear through some financial loophole. When it didn't, I had no idea how to process the disappointment that ensued. Every morning as my Bible lay in my lap, I'd flip back and forth through the Old Testament prophets then to the words in red, knowing I held Truth in my hands—Truth that superseded whatever our circumstances wanted so badly to convey. Yet none I read directly addressed the resounding cry of my heart, *Why, Lord?*

I just didn't understand. The religious side of me held on to my internal checklist wanting to present it as evidence that since I had done what He asked, none of this should have been allowed to happen, as if my family and I should be spared from such disappointing setbacks. And, while our obedience to Biblical principles inherently keeps us under His spiritual protection, it doesn't always keep the effect of the human experience outside our door. None of us, believers or not, are above setbacks and disappointments. Sometimes, bad things just happen.

I didn't fully understand all that then. In the midst of that particular wrestling match unseen remnants of who or what I thought God was like became fodder for the enemy's maligning whisper. Capitalizing on my frustration over watching Anna's pain or even wondering how we would pay for everything was just the beginning of my battle but never truly the epicenter. Rather, as time passed and those issues continued to swirl in an increasing whirlwind of confusion, it became progressively apparent that what the Father *really* longed to deal with is what was surfacing in me as I stood in the midst of this intensely hot circumstantial fire.

Those specific impurities—those unsanctified or unholy belief systems were the breeding ground for the enemy's whisper to find a place to land. Whether it was the doubt over provision, feeling betrayed by the injustice of it all, or the overwhelming feeling that I was once again on my own evidenced by my, "What are *we* going to do?" question. Each of them in their own right enough to sideline any believer's faith, but all three combined were growing in their ability to not only tranquilize their prey but take her faith completely out as well.

Daily, I wrestled taking to heart Paul's writing, " . . . work out your salvation with fear and trembling," (Phil. 2:12). I didn't want to believe what the voices in my head continually whispered. Instead, I wanted Him to reassure me as He always had, to tell me who He was again and that what I had believed wasn't foolish after all. But He didn't. On the contrary, He wasn't very quick to respond at all.

In fact, in some ways initially He never did. I suppose sometimes His silence is an answer unto itself; after all, Jesus offered no defense when He stood before Pilate's accusations, leaving him free to believe whatever he chose. The same was becoming true for me. For though I battled to believe the best, something deep inside sensed that if I weren't careful my ongoing doubts would somehow create a type of gateway into bloodier battles for my faith.

I couldn't hear the additional rumbling that was building just beyond our current storm; it was taking most everything I had to weather the current one, and I desperately needed the ground underneath me to stabilize. There had been too much upheaval the past ten months—too much change. I yearned to have my family back as I once knew it, long before Matthew left for Wheaton and Anna transferred high schools. *Those were simple days,* I reminded myself as my heart ached and cried out for the simplicity of what used to be—I was tired of things being different and chaotic and always having to adjust.

Perhaps that's why I was primarily relieved when Anna came to me and asked if we could talk. The stirring had been as evident in her as it was in me, the difference was I had assumed it was due to all the medical intervention. It wasn't. Nearly ten months had passed since she had transferred to the new school, and although she wasn't overtly social, she equally didn't appear to be unhappy. She had made a few friends and played shortstop for the softball team, yet the majority of her time and investment had slowly been made at a youth group at one of the local churches. It was there we saw her begin to flourish and relax within herself, so when she began to share her heart about how she had grown and everything God had done in her, my heart leapt at the realization that we were seeing the same things.

Rather than chime in agreement, I felt led to intently listen unable to deny the, "But" I heard in her voice. "My new school is a great place, Mom, but I don't need it to keep me out of trouble anymore. I'm growing in my relationship with God, and I have my friends from the youth group who hold me accountable and none of them go to school with me. Funny thing is Mom, they're all back here right where I left them . . . ." her voice trailed off.

Her awareness of self blessed me. For a fleeting second all I wanted to do was take her in—I marveled at her . . . at her maturity . . . and at the young woman I was seeing her become. She looked at me sheepishly as if she was trying to read my silent thoughts, then merely asked, "Mom, would you just pray about letting me transfer back?"

My heart skipped, not as in missed a beat, but as in it grew feet and literally skipped, excited at the thought of some level of normalcy returning to our home once again. Remnant thoughts of how odd it felt, even now, to pull into the unfamiliar circular driveway mentally flickered, quickly followed by relief from the possibility of not feeling that anymore. A split-second later I rejoined our conversation wanting to blurt out, "YES! Of course, you can transfer back. I don't even need to pray about it," but Self-Control held my tongue. Instead I grabbed a quick deep breath then leaning forward, reached for her hand across the table, smiled and said, "Absolutely."

I thought long and hard about that conversation and reflected on Randy's question last summer about how this community may have been what I needed but not necessarily what Anna did. I sat in silence a long time trying to sort out the "me" part of this equation versus the "Anna" part. I couldn't deny the fact that as soon as she asked me to pray I immediately sensed she was coming home. But I had to know if "coming home" was really the best thing for her and not just because I felt so out of place where she currently attended.

Replaying the past eighteen months or so, all that she had already been through as well as what she still had yet to face wasn't lost on me. "She's going through a lot, Lord. I'll keep her there if You want, but is there freedom for her to come home?" I asked.

Thoughts of the Israelites and how they had wandered through the desert played in my head and with them came the gentle reminder of how He taught me about daily provision and manna so many years ago. I couldn't help but smile at the memory, realizing it only takes Him to speak a word, just one, and all the chaos and confusion ceases just because He spoke.

"Speak to me, Lord. What would You have us do with her?"

I closed my eyes and centered my spirit in an effort to discover His presence. Like pieces of a puzzle, I needed to make sense out of what was she was asking by starting with what He had just reminded me of. I quickly flipped to Exodus and scanned the headings, waiting on His Spirit to stop me. Then I worked my way over to Deuteronomy until I found Chapter 28 and reread the "Blessings on Obedience," praying each of them as I read.

"So good, Lord," I whispered, sensing we weren't quite done. Looking back down, I continued to scan the pages until I came upon Deuteronomy 30:19-20.

> *I call heaven and earth as witnesses today against you, that I have set before you life and death, blessing and cursing; therefore choose life, that both you and your descendants may live; that you may love the Lord your God, that you may obey His voice, and that you may cling to Him, for He is your life and the length of your days; and that you may dwell in the land which the Lord swore to your fathers, to Abraham, Isaac, and Jacob, to give them.*

I read it again and again until slowly it seeped down into my spirit, settling in with previous deposits. Jesus words in Matthew 7, *"Therefore, you will know them by their fruits,"* (v.20) coursed through me reminding me that at their core He's saying the fruit of one's life is evidence of the relationship they share with the Father. Based on the past six months or so of Anna's life, it was increasingly clear that she was developing a deep love for the Lord her God. She was passionate about spending time with Him and in deep relationship with a number of girls from her youth group. In other words, she had already chosen Him, just as Joshua had commanded before the end of his life. Her love and obedience to Him was evidence of that, and for those reasons alone He was now giving her the freedom to choose for herself.

She could either choose to remain obedient and in relationship with Him or not, but no longer did she need hemmed in by external parameters for He was doing an internal work. As a result He was enlarging her territory, and she was free to come and go as she wanted because He knew He could trust her. Somewhere in the past six months she had chosen to surrender herself to Him.

And in the end that's all any of us have.

Choice.

The choice is ours whether or not we'll allow circumstantial evidence to sway our belief system. Just as it's ours to choose whether we'll allow the enemy to use those same external circumstances as an indictment on the Father's character. It's ours because only then is our relationship with Him built on trust and confidence. Circumstances are the very things He uses to invite us in so that we begin to know *Him*—not just His word or what He says—it's actually *Him* we get to know. It's why Moses once said, "*. . . . show me now your way so that I may know* **You** *. . .* " (Exodus 33:13, bold added).

Moses understood the secret to experiencing the Father's heart is to draw near to Him in the midst of our setbacks and disappointments. It's those moments, when our hearts are torn and conflicts are high, when our choices are actually the most paramount. Who and what we choose to believe and partner with in moments of crisis matters. Moses chose and he remained. It was through his choice that he came to understand that only when we get up close and personal with the Father are the wounds of our soul healed, ultimately denying access to the accuser of the brethren.

CHAPTER THIRTY-ONE

WOUNDS OF THE FATHERLESS

I will not leave you as orphans; I will come to you.
—John 14:18

Piece by piece, life seemed as if it was falling back into place. The panic that had once ensued as a result of Anna's diagnosis was easing as the specialist's treatment was proving successful, the bills were being paid, and our budget was slowly adjusting. The end seemed to finally be in sight, both physically for her and financially for us.

My wrestling matches with faith and God's goodness still occurred though their intensity wasn't quite so fierce. An inner resolve had occurred that helped me make some kind of peace with the events of the past eighteen months, and for the first time in quite awhile hope began to return.

Both Matthew and I were wrapping up the final weeks of our respective spring semesters—his would soon bring him home from Wheaton while mine carried me to the School of Education's front door. Things were finally jockeying themselves back into position, especially when I shared the news of Anna's pending transfer with Lori.

Ten months after deciding that Anna could transfer schools, I sat in Lori's car excited to talk about Anna's decision to return "home." Being able to share and compare our daughters' school schedules along with discussing their upcoming tenth grade teachers confirmed in me how very much I missed being a part of everything. *I've missed feeling like I belonged,* I thought as the comfort of being reattached washed over me.

Leaning back in the passenger seat I absorbed the ease of our relationship as it filled the car with chatter. We spoke of family and of our daughters' youth group and had just started discussing how Randy and I were doing with regard to Anna's treatment when the subtle vibration of my cell phone indicated someone was calling.

For a split second I considered hitting the Ignore button but when I saw Matt's name my sense told me otherwise, so I quickly glanced over at Lori, whispered, "Sorry, it's Matt," then redirected my attention and answered, "Hey, Bub, what's up?"

Typically upbeat and energetic, Matt's tone was uncharacteristically tentative, almost reserved, as he fumbled and stuttered his way around the introduction, unsure of what words he wanted to use. Cause for concern rose in the face of such awkwardness as various possibilities began skirting across my mind. Images of car accidents faded into phantom discussions of academic failure to wondering if his hesitancy had anything to do with his working at a Christian camp for part of the summer. *Maybe he's called to say he didn't get the job after all or that he doesn't want it.*

Each speculation gave way to the next as his unusual stammer and fight for language continued. Sentences started then were abruptly self-interrupted as he said, "Mom, I've really been thinking," then another thought rolled on top of the first, "No, really, I've been praying," then he'd stop as if he suddenly recognized he was sharing what should only have been his inner dialogue and then he'd start all over again.

Each new attempt gave me a bit more information as to what was troubling Matt, and one by one I dismissed my previous assumptions. Until after four or five restarts I finally heard him share one consecutive idea, "Okay, Mom, let me try again. I've been praying about some things and . . . " his voice trailed off momentarily. "Mom, I'd like to meet him. I think I'd like to meet my biological father."

For the briefest of seconds my eyes closed while everything in me fought to maintain composure. Randy and I had always wondered when this day would come; in fact we suspected when Matt left for Wheaton that it was waiting as if right around the corner. But now it was really *here*, and suddenly I wasn't ready. I wanted it to feel as it had always felt—*out there*, far off in the distance—one of the those things that we would always be waiting for to happen, but never certain if it really would.

Then just as quickly I realized that this, Matt's need, wasn't about me or what I wanted; it was about Matt and what he needed. Instinctively and without a cognitive awareness I heard myself say, "Oookay, I can see that," then more silence as I struggled to collect my scattered thoughts from far-off places. I glanced over at Lori who had just put the car in park and was looking at me with a half curious, half concerned look on her face. I rolled my eyes in a "you're never going to believe this" way and held my finger up, sending her a silent "hold on for a second."

"I just think it's time, Mom. I've been thinking more and more about him and I . . . I don't know . . . I want to see him. I want to know what he looks like and if I look like him." Another brief pause before he finished, "And . . . and I have some things I'd like to ask him."

He's ready, I thought, shrugging my spiritual shoulders, *and he's nineteen.* "Okay, Bub, I hear that, and I understand," I quietly responded, trying to reassure him.

Silence could have skipped from Indianapolis to Wheaton and back again before our conversation continued. Then suddenly out of nowhere came ideas and counsel that given any other circumstance would have taken me a lifetime to formulate. But once I started talking things just rolled out, "There are just a couple things I'd like you to consider," I continued.

When he didn't respond I knew he was listening; it's just Matthew's way. "I need to talk to Dad, but off the top of my head here's what I think. You're going to camp for six weeks, right?"

A quick and mumbled "Mmm-hmm" came across the line.

"Then let's take that time—you, me and Dad—to pray about this, to make sure it's God's timing. Then secondly. . . " I paused, swallowing hard because this was the most difficult thing to acknowledge and accept. With my head leaning on the headrest and Lori's hand now covering mine, I continued, "Let's pray and ask the Lord who should go with you."

The bile in my stomach crept upward at the thought and my throat burned as I continued, "Matt . . . you need to have the space and freedom to react as you want so, honey, it can't be me and it can't be Dad."

It's always been me, Lord; I've always been the one who was there.

I shook my head in a futile effort to clear the image of holding him in the hospital room when he was first born, watching his little hand clasp mine, realizing for the first time his biological father wouldn't be coming to Indianapolis after all, and that naming my son would be something I would have to do on my own . . . me and Silence.

A blink later I heard Matt, "Mom? You still there?"

"Yeah, I'm here," I replied, barely audible. "Do you understand?" I asked, not really wanting an answer. "I don't want you going alone so let's see who God has, then after you come home from camp we'll see what we have to work with . . . sound okay?"

Without hesitation he responded, "Yeah, Mom! It sounds great!. . . Thanks."

I couldn't help but smirk at his gratitude, as if he needed my permission to do what his heart has always known he would do but the timing was never right.

"You're welcome, Matt," I replied, quietly grateful he was none the wiser to my internal hesitations, then explained I was with Lori and slowly drew the conversation to a close.

Silence sat in the car with us as Lori tried to help me come to terms with this most recent development. "Well, I didn't see that one coming quite yet," I told her.

"You okay?" she asked, still gripping my hand.

"You know, strangely, I am. I just feel a grace on him . . . that it's time," I said shrugging my shoulders. "What else you going to do? The hardest part is letting him go into the unknown to meet someone who has a history of being less than trustworthy and not being entirely convinced that we've fully prepared him for everything that could happen."

Offering me a half-hearted smile as a source of consolation, Lori, reaching for my other hand, said a quick prayer lifting Matthew and his desires up to the Lord. I listened carefully, wanting to remember everything she said but my head was still reeling from the complexity of it all. Yet something in the simplicity and the genuineness of her prayer worked because Peace came and washed over me in gentleness and mercy.

The weekend following Matthew's phone call Randy and I moved Matthew home from Wheaton, excited to finally have him back, even if it was for only six days. Time passed too quickly as we took deep enjoyment hearing his stories about college life and Wheaton football and re-immersing all of our children back into our family structure, for that is when we were complete and fully functioning at our very best.

We had six days together. Six days to unpack and repack, six days to laugh at Matt's storytelling, and six days for our three children to reconnect and bond with one another all over again before it was time for him to leave for camp where there would be no communication, no phone calls and no interaction. The camp was too remote.

We spent every available minute together talking and playing and talking some more until the day came when the last of Matt's gear was loaded in his trunk and every detail of his route had been reviewed for the umpteenth time. Standing on the curb I breathed deeply as Randy's hand squeezed my shoulder and we watched, waiting for Matt's car to turn the corner and drive from our view. In so many ways his freshman year at Wheaton made it easier to let him go, yet there was still a huge part of me that didn't want to do anything but hold on to him even tighter.

Letting him go isn't easy, Father, even if it is into Your hands, I thought as I reached for Randy's hand.

Memories of standing in the driveway watching a much younger Matt board the school bus replayed in my head, bringing with it the all-too-familiar feeling of fearing the unknown and wanting everything to stay just as it was.

"You okay?" Randy asked, looking down.

I slowly nodded my head then quietly said, "Yeah . . . just wondering what things will look like in six weeks when he comes back home."

"All we can do is pray, Kelly. The rest is up to Him," he said as he gently squeezed my hand then turned to walk us up the driveway.

CHAPTER THIRTY-TWO

FINDING THE HEART TO SURRENDER

*One does not surrender a life in an instant.
That which is lifelong can only be surrendered in a lifetime.*
—Elisabeth Elliot

I followed Randy's lead throughout the next weeks about as closely as I followed him up the driveway that day. Thoughts of biological fathers and looming surgeries occupied most of my attention while double-mindedness fought to plague my approach. Randy remained steadfast while Fear persistently distracted me, and as my husband set his face like flint before the Lord, my faith played hopscotch most days rather than stand still, assured of what it knew to be true.

I hadn't seen this much uncertainty swirl around me since the days of my adolescence when moving from Ohio to Indiana back to Ohio again had altered nearly every facet of my existence. But something about this moment and these days made it seem that much more daunting. The landmines of change were so much easier to charter when I was the one at risk. But now, with my children being the ones who lay subject to the hands of change, the collateral damage seemed so much more pervasive—as if risk becomes inherently greater as children mature despite how meticulously we may work at building walls of containment. Life had found a way of breaching those walls, and I was learning there was little to nothing I could do about it.

As a result my heart pounded with curious doubt as I dreamt about surgical procedures and role-played my way through relational inquiries. The idea of seeing either of my children hurt physically or emotionally haunted me despite my acceptance that for both it was a necessary evil. Truth was, the upcoming mountains they each had to climb were unavoidable.

Knowing their climbs were inevitable was challenging enough; accepting the limitations that come with being reduced to an encouraging observer was an altogether different issue. For each of my two eldest children the physical and emotional requirements that are an inherent part of scaling mountains were going to solely be theirs to shoulder. I could encourage and I could advise, but I couldn't actually protect their hearts or make their physical bodies respond to the extraneous demands that would be placed on them as a result of their respective climbs—those alone were theirs to shoulder.

Conceptually that was the heart of Fear's greatest taunt. I could ask God to guide each movement of the surgeon's hands just as I could ask Him to protect Matthew's heart from destruction, but it did little to hem in my vain imaginations of what *might* be or what *may* happen. In that regard, my spirit knew no rest for those things remained out of my control. And while Anna's circumstance clearly had some measure of a silver lining, Matthew's remained completely in the land of the unknown. In large measure his heart would be entirely at his biological father's mercy, and memories of the danger that represented shook the deepest part of me.

I'm frightened, Lord . . . I know the wounds You've had to heal. How do I freely let Matthew meet with someone who represents such a potential threat?

My heart raced at the thought. "It's not the meeting him that bothers me, Father . . . well, not really," I admitted. Then another moment passed in reflection before more truth surfaced, "I don't trust him, Father, and I'm afraid. I don't want Matt hurt, and . . . how do we know?" my voice trailed off along with the thought.

The memory of my eighteen-year-old self holding my newborn son flashed through me once again, but more than the memory was how real the feelings to defend and protect him still were even all these years later. It didn't matter that Matthew was nineteen any more than it mattered that I realized the time had arrived for him to come to terms with some things for himself. In that regard my heart was still eighteen—back in a hospital room where the realization that I was young and completely alone had provoked me to make a vow of personal responsibility. With no one next to me and no one to share him with, the role of defender and protector had rested squarely on my shoulders, even if that meant shielding him from someone who *should* represent the smallest level of risk.

The irony that I had come full-circle didn't escape me. "Funny that the one person I thought would share that responsibility with me is now the person I feel the need to protect him from," I whispered. Initially, nothing much was said in response. On the contrary, the Father's response didn't come until much later, as if He knew I needed time and space to wrestle with the doubts and uncertainties that buoyed to the surface without any effort—the familiar things the Hebrew writer says so easily entangle us (12:1). Those were the things He allowed me to untangle myself with Truth and process. It was the question that lay much deeper within me, the one I wasn't able to recognize at first until one day, sometime later in the midst of quiet pondering and reflection, His familiar tender voice whispered, *"But do you trust* **Me** *with him, Kelly?"*

A quick, mindless, almost dismissive "Of course, Lord" instinctively rolled off my tongue. Then just as quickly, images of the past weeks panned across my mental eye. Moments when I paid more attention to Fear than Faith, wondering what *I* could do to keep my children sheltered from the pain that threatened to greet them, as if it was all up to me—as if I was still that young woman alone in the hospital room solely responsible for the one whose life lay in my hands. The reality that deep within me there was still a little girl who was deeply afraid of being left alone washed over me all over again.

"Oh, Lord," I sighed, disappointed. "I'm so sorry . . . " The feeling of abandonment as recognizable to me that day as it was when I was three and I was told my dad had gone to heaven, and that I wouldn't see him anymore.

The memory of standing at the storm door, looking out over the field watching the excavator lift its bucket of dirt far above the cab of the tractor, wondering if that's how my dad went up to heaven. *Did the excavator lift him up to take him there?* my toddler mind wondered.

I sat for a long time reconciling what I felt then with what I knew now, realizing that although the Lord had been true to His word when He promises to be a Father to the fatherless (Psalm 68:5), in many ways my involuntary reaction to difficult circumstances was still that of an orphan. "In so many ways Lord, I don't understand what it means to be a daughter . . . my initial thought isn't 'my Father has this.' Instead, it's "What am *I* going to do?' As if Lord, it's all up to me," I whispered back to Him.

My heart's disappointment was authentic and transparent that morning with the Lord, and it didn't take long before Silence ushered himself into the room and a subtle rest began to take hold in my spirit. Gone were the days of hiding and covering myself when my heart faltered; somewhere along this journey of faith I had stopped cowering to shame and cooperating with Hiddenness. Instead I sat openly in His silence, wading in His grace until the release came to discover more.

As if Truth Himself was summoning me, His word, verses I knew so well, began to course through me until the time came to find them on the paper. The ones written in red were the first ones I rediscovered—the ones where the heart of God is so vibrantly displayed. Then I flipped back to the stories of old: the faith of Abraham, the repentance of King David, the prophet Isaiah. Each encouraging and strengthening in their own right, but none of them fully resonating with where I was at. *What is it, Father?* I silently inquired. Back and forth I went, Old Testament to the New then back to the Old, scanning, reading, referencing until I turned to the Psalms and began skimming my way through Psalm 10:

> *But You have seen, for You observe trouble and grief, to repay it by Your hand. The helpless commits himself to You; You are the helper of the fatherless . . . LORD, You have heard the desire of the humble; You will prepare their heart; You will cause Your ear*

to hear, to do justice to the fatherless and the oppressed that the man of the earth may oppress no more.

One word more than any other stood out, telling me once again that it is *He* who sees, *He* who repays, *He* who is the helper to the fatherless, *He* who hears, *He* who prepares, and *He* who brings about justice on behalf of the fatherless. *He does it all.* Sitting in that truth, I asked Him to let it wrap around me, to strengthen me, to undergird me so that, in the light of His truth, the root of the enemy's lie couldn't help but be exposed.

If You really do it all then it isn't up to me, is it? I silently pondered. *It really is all up to You.*

Instantly, a new wave of His peace fell in the room as I repented for responding like an orphan, then began praying the truths I had found in that passage. I prayed them then I proclaimed them . . . out loud . . . as truth. I declared the Lord's promises over my son, then using His word as the foundation I clung to the Lord's promise that He would help the fatherless. I asked Him to prepare Matthew's heart and bring about His justice in the places where injustice had had free reign for so long.

Then, like waiting for the waves to roll ashore, I watched to see what would appear once the tide receded. I could sense the season of surrendering my children was imminent—frankly, it was already here. I had been rendered helpless to do anything but surrender them. *But how do I do that, Father, when protecting and shielding him is all I've ever known?*

Silence shared in the images of Matthew's childhood as they scrolled across my mind then remained with me as moments of joy and turbulence for both of my children replayed once more. But this time Silence wasn't the only one sharing my reflections. Somewhere along the way the Father had woven His presence into each and every one of them, as if He wanted me to know He had always been there in the very fiber of their experiences, rejoicing and weeping right along with me as only a paternal partner can do.

His heart overwhelmed me, and for the first time I realized that although I may have spoken a vow of sole responsibility, I was never truly alone. On some level, whether I knew it or not, God had always been shielding and protecting Matthew right alongside me . . . the whole time.

Earlier memories appeared like flashes of light—the plus-sign of pregnancy, the desperate fear, the logical arguments to reclaim my future from a world of statistics. The reality of His hand resting, shielding and protecting the unborn life I carried took my breath away. *Your role began long before mine ever even started, didn't it?* I asked.

"I knew him in his mother's womb, Kelly. Even then he was Mine . . . I brought him forth and I know the plans I have for him."

I closed my eyes and focused on trying to absorb the enormity of it all—the expanse of Matthew's story and how some nineteen years later chapters were still being written. *This story isn't over yet, is it Father?* I silently wondered. *Not Matt's, nor mine, not Anna's nor Randy or Aaron's—You truly are working all things together for the good, aren't You?* I asked rhetorically. And, with that I reminisced over the first time He had ever made me such a promise then marveled at how truly good He had been about keeping it.

CHAPTER THIRTY-THREE

RECONSTRUCTION

To console those who mourn in Zion,
To give them beauty for ashes,
The oil of joy for mourning,
The garment of praise for the spirit of heaviness;
That they may be called trees of righteousness,
The planting of the Lord, that He may be glorified
—Isaiah 61:3

The goodness of God is the only thing that can lead us into the land of wonder. The wonderment of how only He is able to take life's disappointments and setbacks and weave them into something altogether beautiful. After nearly three years of endlessly battling for Anna's health, we now stood on the precipice of seeing His hand work once again on our behalf.

"We'll almost there," I whispered, "Though I'm not sure exactly how."

Flashes of my seventh grade, pony-tailed daughter dismissively mumbling something about her jaw hurting drew to a close marked by gasps and pounding hearts as we listened to her doctors try and explain their approach to reconstructing our daughter's once perfectly constructed jaw.

Anger could still make its appearance if I allowed myself to focus on the injustice of it all, but with so much already on our plates it didn't seem as if that was the most useful emotion to entertain. Which always led me to reflect on how many different emotional roller coasters we had all rode throughout this particular journey—Randy, me, our children. Each of us had experiencing different emotions at different times for different reasons, making it seem as if getting to 'the other side' was never really going to get here at all.

Looking back, however, has a way of changing your current perspective, and although the clock *felt* like it ticked quite slowly through our most recent moments, the reality was the past six weeks were marching on without really stopping by to say hello.

Instead the days felt like they were over before they even got started, swallowed in heart preparation for welcoming one son back home and escorting our daughter one step closer to wholeness. Anna's doctors' appointments increased in frequency as the scheduled surgery grew closer and closer. Liquid shakes, DVDs and library books began to find their place right alongside her cheerleading pompoms and high school transfer records; it was as if her room itself housed two different worlds—the one that was waiting for her and the one she hadn't yet departed.

After what seemed liked endless months of speculation, then discovery and now weeks of planning, Anna's opportunity for healing and wholeness was upon us. A cool morning in June would mark the end of wrestling with fear of the unknown, along with the unanswered *whys* and *what ifs*, for they served no purpose other than to teach us that Regret plays no part in winning wars with reality. Our victory march only began once we learned to accept things for what they were and chose to focus on being grateful for the medical team who now held my daughter's jaw literally in their hands because they possessed the ability to make her whole.

Which all sounds lofty, ideal and noble until my humanity as a mother would resurface, bringing with it memories of my pre-teen, brace-filled daughter and how quickly the past three years had really gone. Pacing the waiting room, I thought about the first time she came to me, rubbing the right side of her jaw, saying, "Mom, my jaw hurts," and me very casually dismissing her pain. *Who would have thought three years ago would lead to this?*

I wondered as I turned, counted the ten block tiles on the floor, then turned and paced the other way until I got to ten again . . . mindless attempts at distraction while we waited.

Breathe . . . walk to ten . . . turn . . . breathe. Intermittent glimpses of the TV would momentarily catch my visual attention but failed to keep my auditory one—hard to listen when everything sounded garbled. I was too far inside my own head to pay attention anyway. Bouncing eyes took in the faces or the tops of heads of the people I knew who had gathered there to support us—friends, family, the four women who represented the YaYa's—everyone. Still the oddest silence hung in the air. No bellowing laughter came from Pam's presence nor did the sound of Kerri's infectious giggle roll across their seats. Rather a reserved, intentional quietness lingered as I paced the time away waiting for the surgeon to come out and say my daughter was well along with the infamous, "You can see her now."

I suppose in light of the numerous phone conversations explaining procedures and doctors' appointments where pictures of reconstruction were skillfully painted, Randy and I should have been more prepared for what we would see when we entered Recovery Room 104.

We weren't—I don't know how any parent ever is.

For a mother who was studying secondary education English and a father who had only known a white-collar business job, we had no reference point for hoses and oxygen tubes and the rhythmic beep of machines we didn't know how to read or what their numbers meant. Nor did we have any coping mechanism for seeing our fifteen-year-old daughter curled up on her side, hair matted down, her swollen, puffy face trying to find comfort despite the thick-walled cylinder hose protruding from her now wired shut jaw. She lay lifeless while deep crusts of burgundy crackled on both sides of her nose alongside a small pool of blood trying to find its way down the outside of her mouth.

At the first sight of her, air instantly drew short and the rage I thought I had laid at His altar months ago came back with a fury. I was stuck in that doorway; for some reason my legs rendered immobile as my hand gripped Randy's with a force I didn't know I had. My knees buckling under the strain as my throat began to burn in an effort to contain both my emotions and the bile curdling in my stomach.

With our hands still clasped and his arm stretched practically horizontal, Randy glanced back at me and quietly said, "Come on. We need to do this."

I looked at him then over at her then back at him, eyes wide in disbelief. My brain told me I had to move, but all I could do was shake my head in sheer horror and dissonance at what had been done to my daughter, certain any words I tried to say would be unintelligible. Randy stepped toward me in comfort and consolation but my vision became blurred by the tears of frustration and heartache that uncontrollably formed.

I knew she was there, and I knew she was nearly grown, but when I looked at her all curled up and piped full of hospital tubes, all I saw was her in the bassinet when she was a newborn—then I blinked and she was three getting her tonsils out. Then she was twelve, innocent and vulnerable, and the sound of her constant cries for help over the past few years muted the incessant beeping of the monitors.

For the second time in just weeks I was helpless—rendered powerless by circumstances I couldn't control and things I had absolutely no control over. It didn't matter how much resolve I displayed or how badly I had wished things to be different. In that moment, standing in that doorway I knew nothing else but a paralyzing numbness caused by the sheer inability to understand how this had happened at all. I was living the moment, but the moment didn't feel like it was mine to live. My brain couldn't process what my eyes were required to see.

A squeeze from his hand marked one jagged deep breath, one baby step forward. Then another breath, a bigger step. Two more and I found my place alongside Randy who stood holding the rail of Anna's bed, white knuckle himself, control etched across his face as pools of water filled his eyes.

The tender brush of my hand across her hair caused her to moan. With a tip-toed stance, I leaned over and kissed her forehead then whispered, "Were right here Re, Dad and I are right here."

From that moment forward, I never left my daughter's bedside. I grew skillful with the suction tube when she woke up sick from the anesthetic and meticulously dropped ribbons of water from straws whenever she grew thirsty, and through it all never once did she shed a tear. Instead, she blinked her eyes at me in a way that conveyed, "I'm going to be okay, Mom," all the while holding my hand. In that, I believe that not only did we draw strength from one another, we also learned how to draw strength from the Lord for we knew without saying that we both had spent the majority of our time praying our own silent prayers.

Desperation marked me that day. Seeing Anna in that condition became the impetus for spiritually understanding that after a lifetime of protection and nurturing and guarding those whom He had entrusted to me, in the end all I can really do is lay them back at His feet for they are only given to us for a season. Just like the talents in Matthew 25:14-30, stewarding them and their value is our responsibility until at some point the Father comes to claim them for Himself—to love them, to be in relationship with them, and to be a Father to them in ways that only He can.

So, it was with both of our elder children that summer. Their pain had become one of the ways He could show Himself faithful. For Anna, it was through one strategic plan of attack, and while the first week of her recovery was physically excruciating and emotionally exhausting, it didn't take her fifteen-year-old self long before she began to turn the corner. Then when Matthew returned home a week or so after Anna's surgery, he was the one who got her to walk around the perimeter of our small backyard for the first time.

Those were crucial steps for both of them—steps for one child that in effect declared the worst was all behind her, while Matt's silently whispered his journey had just begun.

CHAPTER THIRTY-FOUR

One Down, One to Go

*The brave man is not the one who has no fears,
he is the one who triumphs over his fears.*
—Nelson Mandela

With the scales of adversity coming into balance now that Anna's surgery was behind us, watching her walk on the road to recovery brought an ease into the atmosphere where once there had been nothing but strife and worry. It was as if her moments of marked improvement were creating space allowing for our focus to shift more toward Matthew's meeting with his biological father than we had in the past few weeks.

Holding fast to the promises of Psalm 10, I greeted Matthew's desire to meet his biological father with a different expectancy than I had when he had left for camp. Gone was the apprehension as well as the overwhelming need to protect him. Something from my most recent encounter with the Lord lingered—an unexplained peace remained and brought with it the courage to consider that perhaps the waters of Matthew's journey weren't quite as menacing as Fear had originally wanted me to believe. *Maybe he really will be alright* was a reoccurring thought.

Then once I saw Matthew's demeanor when he returned home from camp—confident and at peace himself, more than I had ever witnessed, an entirely new ease ushered us all into the process. No longer was he the nineteen-year-old on the phone stammering to find his words, reflective of one who wasn't quite sure of what he was about to ask. Rather, his speech was strong, his language precise and the recapturing of his own events of the last six weeks was delivered with more assurance and authority than I had ever known him to have.

Matthew had been home from camp for just a day or two, when the three of us, Randy, Matthew and myself gathered in the kitchen after a long day. Finally able to relax, I watched as Matthew placed his glass on the table, walked toward the pantry and said, "You know, when I left for camp I wasn't completely convinced that I really wanted to go," he explained to Randy and me, "well, after being at Wheaton and everything that was going on with Anna, I wasn't sure I wanted to leave."

A maternal smile of understanding along with a pregnant pause passed through the room before he made his way to the table then continued, "But then I got to the camp and since we all had to be there early, they wanted the counselors to have time to get to know each other and familiarize ourselves with the camp theme for that session."

A curious thought of direction flew through me as I tried to make sense of where his story was heading. "You guys are *never* going to believe this . . . " he said as he repeatedly spun the napkin. His speech sped up as his fingers spun faster still then he repositioned himself in the chair, crossed his arms on the table, then locked his eyes on mine. He paused for just a second then redirected his gaze Randy's way and said, "The first day of counselor orientation was hard. I didn't really want to be there. I wasn't even sure I was supposed to be. But then," he paused as he glanced back at me again and started to grin. "But then the Camp Director came up to the mike," seconds of silence filled the atmosphere as his reflection of that moment surfaced in his eyes. "Mom, the theme for the six-week session of camp was the 'Wounds of the Fatherless.'"

His speech fell silent once again as if he knew to allow the weight of his words to fall on the room. With one snippet of information, the three of us instantly recognized the theme wasn't just coincidental. The goodness of God and His absolutely unwavering authorship of our collective faith had just been put on full display. It is what we have since learned to call, a 'stumbling into glory' moment. Those priceless, unpredictable times when the glory of God appears in the midst of a circumstance in a way no one would ever expect. Sitting there, listening to Matthew's recitation of the camp's theme caused all of the concerns of the past six weeks to crumble into countless little pieces.

The urge to not laugh out loud was hard to resist. Here I had spent so much time worrying and wondering if Matthew was ready and how I was supposed to help get him there when the whole time, and without my knowing, God was already working on it. And for the second time in my life I was struck by the revelation that God doesn't like boxes no matter how big of one I may make for Him.

I breathed deeply, wanting to stay in the joy of His provision, but Matthew's story didn't wait. He continued and while I was still digging out from beneath the rubble of my now blown apart container of control, I fought to refocus on his animated retelling of the many ways God had ministered to him throughout his time at camp. He spoke of different camp counselors and how amazed he was at how they offered to pray with him and minister over him once they heard his story. "It felt like that was the whole reason I was supposed to go. Even Joe White, the owner of the camp, prayed for me." Then he grew pensively quiet before looking directly at Randy and I, his eyes misty, and quietly said, "It was so cool you guys. I've never had anything like it."

A silence filled the room as the revelation of God's heart behind Matthew's journey fell. Like building blocks sent from the Throne Room I thought about how many times God had said, *"That child is mine . . . "* or *"I know the plans I have for him . . . "* Then, assembling all the pieces, I thought about the recent moment of discovering that God had been protecting Matthew since his first moments in the womb. Every detail rolled in front of me as if God Himself was on display wanting me to see just how deep and how wide and how high is the love of God through Christ Jesus. The reality of it all took my breath away as His revelation continued, *"Look, Kelly, this is my heart for the fatherless—to love them like no one else does and to move on their behalf in ways that no one else can. That child has always been mine. All of this is just proof of that."*

The intensity of the moment lingered long enough that involuntary reactions had to become voluntary and although I could hear Randy and Matt talking, I wasn't capable of listening. Caught up in the moment, I wasn't ready for Him or His truth to lift quite yet. I wanted Him to remain for His words had burned within me, just like they had in the men on the road to Emmaus, (Luke 14:13-35).

I centered myself once again in the chair, looking to find a way to flawlessly reenter Matthew's conversation. Still hazy from my momentary departure, all I heard was, "So, have you been praying about this and who should go with me?"

I blinked twice, hoping to clear away some of the remaining haze that comes with reentry before shifting my gaze toward Randy as I waited for him to respond. As Matthew's father it was his question to answer, if for no other reason than Matthew needed Randy's covering just as he much as he needed to follow Randy's lead. Therefore, I remained silent, content to watch the scene unfold as Randy's subtle grin gently reminded me of who we believed should be Matthew's traveling companion—Randy's brother John.

We trusted John, we always had. His heart of selflessness and love for our children had been proven over the years, establishing that in every way possible he had become a second father to them. *Matthew will be safe with him,* I remembered sharing with the Lord.

"Well, who?" Matthew asked again, this time with more excitement.

Randy briefly glanced back at me before redirecting his attention toward Matt, clearing his throat and turning his answer into a question he said, "Well, how do you feel about Uncle John going?"

Matthew threw his head back in delight as his infectious laugh filled the room and said, "That's exactly who I thought God gave to me . . . "

With that the three of us went on to share the different ways God had shown Himself to each of us over the course of the past six weeks, then marveled at the way He had moved on behalf of our family. We spoke of

His faithfulness and how He tends to love the element of surprise. Then we sat back and discussed at length the different approaches Matt could take in preparation for the next step of his journey—the most obvious being how to contact him.

Years had passed since *that weekend* and my botched-up phone call to Matthew's birth father, and I no longer had any idea where he was located or how to reach him. Therefore, Internet searches launched Matthew's fact-finding mission, followed by introductory phones calls to a list of men who shared his biological father's common surname. Multiple "hello's" spoken by unfamiliar voices were consistently met with a silent negative shake of my head in Matthew's direction as he went on to dial number after number, exhausting nearly all the names on his list. That was until he dialed one of the last numbers on the printout, and despite the knot in my stomach or the pounding in my ears, as soon as the sound of his voice flowed from the phone I *knew*—one quick glance toward Randy and an affirmative nod of the head in Matthew's direction was all it took for whatever was left of my containment walls to come crumbling down. Matt was no longer under my protection. The process had set him free. Now, *he* would choose.

I remained frozen in place, unsure of whether to stand guard and listen or offer privacy and leave. I chose the former. Their conversation was brief, their meeting tentatively scheduled. I closed my eyes desperately wanting to be happy for Matt but skeptical about him getting hurt. *I don't trust him, Lord,* I silently told Him. To which came the reminder, *"You don't have to . . . trust Me."*

An audible exhale, then Silence took over—the rise and fall of my chest shallow in the face of one of my life's greatest fears. Clearly it was happening because while my walls of containment had crumbled, Randy's paternal guards had begun to fall gently into place. Where I would have given mandates, he offered questions, and instead of providing a blanket stamp of approval, subtle cautions were covertly offered.

"Dad, do you think I should drive all the way back there?" My eyes darted from one man to the other, glad that the question was Randy's to answer.

"How about you meet him halfway, Son, in Columbus?" Another exhale led to another breath. Content to watch Randy steer the conversation without ever demanding control, I marveled in the way grace seemed to just flow from him. Nothing in him needed to order Matthew's steps—as if empowering Matthew was as important as protecting him.

I walked away from the conversation that day with little to say. For so many reasons I felt like the baton had been passed. Randy would now be the one who prepared and guided Matthew through the ins and outs of all the details, just as it would be Randy who held my hand one early Saturday morning a few days later as we watched Matt back out of the driveway as he and John left for Columbus, Ohio.

Letting Matthew go that day was surprisingly easier than I ever expected. Perhaps that's because the work of releasing him had already been done in the spirit. The Lord's words to Joshua resurfaced within me, *"Every place that the sole of your foot will tread upon I have given you, as I said to Moses,"* (Joshua 1), reminding me that we can only succeed in the places the Lord has already been. *That's why there's two verb tenses, isn't it, Lord? You carve the path ahead of us and we just have to follow.*

I breathed deeply, praying the same would be true for Matthew; I wanted him to walk victoriously on the ground God had laid out for him. *Give him eyes to see, Lord,* I asked as Randy and I made our way back to the front porch. Remnants of my earlier time with the Father revisited me as I thought about the breadth of Matthew's trip. Today was a turning point for him in ways he had yet to understand, and although I had no freedom to share, the Lord had already shared with me, *"Today Matthew will choose who his father will be. I gave him the one I wanted him to have, but from this day forward the choice will be his."*

I thought about how I felt the day in the restaurant when the reality of my father finally collided with my idyllic version of who I had created him to be. *Pave the way, Father,* poured through me. Then I wondered if Matthew meeting him would somehow level the uneven playing field that had always existed between he and Randy—the absent biological always having the slight upper hand over the adoptive parent because the conceptual paternal figure wasn't physically here to hold the line or to say no when no needed to be said or to require something out of someone who would rather be left alone.

Randy was the one who had always played that role, just as it was Randy who kept the wall of protection securely around Matthew ever since he was four. But walls don't just keep things out; they also prevent things from coming in. And until now the barrier of protection that had always been there to shield Matt had also kept him from seeing the true nature of his biological father. Once Matthew stepped over the rubble, Randy would no longer have to compete against a glamourized paternal concept—*which means You're right, Lord, the choice is now Matthew's to make,* I silently whispered back.

I clung that truth tightly to my chest over the hours that framed that particular Saturday afternoon while we waited. Those of us who remained—Randy, me, Anna and Aaron—were as aware as anyone could be of the moment Matthew was seizing. As silent moral supporters, none of us ventured very far from one another. Instead, we passed those ten hours the only way we knew how—as a family deeply woven and united together— until late that afternoon when we saw the silver flash of Matt's car glint in the sunlight silent declaring their return.

Wait, Kelly, I reminded myself as I fidgeted on the porch bench, mentally willing Matthew to hurry up, my leg bouncing with nervous energy. I glanced at Randy who gave me one of his "What am I going to do with you?" looks but I couldn't help myself. I fidgeted in response, then rearranged my seated position in hopes of appearing calm and cool, as if everything was under control as I waited for Matt and John to exit the car.

First impressions would indicate they were as relaxed as I've ever seen them; nothing indicated they had done anything more than gone out for a bite to eat. They appeared to be chatting casually and laughing as usual. *Am I the only one who thinks this is a big deal?* I wondered, looking at the three men who now stood on the porch. They laughed as Randy seamlessly joined in their conversation while I struggled to figure out what they were talking about.

Again I shifted my position then endured an eruption of male laughter before I offered a relatively loud "Ahem" in hopes of bringing their attention back to the matter at hand. Matt's head turned first, then Randy's, before John's finally turned to look at my silent, "WELL????"

Matt just smiled as he sat and said, "Sorry, Mom . . . " then turning to look back at John, grinned and said, "Ya know, Mom, it was pretty uneventful." He paused a second to collect his thoughts, then continued, "He was on time, we ate . . . *he* talked, and then it was time to go," he finished as he shrugged his shoulders. "Really . . . there wasn't anything to it."

I scanned his eyes, unsure that it was as simple as he conveyed, eyeing him quizzically and hoping he would elaborate.

"Really," he continued, "there's not much to tell. I know where I get my height or the lack of it now though," he said lightheartedly.

I'm not sure if I smiled *at* him or *over* him as he continued to share his thoughts. He spoke of what he saw when he looked at the life his biological father had led—the hardness of his eyes . . . the weariness on his face . . . the heaviness of his steps. "He carries a heavy load, Mom. I wish it was different for him, but he doesn't seem interested. I tried."

Listening to Matt, it suddenly occurred to me that although I had prepared myself to watch my son wrestle with the torrent of emotions that would result when meeting such a large mental enigma, the reality was they weren't the source of his wrestling match at all. The biggest conflict Matthew faced when he left Columbus was rooted in leaving his biological father in Ohio without him ever truly experiencing the grace of God. Matt didn't have any place to put that reality because he didn't come from it. All he had ever seen was grace and redemption in action.

Perhaps that's what gave Matthew a new appreciation for the father God had given to him; he saw firsthand how differently a life redeemed by grace looks from one that had not yet been ransomed. However, appreciation is far different from acceptance and while Matthew was grateful for what he had been given, his heart still ached for what lacked.

He processed, he prayed, then he asked questions . . . a lot of them, all the way up until it was nearly time for Wheaton's fall semester. To which end all Randy and I could do was encourage him and reinforce the idea that God is faithful and often pursues even those who don't necessarily want or even know they need to be pursued. "It takes Him but a moment, Matt, and all things are made new," I reminded him one last time before he left for football conditioning.

Not long after we moved him back to campus and school started, my phone rang and Matthew, sounding more like himself—excited yet a bit taken aback—began describing the requirements of an English essay he had just been assigned. "I have to write about a non-academic lesson I learned over the summer and it has to be non-linear, meaning it has to start in the middle of the story."

"Okay . . . " I replied tentatively, not exactly connecting all the dots.

"Mom, if it's okay I'd like to write about what I learned when I got to meet him—what I learned about me . . . and about him . . . and about God," his voice trailed off as if it reflected the scope of his wandering thoughts. Then, regaining momentum, he continued, "I want it to begin with me standing at the door of the restaurant trying to find the courage to turn the knob when all I really wanted to do was run the other way."

He paused for a split second before he said, "'The Day I Became a Man.' Mom, I think that's what I'll call it."

The past months scrolled across my memory: his initial phone call in May presenting the idea . . . my unusually collected response . . . the longevity of God's protection . . . the camp . . . Johnny—all of it, every moment passed in breakneck speed until present day was back in focus with the assignment taking front and center.

Silence found his way back to me as I stood awestruck by how detailed and thorough the Father had been every step of the way. From beginning to end, every leg of Matthew's journey thought out and orchestrated in such a way that it couldn't have been anyone but Him. His fingerprints were all over it.

Matthew's final question drew me back from my spiritual reflection as he, with far more assurance than when he began, asked, "Then, if it's okay,

I could write the rest of the paper using flashbacks based on your story. Do you mind, Mom? Would that be okay?" his questions tumbling out.

What do you say when you stumble upon such a moment? When you realize that the God who has loved you unconditionally and without reservation—the God who crawled into the deepest of life's pits to redeem you—has just systematically covered every possibility, every minute detail and every concern from beginning to end *for your child?* Up until that moment, I had always believed he was just *mine*. Certainly I knew God loved him—but count-the-hairs-on-his-head and number-the-grains-of-sand kind of love? I never transferred the thought; my children had always been that—*my* children. Mine to raise, mine to teach the difference of right and wrong, and entrusted to me to teach or model how to love God with a passion.

That day on the phone, however, I saw just how "His" they really were, and the enormity of His heart overwhelmed me—not just to love, although He does. But more than that was realizing the scope of this faith walk that He had invited me into so long ago was so much greater than anything I had ever imagined. For so long I presumed it was primarily about me learning to love Him, then teaching my children to do the same; never had I considered how jealous He was for them Himself.

I stood in that season of life, those first weeks of Matthew's second year at Wheaton, and realized that I was more at ease than ever with Matthew being away. After the events of the past summer, I had come to accept that he truly was in the best of hands. Then, just when I thought this particular chapter of Matt's life was coming to a close and our rejoicing was just about over, he called again weeks later to share the results of his essay and to say the professor wanted to meet with him. "Mom," Matt said a bit breathless, "he said he'd meet with me every week so I have someone to help process through what I wrote about. Can you believe that?"

My being at a loss for words lasted much longer than just our phone conversation. Few words remain that can adequately express the depth of gratitude when someone moves on behalf of one of your children, let alone when that someone is the Father. Words pale in comparison.

King David once said, *"All your works praise you, Lord; your faithful people extol you. They tell of the glory of your kingdom and speak of your might"* (Psalm 145:10-11). I learned that to be true that summer, and only He knows how very much. The fruit of His labor tells enough of the story. Everything else He already knows.

CHAPTER THIRTY-FIVE

BROKEN PATHWAY

*The pathway is broken
And the signs are unclear
I don't know the reason why You brought me here
But just because You love me the way that you do
I'm going to walk through the valley
If You want me to*
—Ginny Owens
If You Want Me To

Years after that whirlwind season of jaw surgeries and meeting biological fathers, the Lord whispered to me, *"Clay has no resistance, Kelly."* Then He showed me a picture of a ball of clay being molded under the gentle hand of the Master, so pliable and yielding that it nearly melted into its new form.

Ever since that moment I've looked back on various seasons in my life and thought about all the times when I was absolutely certain I was fully cooperating with the Lord in the midst of whatever was going on—convinced I was letting Him have His good and perfect way in me—only to discover the wounded parts of myself that remained so deeply resistant to the necessary process that comes with transformation. Some people call that hindsight. I think spiritual wisdom is more appropriate.

So it was the fall after Matthew's summertime encounter when I returned to life in the valley fully believing that I was clay in the Potter's hands. After all, why shouldn't I be after everything He had just taken us through and taught me about His heart? He had shown Himself trustworthy, faithful and completely willing to move on behalf of my children. Few people had ever experienced such things—we had come to expect them.

Whether it was healing the wounds that came from being fatherless or intervening in the lives of my children or consistent moments of supernatural provision, I was learning that He would put His hands in whatever messes I gave him. And I had given Him a lot—especially financially.

Money, or the power Randy and I ascribed to it, always seemed to be a point of contention for us. We've never found our financial history to be extraordinarily simple—ever. Whether it was the difficulties that came from being self-employed and therefore self-insured and discovering we were unexpectedly pregnant and without sufficient coverage or watching the economic tides of difficulty rise as grace lifted in a home we should have never purchased, finances haven't been exactly easy.

Yet somehow God has always provided—in the most unexpected ways and at the most unexpected times. As if all along He's been wanting us to learn another dimension of the Father's heart that says, *"Rest, child. I have you."*

Which is unspeakably difficult for a girl who has never physically seen a father in action. My flesh is always faithful to remind me that on some level I'm responsible for *something*, even if the Father says, *"No, you're not."*

It's another lesson I've had to learn over and over because for whatever reason my spirit just hasn't been able to get it—not way down deep where Truth resides and holds the power to transform us. Rather it comes on levels and in layers, one onion peel at a time, and for fifteen years He's been in the process of peeling those layers off.

The process goes something like this: we have need, He provides. Then we're good for a while until another need arises, something that is just beyond our ability to manage, and He, in time, provides again. Each provision comes exactly when it's needed in just the amount that's required and though He's pulled through every time, waiting to see *how* remains unbearably difficult. Repeatedly, and despite His faithful track record, the Orphan Spirit inside of me cries out, convinced I'll be left holding the proverbial bag and that this is the *one time* He won't deliver on His promise to be there. It's been an unrelenting, overwhelming fear of mine. Then just about the time I'm sure I'll BUST, He shows up in His gentle way, exactly like He promised and I am left to wonder all over again why I ever worried in the first place.

The process is cyclical and each time it seems His provision won't come until the eleventh hour, but it *always* comes and He has *always* provided exactly what we needed. It was a way of life Randy and I had come to expect and were learning to grow fairly comfortable with, especially after the summer of such of monumental moments.

We had seen God's hand move in unprecedented fashion, which resulted in an almost euphoric level of faith. As a family, we floated on the recent victories—being able to pay cash for Matthew's first year at Wheaton, withstanding Anna's fifty-five-thousand-dollar jaw surgery, and Matthew's journey of meeting his biological father—

certain that whatever future obstacle or mountain we encountered, our God was strong enough to overcome it.

Like hash marks on a growth chart we could measure how much our faith had grown. Perhaps that's why we weren't overly concerned with how we would pay for Matthew's second year at college. Experience had taught us scaling mountains this size required more than the equipment we naturally possessed. God would have to show up, and undoubtedly He would since He was the One who called Matt to Wheaton in the first place.

But waiting is when Doubt tends to throw a few punches at our faith. It was on those days when Doubt lingered in the valley that Scriptures would speak life back into me. When I doubted or feared, I grasped Jesus' words in Matthew 17, "*. . . for assuredly, I say to you, if you have faith as small as a mustard seed, you will say to this mountain, 'Move from here to there,' and it will move; and nothing will be impossible for you*" (20).

With that verse tucked away in my satchel, I would pray, then declare, then pray again until my fear that He wasn't going to provide would vanish. And once again I would be steady on my feet, ready and waiting for another "God story" to emerge.

It was the only way I knew to do life.

But days turned into weeks and the numbers remained the same. In response, I increased my grip and held tighter to my most recent revelation—the three-way grid of truth: Scripture, prayer and wise counsel. It became almost a check and balance type of system as I reflected on what I believed He had spoken to me and compared it to the reality I was living.

When I prayed, my spirit didn't hear the soft gentle sound of caution; instead all I heard was, "This is the way, walk ye in it." Then the faith verse from Matthew would flow through me again. On the days when I needed more, Joshua 3 and the waters of the Jordan River would illuminate and I would remind myself that just as He had parted the Red Sea to create a pathway for the Israelite captives, so too He made a way for the next generation to cross into their Promised Land. In essence, miracles can and do repeat themselves.

Like faith-filled nuggets of nutrition I took those truths and allowed them to guide my faith through the valley. Resting on the countless times in my own life when the Lord had miraculously provided a pathway across my own Red Sea, I trusted it was only a matter of time before He showed us the way across this particular Jordan.

Most days I navigated things quite well. I was confident—secure in what I believed to be truth despite the mounting pressure of unpaid tuition bills and persistent phones calls from the bursar's office. On the days my faith faltered and I stumbled in the divots Doubt placed in front of me, invariably someone would unexpectedly come along and encourage me in the same way they did during the six months of trying to sell our house in "Egypt." But instead of "You're house is beautiful. Just be patient; it will sell," this time encouragement sounded more like, "Don't worry. Just be patient; God will provide."

So wait we did. But bursars' offices don't really have a place to put "I'm just waiting on God for the money," not even Christian ones. Instead, spurred by deadlines, they propose ideas like Parent Plus loans and student debt to pay for things, all of which caused Randy to question, "What glory does God get if I borrow the money?"

To which no one had a good answer. The usual reaction was a quizzical look of bewilderment while Randy remained steadfast and fixed on walking out his faith. After all our years together and all our financial ups and downs, Randy's faith slowly emerged with a tenacity and resolve I had yet to ever witness. It was as if he was laying everything he believed about the Father's provision on the line. He literally was putting God to the test just as Malachi 3 called him to do, and this was his moment when his theology was going to meet his reality, much like mine had so many years ago.

Since then, I've intermittently wondered whether either of us had experienced a check in our spirit—something to indicate that somewhere along the way we had turned off the beaten path or misunderstood God and what He had called us to do. To our knowledge, neither of us ever had. Instead, because I had spent much of my adult life learning about manna and the miraculous daily feeding of the Israelites, my faith had grown to expect nothing less. Most of our life together had been spent doing just that—learning to be fed daily by His hand and content with the provision for that particular day. We never really had extra to store; most days I wondered if we were even supposed to. Dependency was what we had to learn. To depend on Him . . . to trust Him . . . and to relax and know that we know He *will* provide.

To a woman raised in a fatherless home and never having seen a father's hands actually provide for me, believing those truths doesn't come easily. And confidently stepping out on them is an altogether different story. In all reality, for those of us who have grown up fatherless, the challenge that faith coupled with works represents stirs up every ounce of our survival instinct. The unhealed orphan spirit within us diametrically opposes the free-fall feeling that comes from taking risks, not because of a lack of adventure but rather in the depths of our souls we're not convinced anyone will actually be there to catch us. Releasing control is the last thing we know how to do because we've spent most of our formative years finding ways to feel secure and governing aspects of ourselves that should have been entrusted to our fathers. As a result we learn to embody traits we were never created to possess. Leaving me with one persistent and exhausting thought—*Fatherlessness wreaks havoc on the soul.*

I'm not sure whether that awareness came into the valley with me or not; I just knew that as Randy and I traversed the hills of provision and faith, there were definite moments when I knew the only way I would withstand the current was if I jumped on His back and He carried me. Left to my own devices, I would never find my way.

So follow I did. In my own quiet place I'd either find a Psalm that spoke the language of my heart or I'd reflect on all the times God had shown His faithfulness to me. Like a voice in the distance I'd hear the Hall of Faith as recorded in Hebrews 11, "By faith we understand . . . by faith Abel . . . by faith Enoch . . . by faith Noah . . . by faith Abraham . . . by faith Sarah . . . by faith Isaac . . . by faith Jacob . . . by faith Joseph. . . " On and on went the list, honored ancestors and their historical landmarks of great acts done in great faith—all of whom knew that without faith, it was and is impossible to please God.

Slowly I began to identify with them, but not because the challenge before me was great like theirs. I simply couldn't help but believe that this was our time to extol great faith in the face of impossible circumstances. This was our moment, and I so desperately wanted Him to be pleased. We took daily accounts of all He had done for us, then—as an extra measure—sifted everything *again* through the three-way grid of truth while we asked Him for clarity. When silence was our only answer, we relied on the unity of counsel we received from our inner circle and most trusted confidants. Then with the purest hearts we knew how to present, along with our great cloud of witnesses, we stood steadfast and committed to trusting that Wheaton was where God wanted Matthew to further equip him for what he was created to do.

Believing came easier in the midst of the community the Father had given us. But as more time passed and the waiting fought to dampen our spirits, the no response began to take its toll. For weeks ago life, though lived in the valley, still had moments when the villagers come alongside us to edify and encourage—but what grew in the quiet? What about then, when we find ourselves like David facing Goliath and all we could hear were the taunts and heckles of the enemy shouting, "Are you sure? Are you really sure? You know you're crazy? You know only crazy people believe this way, don't you?"

Round and round it went till finally, days after Wheaton's deadline had passed and our collective faith was stretched to the limit, Randy sat at lunch reading the latest Larry Burkett book on financial management and someone unexpectedly came up to him inquiring about the principles in the book. After inviting the stranger to sit with him, Randy shared that Burkett teaches of the intricate balance that exists between self-management and trusting God for your needs. When Randy was finished and all of his "God stories" had been shared, the man sat quietly for a second before asking one simple question: "What do you intend to do about Wheaton?"

Knowing Randy, I'm sure he smirked before ever replying, if for no other reason than being struck by the reality of just how far out of the box his response was going to sound. A man who rarely feels the need to put a public voice to his faith, Randy simply handed the stranger his business card then without hesitancy said, "Call me in three days and I will tell you how my God provided. He is faithful and *will* show up, that much I know." He was as far out as I had ever seen him.

It was the one and only time Randy ever spoke with the man.

Curiosity has often caused me to wonder if the stranger was an angel sent to test Randy to see if he would stand true to his faith; I doubt I'll ever know this side of heaven. Time and seasoning have allowed me to accept the fact that where faith is concerned, there are some things that during this lifetime will remain a mystery. Until we're on the other side of the earthly experience, we're called to give thanks in all things. We've had to learn how to do that, and that lesson hasn't come easy.

To this day we remain thankful the man never called, because those three days passed uneventfully. Though we waited on and fervently sought the Lord in every way we knew how, for the first time in our married life we never received any miraculous provision or supply.

In fact, once those three days fully expired and the deadline for payment had long since passed, Wheaton called one final time and presented us with the option of either paying Matthew's fall semester bill or withdrawing him from the school. Regardless of what we decided, they couldn't wait any longer.

In retrospect I wish I had walked in confidence in all the Lord had done for me. I didn't. Just as in retrospect I wish I could have persisted in my faith like the apostle Paul had, despite shipwrecks and beatings and stoning. I didn't do that either any more than I remembered like King David *all* the great things the LORD has done for me.

Instead, as if the stress of the past months had been unknowingly accumulating and the deepest darkest most inner part of me manifested once again as we confronted the reality that we had no way to pay for Matthew's education short of taking out a loan. The feeling of being trapped washed over me just as it had when I first heard the specialist detail his plan of attack for Anna—as if Wheaton's tuition was the second punch in an unseen one-two punch scenario. Only this blow somehow caused the things of God to no longer make any sense to me. Deep within the recesses of my spirit, the past year's events wanted to confirm that my worst fear had finally come true. In the end, no matter how long I journeyed, I really *was* all alone, as evidenced by the completed paperwork that now lay in front of me, seemingly declaring that this was indeed the one time when God had chosen not to "show up."

The vacuum of space my unanswered questions created felt as if it would suck me into its chasm, uncontrollably spiraling downward into the endless pit of rationalization and need for answers. Yet regardless of how many whys were uttered or reexaminations were made of the three-way grid of truth we had sifted Wheaton through, the one fact that continually remained in front of us was the tens of thousands of dollars of educational debt we would incur with just one signature.

"I don't understand Lord, we've done everything You've asked. Did we miss You? Are we not supposed to do this?" My questions sounding more like begging than asking.

Rarely do those questions ever receive an answer. Rather, Silence seems to be the only one who ever joins me in those conversations. Yet I continually have them, and although the loan was taken, and Wheaton's payment was made, it was in the presence of silence where my faith plummeted— the fall from the previous mountain peak nearly fatal.

Somewhere deep inside, despair had found a place to take root. I struggled with reconciling the God I knew to be true with the experience I just had. Never before in all the years that I had walked with the Lord had He ever just not shown up—not in answers or in reflection or in showing me the waywardness of my own thinking. My inner battle became fixated on one thought, If You had shown me otherwise along the way . . . *if You had led me in another direction, it would be different. But You let me believe . . .*

Eventually the thought would trail off unresolved, unanswerable giving way to a slow, growing sense of what I would come to learn was a bitter root judgment, which would have been easier to uproot with if it hadn't been directed toward the Lord.

Yet it was, and with each passing day my heart's agreement with the heaviness my internal argument caused compounded its rate of growth feeding the root of bitterness while I continued to grow increasingly resistant to the concept of a God who was altogether good.

Recognizing we were both in a spiritual quagmire we couldn't get out of, Randy began to seek counsel telling me, "We're in over our heads, Kel, and I don't know what sense to make of all this. I need to talk to somebody," he said.

His tenderness toward the Lord admirable even if it did serve as an irritant. Months after all that had happened, I *wanted* to be angry. Yes, my daughter was healing and yes Matthew had remained at Wheaton, but at what cost? The numbers wreaked havoc in my head as tens of thousands of dollars stacked up in organized piles in my brain. Tormented by such amounts, I needed a place to direct my anger and frustration—the indignancy I felt was inescapable. New chains of financial bondage seemed to have found their way to secure us to their grasp regardless of our intention to live debt free.

My frustration simmered just below the surface; all the while, Randy stood. Confusion swirling around him in its own way, but that doesn't mean he didn't stand. Instead, he remained willing to go where he sensed the Lord had called him. Therefore, he remained pliable before the Lord, and to my own confusion never grew angry. Much like the evening years ago when the lady totaled the last working car we had and we were months behind in our house payment, Randy remained committed to his core belief that God knew our needs. It was his own personal center point.

I yearned to learn from him—to believe as he did, to exercise my faith with the same simplicity that he walked in, but instead it exasperated me. Like a magnifying glass, his resolute commitments only served to enhance my own internal wrestling match as if they were being used to put mine of full display.

Like a sideline participant, I watched as Randy worked to fight against the disappointment that wanted to take root and gnaw away at his faith. He countered the assault by seeking counsel from various pastors regarding the disconnect between his reliance upon God and what appeared as unfaithfulness or abandonment, and with bated breath I waited for one answer that would help me make sense of our situation—but none ever came, at least not a viable one. Instead, failed attempts were made to try and cushion the blow with phrases such as, "God's just a mystery and His ways are not our ways" or "These are the times that try men's souls," but never insight as to what Holy Spirit might be trying to teach or touch or do through our circumstance.

"Try men's souls? Really?" I blurted out in such a way that revealed how annoyed I was with the empty, calloused answer. "We believed . . . we trusted

. . . we prayed . . . we did it all, Randy. And that's the answer? Our souls are tried?" My fury escalated and I wanted to explode.

"I know, Kel," Randy said in a hushed tone, that sounded more like defeat than I had ever heard him utter.

"Did you ask him what God was doing in the midst of all this? Did he even ask questions to find out?"

Randy just shook his head no, his shoulders slumped.

In normal circumstances, seeing Randy that way would have caused deep wells of compassion to begin to stir within me. It didn't. Despondency had expanded its territory within me, and all I felt was the same overwhelming sense of abandonment that I did in high school. Standing in the kitchen, the fear and anxiety I hadn't felt since I was a teenager washed over me, drowning me with the force of its appearance. I couldn't breathe.

Gasping for breath, I leaned back on the counter, vowing to myself that I wouldn't cry and said, "I don't understand, Randy," I mumbled, "I just don't get it."

"Yeah, I understand . . . me neither," he said as he made organized piles out of the clutter that lay on the table.

I stood there for a moment longer, feeling the last bit of hope dissipate from the room before I finally turned and walked away.

CHAPTER THIRTY-SIX

BREAKING POINT

*He is no fool who loses what he cannot keep to gain
what he cannot lose.*
—Jim Elliot

Living in the ongoing spiritual state of distrust and despondency took an exorbitant amount of emotional energy because they are conditions the Lord never intended any of us to walk under. Rather, they are the fruit of the enemy whose sole mission is to steal our joy, rob our relationships and destroy our faith while Jesus came " . . . to give life and life more abundantly," (John 10:10). These two truths are at war against each other and the only way we can gain the victory is to appropriate the work that Jesus did on the cross, thereby destroying the very things that stand in opposition to what is rightfully ours to inherit.

Some of the problem was I didn't know or even understand that principle at the time. Instead, my faith was simple, like a math equation: I depended on Him to provide . . . He didn't . . . conclusion made.

Partner that with not being one who can accept blanket answers such as, "This is God's will for you," especially when the "this" didn't line up with anything I had ever previously experienced or known about His character, and I was somehow walking on barren land with Despair and Abandonment as my personal escorts. My faith lay in Uncertainty's hands and it felt as if a black expanse had gradually consumed every place where light and purity of heart had once existed—I couldn't "see" my way clear through anything. Instead of experiencing the joy that comes from *knowing* God was walking with me, Doubt had all but convinced me that somewhere along the way He had left us stranded in this particular valley causing my steps to grow as heavy as my heart felt.

With each worn down moment, intolerance to anything "spiritual" began to take hold. Subtle mocking phrases would emerge from my heart whenever one of the YaYas would declare a particular way God unexpectedly "showed up" for them, and inevitably my inner self would cry out, "Why, God? Why do you show up for them and not me?"

The only true source of fellowship I found was with Silence. Only in the company of my own head could I find solace even though I never found any answers. At least people couldn't reach me there, and I could discover momentary escape routes from the torment that came from not having eyes to see what exactly God was trying to uncover in me through the process. Whispered lies of the enemy had begun to look too much like truth, so much so I struggled to differentiate between them anymore. The only tangible consistent thing I felt was the growing sense of righteous indignation I believed I was entitled to hold onto and carry with me like a decorated war veteran.

It became a badge of honor in a way. God had offended me, and I viewed that offense as unjust for I had done nothing to warrant it, only what He had asked me to do—believe. In essence, I had fallen victim to my own faith and even though we sat in church and did "churchy" things, Silence was the only one who really knew of my contempt—Silence, and on some level, Randy. God certainly didn't, for it had been weeks since I had spoken to Him. The only thing on my radar regarding my spiritual life was to try and starve it to death. I didn't want to have anything to do with it anymore.

Yet I remained cognizant enough to value the importance of setting an example before my children and maintaining our attendance at church was a priority. Nothing in me wanted to compromise their belief system, so to church we went and out of some distorted sense of submission I let Randy talk me into continuing on at Sunday School. I was resistant at best to anything more than what was absolutely necessary but if there was any crack in my armor, any hole in my defense, it was that I knew Pam and Ted would be there. Everyone else would require me to don the Christian mask and pretend like all was spiritually well in the Williams household.

But I'm not a very good mask wearer, especially when my indignation is at an all-time high and it takes every ounce of self-control I have to contain my emotions. Inevitably those are the moments when the mask slips and falls off, sending a clatter so reverberatingly loud that everyone can hear it, and the very ugliness I had so artfully been trying to disguise is laid bare for all to see.

It was a late January Sunday morning, and I was particularly highstrung. Agitated at having to be there, hungry and in constant pursuit of a way to ignore my pent-up spiritual fury, I welcomed Pam's conversational distraction from the mindless droning of class announcements. Like two adolescent girls, we whispered, I giggled then, as covertly as possible, we started all over again until Randy leaned over and quietly whispered, "Can you write down the prayer list so we know who to pray for this week?"

Enmeshed in my hushed conversation with Pam, I glanced over at him while I simultaneously shook my head no and batted the pen in his hand away.

Another giggle, another "Shhh," before he repeated, "Kel . . . would you please record the prayer concerns?"

Remnants of the people's concerns bounced around the room, something about so and so's sister or Aunt Mary's big toe, all of which just confirmed my disinterest in the class's conversation, so I refocused on Pam's humor and slightly shook my head no again.

"KEL," he whispered more insistently and authoritatively than usual, "I want you to list the prayers, okay?"

I can't really say when I felt Tolerance vacate the premises or exactly when Exasperation took its place, but I can say that it didn't take more than a split second for the hair on the back of my neck to rise. With a sense of sheer finality and louder than I ever intended, my head spun around and I seethed, "I DON'T EVEN PRAY FOR THESE PEOPLE, WHY WOULD I WRITE DOWN THEIR PRAYER REQUESTS!?! You write them down if you want to pray!"

The whole room stopped . . . frozen in time except for the thirty heads that turned like dominoes falling in slow motion to see what all the fuss was about. I immediately began looking for the internal rewind button, but there wasn't one. The heat of embarrassment rose until it could be seen in the flush of my cheeks. With no place to hide and no tactful way to pick my mask back up, I slunk down in my chair, hid my face and wondered what exactly I had become—I was mortified. Thoughts of standing up to say, "Wait, that didn't come out right. It's not that I don't pray for *you*; what I really meant was I don't pray at all. I'm not talking to Him right now."

The thought remained just that—a thought.

I left church that day struck by how far down the pit I had fallen. I was well aware that while it had taken years and untold God moments to build my faith, it took only one encounter or lack thereof to nearly destroy it. Realizing the ease with which I fell shook me to my core.

It's not like I instantly plunged into the well of despair; looking back over the past six months I realized it was more like a gradual descent into oblivion. Truth was, directly or indirectly I had been crying out to the Lord, begging Him for understanding, pleading with Him for answers. But I couldn't find Him. Just like the provision for Wheaton, He was as absent from me as I had ever known. In retrospect, that was the most difficult part of that entire season—my faith was strong enough to handle the adversity, and I could accept His decline of my supplication. But it was His silence that ripped the innermost part of me into countless shreds because it hit the wound of abandonment that had been inflicted on me the day my father died.

I didn't know it at the time, but that season came to be known as what St. John of the Cross calls the "Dark Night of the Soul"—the season in life when God withdraws Himself as a means to purify the spirit. In contemporary language it's the Refiner's Fire or His own way of purifying us. Much like the process of making gold, the heat of circumstance is the very thing He uses to "bleed" out the worst of our impurities, and they only come out when we the fire is the hottest.

My issues of abandonment as they relate to my father were some of the deepest impurities that needed to bleed. Did I understand that during the process or even have eyes to see that at the time? Clearly not. Most days I felt like the StayPuft marshmallow man at the end of the Ghostbusters movie who, as a result of being incinerated by the three Ghostbusters, explodes covering everyone and everything in globs of ooey-gooey marshmallow. My soul had involuntarily exploded all over the Sunday school class that January morning and no matter what I did, I couldn't collect myself or find a way to put myself back together. I had, in effect, slimed everyone around me.

Remnants of myself remained scattered until nearly a month after my embarrassing eruption, Pam, in all her joy, felt led to knock on my door. Always happy to see her and the ease with which she carries herself, I immediately welcomed her into the house.

Stepping onto the tile entryway, she was unusually apprehensive . . . tentative almost . . . as if she wasn't sure how to present what she so obviously contained. She fidgeted and she stammered, then I watched her silently chose to articulate what she came to say, "Kel, I don't know how to tell you this so just let me get it out . . . "

A guarded skepticism furrowed my brow as I wondered what exactly was going on. She remained silent, looking at me as if she was waiting for permission to continue. So, draped in curiosity I said, "Oookay. . . "

An unusual pool of tears glistened in her eyes as she continued, "I love you, Kelly, you know that," she paused, not overly comfortable with visible displays of emotion. "But I can't do life with you in the pit anymore. I need you how you used to be."

I listened with an unusual poker face as I wondered how or where I could find that person. She fixed her eyes on mine, hesitated, then strengthening her resolve said, "So get your coat and come with me."

Any other time I would have jumped at the chance to go with Pam but something about her intensity, her seriousness, made me not so willing this time. "Where are we going?" I questioned with strong reservation.

Her eyes fluttered around the room before settling back on mine, then she said, "There's a Beth Moore study starting tonight at the church and I think we're supposed to be there." She paused, looking at me in such a way that I knew I no longer had any wiggle room, "So go on, get your coat and let's go," with a nod of her head and one foot out the door as if it was a done deal . . . planned out and fully expected.

My gut reaction wanted to say, "NO, NO WAY!" and return to what I was doing, but something far more subtle told me this was more than just a friend showing up inviting me to your average Bible study. This was a fork in the road—a divine invitation, almost a mandate being given, and I suspected that if I didn't respond positively I would forever re-chart the course of my spiritual life.

I glanced out the door for a split second and watched Pam climb into the car, realizing this was most likely the one chance I had to turn things around. Whispers of, *"Do you want to be made well?"* (John 5:6) coursed through me and I flinched. Then before I could think twice I told Randy where I was going, got in Pam's car and fought myself the whole way to the church.

True to my recent behavior over the past few months, I spent most of the two hours agreeing with the mocking spirit inside me as it scoffed and ridiculed the five main points of Beth Moore's *Believing God* study. She made an early point in her presentation, that it isn't enough to believe *in* God—she asked if we *believe* God? In other words, do we believe the following and live as if we do:

1) God is who He says He is . . .
2) God can do what He says He can do . . .
3) I am who God says I am . . .
4) I can do all things through Christ . . .
5) God's word is alive and active in me.

Their truth, like salt, immediately struck at the heart of the wound, the pain so immediate and so deep all I could do was shriek back. My second reaction was to mock, but not because I didn't believe them—rather because I did.

But what did it get me? I asked rhetorically.

I wanted to scream, "I *did* believe, and I *did* have faith, and look what happened! We ended up looking like fools. So what good is any of it?!"

The contempt in my heart overwhelmed me. There was no outlet or relief because there were no answers—just the enveloping realization that the past six months had been the darkest my spirit had ever known. No matter where or how hard I had looked, I couldn't find Him. I hadn't seen Him since He hadn't 'shown up'.

In reality, He wouldn't be found.

Slouching back in the pew I lowered my head, realizing that despite my best efforts to resist Him and all my temper tantrums over the past months, when it was all said and done, I always ended up right back where I started—I didn't have any place to go other than to Him. It didn't matter that my flesh had fought to leave just like so many of Jesus' followers in John 6. In the end something inside wouldn't let go and Peter's words to Jesus, *"Lord, to whom shall we go? You have the words of eternal life"* (6:68), always ended up escorting me right back to Truth.

Brokenness began to wash over me, "I don't have anywhere else, Lord. You alone are it for me; You *know* that," my inner voice told Him.

Like unseen radar my ears began to tune into something Beth was saying about God sifting leaders and how oftentimes they go through things ahead of others. My head slowly lifted as I clung to every word she spoke. At that moment, every other person in the room seemed to fade into oblivion as if her teaching was directed straight at me. The overwhelming sense of abandonment was gone because suddenly I knew He was standing right there, as real to me in that moment as He had been at the Judith McNutt conference years ago. Overcome by His presence, I couldn't fall on my knees fast enough. So, I crawled my way into the middle of the aisle way and began to drink from the deepest of wells.

I remained in that position for the longest time, drifting back and forth from the throne room to the chapel until I stayed in real time long enough to hear Beth reference Luke 22, *"And the Lord said "Simon, Simon! Indeed, Satan has asked for you, that he may sift you as wheat. But I have prayed for you, that your faith should not fail; and when you have returned to me, strengthen your brethren"* (v. 31-32).

Her words washed over me like a cleansing rain. Over and over, they coursed through me as the force that came with hearing that Scripture for the first time began to take hold. So much truth was embedded in that one verse—the asking, the sifting, the praying—all of it, all at once shone a whole new light on the last few months as if it was music to a parade of the past I had been invited to watch. Instantly I recognized how the days and weeks since trusting the Lord for Wheaton's provision had been a sifting season—a season where the darkest and most embedded impurities were being called up and expunged so that truth of who the Father really is could finally take its rightful place in my soul.

That's when the realization that through it all, through every ugly indignant moment of unrighteous entitlement I displayed, Jesus, the Holy One of Israel, had been praying for me, and I was undone all over again.

Me—the one who had been so unfaithful to Him in my heart and so very pompously angry *with* Him and *at* Him . . . *You never once stopped interceding for me.*

Unable to contain that Truth, I allowed it to open up the inner gates of my soul so that everything—all that I had chosen to believe, every lie, every accusation, could come rushing out in the light of His grace.

The expanse called time didn't start ticking again until hope began to reemerge. Then when I heard the words, *". . . and when you return to me, strengthen your brethren."* Another wave of truth washed over me just as it did Peter when Jesus first spoke them to him. *He didn't say **if**, He said **when**, I told myself . . . He said WHEN!* Suddenly I knew that the eerily dark place where I had dwelt the past months wouldn't be where I would stay; *I too will return to Him.* It may not be fully on that night, but ultimately my heart's return back to the Father was imminent. Of that I surely knew.

Not long after that encounter, Pam and I mindlessly walked out of the church, me a little lighter than when I had arrived. Then after ten exhaustive weeks of faithfully attending that study and allowing the Lord to search me and know me so He could have His perfect way in me, my restoration came much easier than I ever thought it would. My spirit's clay no longer hardening on a shelf, it was growing more pliable with every passing day, and a bit more submissive in part because of that season.

I understand just a little better now what is meant when someone like St. John of the Cross or Beth Moore says it's only when He takes us through the dark night of the soul and we come out on the other side that our spirits possess a Truth that we only cognitively believed when the night first approached. It is only in the darkness of the valley that His word truly becomes Rhema to our souls, because only then is their blood on what we've been through.

For me that Truth is simple, yet according to the Kingdom so very profound:

God *is* good. Not because of the things He does, but rather it's the state of His being. He *is* good just as He *is* love, (I John 4:16). Neither is based on what He does but rather just who He is, therefore, His actions are the fruit and the evidence of His being. And even though circumstances may speak differently, and the enemy of our souls wants to use them to convince us of the contrary, the truth is there is no shadow in His turning (James 1:17). The Father never changes, and never casts a shadow for light is always within Him. Therefore, since He's a good Father that also means that He is a Father who never leaves, and He never forsakes. I've had to learn that He's not capable of it.

Without the Wheaton season, I don't know if I would have ever come to understand that truth or even accept it. Up until then His character had always been, whether I knew it or not, on trial, and the verdict rendered most always dependent upon the outcome of my circumstances. For a girl who understood her father's love through the filter of brokenness and abandonment, learning to walk in spiritual truth rather than the evidence of my natural circumstances has made a huge difference in my life and its perspective.

His Truth continues to bring immeasurable freedom in numerous areas of my life, and while my natural circumstances may not always change, I am learning the power that comes with willfully agreeing with the truth that He is who *He* says He is, and He *will* do what *He* says He will do.

Of this I am learning to be wholly and fully convinced.

CHAPTER THIRTY-SEVEN

STORM CLOUDS ON THE HORIZON

For the eyes of the Lord move to and fro throughout the earth that he may strongly support those whose heart is completely his.
—2 Chronicles 6:19

Learning how to abide in the goodness of God took some walking out over the course of the next few months. There were moments when the enemy wanted nothing more than for me to focus on the mound of debt we had accrued over the past six months, and there were times when the temptation to agree with the voice of Bitterness was routinely overwhelming. Yet, inevitably, just when I thought victory would elude me I would stumble upon a classic like *The Problem with Pain*, by C.S. Lewis or *In the Shadow of the Almighty* by Jim Elliot, and gradually my resolve would strengthen, bolstered by the depth and insight of these pioneers in spiritual formation.

Instead of focusing on our natural circumstances, I was steadily learning how to lift my eyes upward, and even though we had never received the big pay-off, I was learning to be thankful in a new way for daily provision. It was as if there was an unexpected grace on the whole situation because, despite what the numbers said and the fact that Randy hadn't received a raise, we were somehow able to pay on the loans for Anna's surgery and Matthew's tuition without ever really bearing the full weight of either loan.

God's economy remains a mystery to me still because there was and is no way it should have been possible. Yet our life bears witness—as if it was God's own personal way of showering down His goodness to cement the principle I had just learned. Provision was occurring, and though it may not have been in one large miraculous sum, we were learning how to daily rely on the Father's provision realizing that we didn't just have what we needed, we also had most everything we wanted.

Which took us all straight into the end of another school year, including mine. Matthew and I were both facing our junior year in college and the irony that we would graduate at the same time never escaped either of us. It was just another thing in a long line of "things" that made it somehow seem like in some ways I had grown up with him.

Nearly twenty years had passed since Randy and I had first met, and I was awestruck by the fact that I had lived in Indiana for more time than I had Ohio. *And it all went by so fast,* I often thought. We knew we had less time with our children than what we had already spent with them, and now that Anna was also approaching her junior year of high school, we were also aware that college visits and applications were just around the corner.

Then there was Aaron Michael. My Aaron, the tender heart, who just as his name indicated, embodied such a warrior spirit that at times he was difficult to contain. Even at thirteen, he had an energy and a love for discovery that rivaled that of a toddler, yet at times lacked the insight to think through his actions or their consequences.

Just like his older two siblings, Aaron was embedded in the friendships he had known since he was a young boy. His primary relationships revolved around the children of the YaYas, specifically Michael and Christian. Yet as he finished the seventh grade, we noticed something in him started to appear unsettled—conflicted, if you will.

Recognizing the eight-year span between he and Matthew, I never seriously considered the impact of Matthew's shadow on Aaron, if there even was one. Aaron certainly struggled with missing Matt when he first left for Wheaton and no doubt there was a gaping hole spiritually since Matthew was Aaron's mentor. But since then I've wondered just how much unspoken expectation came from being Matthew and Anna's little brother.

"Is that why he's so determined to carve out his own way, Lord?" I would frequently ask.

But all I ever received in response was the reminder of what the Lord had spoken to me years ago about Aaron, *"He is a Son of Thunder, Kelly."*

So to that end I would pray—that the Lord would corral his heart and contain his spirit. I didn't want him rolling around everywhere without a clear direction.

Then came the summer between his seventh and eighth grade years when a bad storm came through the area, leaving us with a damaged roof. I had scheduled an estimate to be given early one weekday morning and asked Aaron to join me on the porch as the roofer climbed down the ladder just so he would know I wasn't home alone.

He was a big man, and by that I don't mean tall, though he was. He was *big*, both in physical stature and spiritual presence, and he lumbered slowly as he approached our home in his faded overalls. But it was his eyes that captured me, the deepest most piercing blue I had ever seen, and they radiated a gentleness . . . a gentleness that defied his stature and presence.

As he approached the porch I rested my hand on Aaron's knee and whispered, "Just stay here."

Aaron looked at me with his still sleepy, puffy eyes and gave me a cock-eyed brace-filled grin as he crossed his arms over his shirtless chest, leaning back on the bench as if he had more confidence than his adolescent body could hold.

Resting on the foot he had placed on the top step, the burly man cleared his throat and began describing all the work that needed done. I tried memorizing everything as he spoke so I could explain it to Randy, but after two or three sentences I realized Randy would just have to review the estimate himself because I didn't understand much of anything the roofer was saying. Suddenly he became quiet and shifted his weight, as well as his attention toward Aaron's direction.

"You, son, are called to your generation," the gentle man began.

The transition of conversation seamless, I listened, transfixed, as he continued, "There will come a day when you will stand on the rock and speak truth, but you will first face many things that God will ultimately use to make you credible to your generation."

Stunned by the man's timing and taken back by his insight, I wasn't sure how to process everything he was saying. Then holding Aaron's gaze, he continued, "You know you will have to choose the Rock before you will ever stand on the Rock and preach the Good News?"

He fell silent as Aaron's body shifted a bit closer to mine, his own uncertainty seeking reassurance. The presence of God on the porch was palpable . . . goose bumps covered every inch of my skin, and I knew better than to speak. I didn't want to; besides, I had no words.

The roofer continued to prophecy, referencing the biblical story of Moses and his older brother Aaron and how Aaron's rod was the one that budded to life as a way to signify his being chosen. It was then I finally found enough voice to ask, "You know that is his name?" as I pointed toward my son.

"You?" he responded, nodding his head in Aaron's direction. "Your name is Aaron?"

"Yes, sir," Aaron mumbled.

"Well . . . " he spoke with satisfaction, then silence, as the magnitude of revelation settled in. We felt the honor and blessing of the moment in what he said next, his voice increasing in volume and authority: "Once a mouthpiece for Moses, you'll now be a mouthpiece for Jesus. You are called, Aaron, that is your name. Don't ever forget it."

Then he handed me his estimate and was gone, leaving just the aroma of Jesus' presence to linger on the porch.

Neither Aaron nor I said much that morning. I think we were too dumbfounded to even find words, but I managed to journal everything I could remember. Little did I know that the roofer's words would become the one beacon that would continue to shine throughout some of the darkest moments of the next three years.

Even after Aaron came home from Christian camp a few weeks later completely broken and repentant for his previous choices and asked his brother Matthew to baptize him, it was the roofer's word—that Aaron must face many challenging things for God to make him credible—that held me and comforted me through future grave disappointments and heart-wrenching decisions.

Unbeknownst to me at the time, that one single prophetic word ultimately foreshadowed a coming season of rebellion and consequences that would forever change the composite and existence of our little family. That word wasn't just for a moment in time, rather it was the roofer's words that God continually used like an anchor as we weathered the storms on the horizon, continually reminding all of us of one thing—that God was good . . . no matter what. And despite it all, despite setbacks and failures, choices and betrayals, He alone would prove Himself capable of bringing about a beautiful redemption.

But this time it wasn't going to just be me He was redeeming—no, from that day forward, He had marked my entire family.

www.ingramcontent.com/pod-product-compliance
Lightning Source LLC
Chambersburg PA
CBHW070140100426
42743CB00013B/2776